God's Country

God's Country

Christian Zionism in America

Samuel Goldman

PENN

University of Pennsylvania Press

Philadelphia

Haney Foundation Series

A volume in the Haney Foundation Series, established in 1961 with the generous support of Dr. John Louis Haney

Published by
University of Pennsylvania Press
Philadelphia, Pennsylvania 19104-4112

www.upenn.edu/pennpress

Printed in the United States of America on acid-free paper

10 9 8 7 6 5 4 3 2 1

Library of Congress Cataloging-in-Publication Data
Names: Goldman, Samuel, author.
Title: God's country : Christian Zionism in America / Samuel Goldman.
Description: 1st ed. | Philadelphia : University of Pennsylvania Press, [2018] |
    Includes bibliographical references and index.
Identifiers: LCCN 2017037678 | ISBN 9780812250039 (hardcover : alk. paper)
Subjects: LCSH: Christian Zionism—United States—History. | Christianity and other
    religions—United States—Judaism—History. | Judaism—Relations—United States—
    Christianity—History. | Religion and politics—United States—History.
Classification: LCC DS150.5 .G64 2018 | DDC 261.20973—dc23
LC record available at https://lccn.loc.gov/2017037678

Contents

Introduction

On March 4, 2002, Senator James Inhofe rose to address the United States Senate on the topic of peace in the Middle East. The occasion was a proposal by Saudi Crown Prince Abdullah, under which Arab states would normalize relations with Israel in exchange for its withdrawal from territories occupied after the Six-Day War and the establishment of a Palestinian state. Inhofe argued against American endorsement of the deal. "If this is something that Israel wants to do, it is their business to do it," Inhofe said. "But anyone who has tried to put the pressure on Israel to do this is wrong."[1]

Inhofe explained that it would be wrong to put pressure on the Jewish State because "Israel is entitled to the land they have. . . . [I]t should not be a part of the peace process."[2] To support that entitlement, Inhofe adduced several reasons, including the record of Jewish settlement in the region, the persecution suffered by Jews around the world, and strategic considerations related to the War on Terror. Less than a year after 9/11, the Oklahoma Republican insisted that "we need every ally we can get. If we do not stop terrorism in the Middle East, it will be on our shores."[3]

Yet Inhofe's ultimate rationale was not based on history, humanitarianism, or strategic considerations. In a final argument, he proposed that "we ought to support Israel" and oppose territorial adjustments because "it has a right to the land. This is the most important reason: Because God said so."[4] Quoting Gen. 13:14–15, in which God promises Abraham that all the land he sees will belong to his descendants, Inhofe concluded: "This is not a political battle at all. It is a contest over whether or not the word of God is true."[5]

Inhofe's view of the relationship between the United States and Israel is not unusual among religious conservatives. Just a few weeks after Inhofe's speech on the Senate floor, the Christian Coalition organizer and GOP official Ralph Reed argued in the *Los Angeles Times* that "there is no greater proof of God's sovereignty in the world today than the survival of the Jews and the existence of Israel."[6] Like Inhofe, Reed denied that theological concerns are the *only* reason "Christians and other conservative people of faith stand so firmly in their support of Israel." Nevertheless, he acknowledged that their "support for Israel derives from the simple fact that its land was the cradle both of Judaism and Christianity. . . . [T]here is an undeniable and powerful spiritual connection between Israel and the Christian faith."[7] It would be easy to cite more examples. In the century's first decade, it was not only elected officials and party activists who explained that their views of international politics rest on divine promises. Ministerial leaders made similar claims. According to John Hagee, pastor of the Cornerstone megachurch in San Antonio, the Book of Genesis is nothing less than "God's foreign-policy statement."[8]

In 2006, Hagee put his beliefs into practice by founding Christians United for Israel (CUFI), which claims membership of more than a million.[9] Beyond its vast mailing list, CUFI's Summits in Washington and Nights to Honor Israel around the country have attracted participation from influential figures in both Israeli and U.S. politics. Christians have also played important collaborative roles with the American Israel Public Affairs Committee (AIPAC) and other pro-Israel groups. In their controversial book *The Israel Lobby and U.S. Foreign Policy*, political scientists John J. Mearsheimer and Stephen M. Walt argue that American Christians—mostly, but not exclusively, evangelical Protestants—are integral members of a coalition that uses a combination of public pressure, voter mobilization, and campaign donations to influence U.S. foreign policy. Like a growing number of writers, they describe these energetic supporters of the Jewish State as "Christian Zionists."[10]

It is tough to define "Christian Zionist." According to historian Shalom Goldman, the term was coined by Theodor Herzl to describe the Swiss banker

Jean-Henri Dunant, who achieved fame as founder of the Red Cross and attended the First Zionist Conference in 1897.[11] Dunant received a Calvinist education but offered primarily humanitarian and moral arguments for a Jewish state.[12] When Herzl described Dunant as a Christian Zionist, he seems to have meant that Dunant was a European non-Jew sympathetic to Zionism.

The Zionist intellectual Nahum Sokolow used the term in a similar way. In his *History of Zionism, 1600–1918*, Sokolow applied it to the British army officer George Gawler, who acted as traveling companion to Moses Montefiore during the Jewish philanthropist's 1849 visit to Ottoman Palestine.[13] In 1845, Gawler had published a tract that proposed the establishment of a Jewish colony there. Although Gawler apparently experienced an evangelical conversion as a young man, his arguments were more political than religious.[14]

For most of the twentieth century, the formulation "Christian Zionist" was rarely seen on this side of the Atlantic.[15] The scholar Stephen Spector finds it was not until 1980 that "Christians who call themselves Zionists" made their debut in the *New York Times*.[16] In this context—a report of the foundation of an organization called the International Christian Embassy in Jerusalem—the emphasis was on religion rather than politics. Reflecting the unfamiliarity of the link, the headline placed the term in quotation marks.

As Spector observes, neither approach to explaining what it means to be a "Christian Zionist" is satisfying. Definitions like Herzl's pay insufficient attention to religious concerns. By treating "Christian" as a synonym for "Gentile," they downplay the role of beliefs about an inextricable connection between Christian faith, the Jewish people, and the Land of Israel. Many non-Jews have supported Zionism and Israel for a variety of reasons. But they have not all been Christian Zionists.

More restrictive definitions, on the other hand, associate Christian Zionists too closely with specific theological commitments. Journalist Victoria Clark, for example, argues that Christian Zionists believe that the Bible is literally true and gives Jews a right to sovereignty over all the lands promised to Abraham.[17] As the quotations from Senator Inhofe suggest, there are Christian Zionists who meet this description. Yet it excludes professed

Christians who support Israel today or have endorsed Zionist projects in the past on the basis of very different understandings of God's word and will.

All definition is, to some extent, arbitrary. The important question is not whether a particular verbal tag covers all conceivable cases, but whether it provides a basis for further inquiry. With that consideration in mind, this book follows Spector in using the term "Christian Zionist" to describe supporters of a Jewish state in some portion of the biblical Promised Land who draw their main inspiration from Christian beliefs, doctrines, or texts. Christian Zionism, in turn, refers to those motives, authorities, and sources. This flexible approach to definition will be vindicated if the book sheds light on the thought and actions of Christians who played an important role in justifying, promoting, and even inspiring Zionism in its more familiar sense.

Where does Christian Zionism come from? Mearsheimer and Walt join a considerable number of scholars who derive Christian Zionism from the theological movement known as premillennial dispensationalism. The basic idea of premillennial dispensationalism is that history is composed of stages that culminate in the return of Jesus Christ to establish the millennium—the thousand-year reign of peace described by the Book of Revelation. This idea was systematized in the mid-nineteenth century by the Anglo-Irish theologian John Nelson Darby and promoted in the United States by evangelists including Dwight Moody and Cyrus I. Scofield.

The anticipation of a personal Second Coming is not what sets premillennial dispensationalism apart from other Christian eschatologies. Its most distinctive feature is the sequence of events that it places in the period preceding Christ's return to set up the millennial kingdom. Drawing on prophecies from the Old Testament as well as Revelation, the dispensationalist timeline includes the return of the Jews to their land, so-called Rapture of the faithful directly into heaven, and an escalating series of upheavals culminating in the battle of Armageddon. Early expositors described these aspects of premillennial dispensationalism in rather vague terms. But they have received vivid and detailed depiction in more recent works, including the 1970s best-seller *The Late Great Planet Earth* and the *Left Behind* novels coauthored by Christian Right activist Tim LaHaye.

John Nelson Darby wrote decades before the establishment of the organized Zionist movement and disclaimed interest in politics. But many Christians influenced by his teachings number the location and condition of the Jewish people among the "signs of the times" that mark steps toward the completion of God's plan. According to journalist Gershom Gorenberg, "for those who accept the dispensationalist doctrine, as so many evangelicals do, it's natural to proclaim love of the Jewish State. Israel's existence gives a believer the warm feeling that the world is behaving as he or she expects it to."[18] As Gorenberg emphasizes, that love has a dark side. Dispensationalists describe the period leading up to the Second Coming as a grim "tribulation." During this phase, they foresee increasing disorder, war, and pestilence. All who are not Raptured suffer these calamities, but Jews and Israel are subject to particularly intense anguish. In some versions of the story, the majority of the world's Jews perish before Christ returns.

These accounts promise Jewish survivors of the tribulation an honored place in the millennial kingdom, but only if they recognize Jesus as their promised Messiah. Although they believe God preserved the Jewish people and guided them home, dispensationalists see Jews as tragically misguided and in need of Christ's love. One function of the tribulation is to separate those willing to accept the divine truth from those sunk in error. It is not only Jews who can find something to fear in this scenario. Christ's rule in the millennium means the end of life as we know it. Premillennial dispensationalism is a complicated movement with several variants, so there are exceptions to any generalization. But it can reasonably be characterized as a socially pessimistic creed that sees civilization as doomed to destruction.

The lurid nature of these expectations has generated something of a critical genre. In books with titles that invoke the battle of Armageddon, academics and journalists alike have attempted to explain how premillennial dispensationalists came to regard themselves as friends of Jews and Israel. Such works typically acknowledge the sincerity of dispensationalists' affection. At the same time, they warn Israelis, Jews, and Americans of all faiths that this enthusiasm could be a mixed blessing. According to theologian Timothy P. Weber, dispensationalists' beliefs "make them skeptical about and sometimes even opposed to efforts to bring peace to the Middle East. Such behavior helps create the kind of world that dispensationalists have been predicting, a world in which they do not expect they will have to live."[19]

Even when they hinge on the meaning of obscure texts, studies of the relation between premillennial dispensationalism and Christian Zionism are not just scholastic wrangling. In practice, they serve as political judgments on Christian Zionism as a whole. To attribute their support for the State of Israel to unsettling eschatological visions is to depict Christian Zionists as a radical and potentially subversive influence on the United States, Israel, the Middle East, and the world. To determine whether that assessment is accurate, we need to evaluate the history on which it is based.

Dispensationalist ideas play a crucial role in encouraging favorable attitudes toward Israel among America's conservative Protestants. Particularly after the Six-Day War, tracking signs of the times in the Middle East became something of an obsession among fundamentalists and evangelicals. This obsession was both reflected and encouraged by the pop-apocalyptic literature that includes *The Late Great Planet Earth* and the *Left Behind* novels. To that extent, the attention they have received is justified.

Yet it is important not to exaggerate the importance of premillennial dispensationalism. Recent scholarship has identified problems with what might be called the standard narrative of Christian Zionism. These criticisms do not deny the influence of Darby and his popularizers. But they suggest that the story is more complicated than most writers have acknowledged.

For one thing, the close association between premillennial dispensationalism and activism on behalf of Israel is a fairly recent development. Dispensationalist leaders expressed abstract approval for the Jewish State before 1967. Yet few considered it necessary to take practical measures on its behalf. This distanced attitude was actually part of Darby's legacy. Although he looked forward to the fulfillment of the prophecies, Darby denied that politics could hasten or replace divine intervention.

Before the Reagan administration, in fact, the most visible American Christian supporters of the Zionist movement and, later, the State of Israel were theological liberals who rejected dispensationalism. Rather than waiting for an apocalyptic future, they argued that Christians had a responsibility to seek religious and political reconciliation with the Jewish people here and now. Reinhold Niebuhr was the most prominent representative of this forgotten strand of Christian Zionism, but his efforts were far from lonely. On the basis of extensive archival research, historian Caitlin Carenen has shown that it was mainline Protestants and liberal Catholics rather than evangelicals or fundamentalists who built the original institutional structure for the alliance between the Zionist movement, the State of Israel and American Christians.[20]

Another problem with the standard narrative is that its key features were not invented by Darby. The idea that the Jews are destined to return to the Promised Land and play a leading role in the millennium—albeit in a converted state—has been widespread among American Protestants for centuries. No less an authority than Jonathan Edwards wrote that "it is the more evident, that the Jews will return to their own land again, because they never have yet possessed one quarter of that land, which was so often promised them, from the Red Sea to the river Euphrates."[21] While he was technically a postmillennialist who expected Christ's return *after* the millennium, Edwards foresaw that a Jerusalem inhabited by descendants of Abraham, Isaac, and Jacob would be the capital of the kingdom of God.

The religion scholar Robert O. Smith has traced this brand of "Judeocentric prophecy interpretation" back to the Protestant Reformation.[22] But the Reformation was partly an attempt to recover themes that emerged in the earliest era of the Christian religion. According to theologian Gerald R. McDermott, "Christian Zionism is at least eighteen centuries older than dispensationalism."[23] In the most basic sense, McDermott argues, the story of Christian Zionism begins with the church itself.

Historical challenges to the standard narrative have placed Christian Zionism in a broader perspective. Rather than an odd and alarming fringe movement, it now appears to be a product of millennia of reflection on the relationships between the Old and New Testaments, Jews and Christians, religion and politics. This observation does not, by itself, amount to a normative defense: not everything old is good. But it does mean that there is more thought and argument behind Christian Zionism than depictions of Armageddon-mad fanatics would suggest.

Theological debates and biblical sources are just one dimension of Christian Zionism, moreover. Ideas linked to Christian Zionism also played an important role in the development of American political thought. Since the foundation of the Massachusetts Bay Colony, many Americans have articulated our collective purpose by means of an analogy with biblical Israel. Proposing a recurring image, John Winthrop wrote: "We shall finde that the God of Isreall is among us, when tenn of us shall be able to resist a thousand of our enemies, when hee shall make us a prayse and glory, that men shall say of succeeding plantacions: the lord make it like that of New England: for wee must Consider that wee shall be as a Citty upon a Hille, the eies of all people are upon uss."[24]

A popular interpretation of this analogy holds that Christian America replaced Israel in God's favor. As the Lord elected Israel to serve Him in biblical times, so He selected America to do His work in the modern age. On this account, a powerful current of American thought is based on what scholars call supersessionism, or (pejoratively) replacement theology. In other words, American Christians are seen as taking over the role of God's chosen people.

Nationalist supersessionism received powerful statements, some of which are still remembered and quoted today. Ezra Stiles, the minister and Hebrew scholar who served as president of Yale College during the Revolution and early republic, went so far as to describe his country as "God's American Israel." But a closer look at the sources reveals the metaphor's limits. Stiles took a cue from Winthrop and other Puritan writers in suggesting that America could be *like* biblical Israel. He did not claim that it replaced Israel in God's favor. On the contrary, Stiles insisted that "the future prosperity and splendor of the United States" was a step toward the time when "the words of Moses, hitherto accomplished but in part, will be literally fulfilled; when this branch of the posterity of Abraham shall be nationally collected, and become a very distinguished and glorious people."[25] For Stiles, divine sanction for American nationalism was premised on God's continuing relationship with the original chosen people.

Stiles's rhetoric shows how American exceptionalism can be intertwined with Christian Zionism. By enlisting the United States in the cause of Jewish return, Christian Zionism helps connect American history and institutions to a biblical narrative in which they do not directly appear. Not all Christian Zionists, let alone all Christians, are comfortable with this entanglement. But the popularity of belief that God has organized history around two peoples, the biblical Old Israel and the analogical New Israel, is among the reasons Christian Zionism continues to flourish in America while it has virtually disappeared from former strongholds like the United Kingdom.

Rather than a unitary movement defined by specific articles of faith, Christian Zionism is best understood as a kind of elective affinity among theological, historical, and political themes. The first of these themes is covenant. In exchange for a commitment to obey Him, the biblical Lord promises to make Abraham's descendants a great people and to provide them with a geographic home that extends, at maximum, from the Nile to the Euphrates, and at minimum, from the Mediterranean to the Euphrates.

Not all Christian Zionists interpret God's covenant with Abraham in the same way. Especially controversial is the issue of whether Jews must convert to Christianity before they enjoy all the blessings they were promised. Despite disagreement on this crucial issue, Christian Zionists take covenant seriously. Even when they believe that Jewish conversion is inevitable, they insist that God maintains an ongoing relationship with the people and the Land of Israel. Many find a source for this belief in Saint Paul's vehement denial that God "cast away His people" after the advent of Christ (Rom. 11:1).

A second theme in Christian Zionism provides a link between the biblical past and times yet to come. The people of Israel never possessed the entirety of the Promised Land and were, for many centuries, substantially removed from it. Prophecy extends covenant into the future by suggesting that God will bring back the Jews from exile and restore them to their appointed home. Before the nineteenth century, this was very much a prediction. Since then, successive waves of Jewish emigration to Ottoman Palestine, the organization of the international Zionist movement, the establishment of the State of Israel, and the conquest of additional portions of the Promised Land have seemed to fulfill ancient visions. As with covenant, there is controversy among Christian Zionists about how these developments should be interpreted. But they agree that the events of the last century or two suggest that God is guiding history toward the fulfilment of commitments recorded in the Bible.

A third theme in Christian Zionism, particularly as it has developed in the United States, emphasizes the present. Even if they doubt the truth of the Bible or the reality of divine providence, many Americans retain an affinity for Zionist aspirations and the State of Israel based on an ostensibly shared heritage. They see the Jewish State as a refuge from persecution, an outpost of Judeo-Christian civilization and a bastion of liberal democracy. Niebuhr called on this theme when he urged Americans to answer threats to Israel with an affirmation that "we will not allow 'any nation so conceived and so dedicated to perish from the earth.'"[26] The reference, of course, is to Lincoln's Gettysburg Address, which culminates in a description of the United States as a nation under God, called to ensure the survival of government of, by, and for the people.

Appeals to cultural and political resemblance may exceed the bounds of *Christian* Zionism. Rather than evoking traditional faith or theology, they sound more like expressions of an American civil religion. The legitimacy of Christian Zionism in its more expansive dimensions is a subject of vociferous debate among writers of various denominational and theological perspectives. For some critics, the distinctively American version of Christian Zionism even represents a heretical departure from core Christian doctrines.[27]

The argument of this book is primarily descriptive. Whether or not it is doctrinally justified—which is a question for qualified religious authorities—the claim here is only that belief in a unique connection between these two peoples and their states is deeply embedded in the American imagination.[28] And not only among conservative evangelicals. In *Honor the Promise*, an appeal for Christian support of Israel published in 1977, the Catholic priest and liberal Democratic congressman Robert Drinan asserted the existence of a "profound bond" that extends from the shores of Massachusetts Bay to modern Jerusalem.[29]

The themes that comprise Christian Zionism are more like the tributaries of one river than independent currents. Sometimes they flow away from each other. Farther along their courses, they overlap again. These intersections make it challenging to impose sharp boundaries between schools of thought or political movements but do not belie the categories themselves. If the politics of the Middle East teach us anything, it is the difficulty of imposing legible maps on challenging terrain.

This book is an essay in the history of ideas, not a policy brief. Even so, readers are likely to wonder where its author stands in the fraught landscape that he attempts to chart. Because suspicion of bad faith is a perennial obstacle to discussion of the vexed connections between religion and politics, questions about the perspectives that inform this book deserve explicit responses. To answer succinctly, the author of this book is not a Christian or a believer in the literal fulfillment of prophecy. Instead, he is a minimally observant Jew who admires Israel but considers America his country. In international relations, the author thinks that Israeli and American interests, while frequently allied, are not identical. A mature relationship demands that citizens of each state acknowledge, and respect, the possibility of divergence between them. Regarding the disposition of territories over which Israel won control in 1967, the author hesitates to join the ranks of armchair diplomats. Although he regards different states for different peoples as the most desirable outcome, he has no brilliant plan for achieving a goal that continues to elude the parties directly concerned.

The author can be described as conservative in several respects, but these opinions place him to the "left" of many, although not all, Christian Zionists. So why write about them? To begin with, this book is a contribution to what the scholar Stephen Prothero calls "religious literacy."[30] Despite religion's central role in our national life, Americans are astonishingly ignorant of the textual sources, historical figures, and key concepts that constitute even the most influential traditions. Lacking important information and a shared vocabulary, we tend to get confused and alienated when we encounter unfamiliar practices and beliefs. This tendency seems particularly acute when it comes to Zionism and the State of Israel. In many cases, secular and religious Americans, Zionists and non-Zionists, Jews and Christians, mainliners and evangelicals confront each other in mutual incomprehension and even hostility.

Common knowledge is no guarantee of agreement. Yet understanding where our interlocutors are coming from can assist us in civil discussion. In a pluralistic society, we are unlikely ever to speak the same language of politics. We have a better chance of resolving our disputes—or reaching respectful acknowledgment of our differences—if we become at least conversationally multilingual.

On one level, then, this book is aimed at readers who want to learn more about Christian Zionism but have little background in theology, history, or political theory—let alone all of these fields. In trying to anticipate and address their concerns, it draws liberally and gratefully on an expert literature without which it could not have been written. Academic incentives point toward specialization and novelty, while public discourse calls for synthesis and generalization. Intended to accomplish a civic purpose, this book risks erring in the latter direction.

At the same time, the book advances a suggestion aimed more directly at scholars. The proposal on this level is that Christian Zionism is an exercise in the style of thought known as political theology. According to theorist Mark Lilla, political theology is "a discourse about political authority based on a revealed divine nexus."[31] In other words, it is a way of thinking about the order and purpose of politics oriented by God's will.

Political theology was the basic form of political thought for much of the history of Western civilization. Since the nineteenth century, it has become less familiar to scholars—partly because a Ph.D. is no guarantee of religious literacy. But the reduced prominence of political theology in academic circles does not mean that it is a relic of the benighted past. Outside universities, it remains very much alive. The legal scholar Paul Kahn notes that "political theology must be more than a genealogical inquiry if it is to be more than a passing curiosity. It becomes interesting just to the degree that these concepts continue to support an actual theological dimension in our political practices."[32] The persistence of Christian Zionism shows that we need not look far for such a dimension.

Last but not least, the author wrote this book for himself. Confronted with a phenomenon that he found at once provocative and confusing, he set out to understand it better. Unable to find the guide for the perplexed that he was looking for, he decided to write one, learning as he went along. Whatever success he achieves, he hopes that the same spirit of inquiry will encourage further and doubtless more skillful attempts.

PART I
The Wilderness and the Eagle

On a Thursday afternoon in the spring of 1666, Increase Mather took his place before the First Church of Boston. The oldest and largest congregation in town, the church was established in 1630, the first official act of John Winthrop and the company that joined him on the *Arbella* and its sister ships. Since 1640, the congregation had been meeting near what would become Faneuil Hall, in a building distinguished by a majestic ceiling that resembled an inverted ship's hull. In other respects, the First Church looked much like Calvinist meetinghouses elsewhere in New England: unadorned by ritual objects, furnished with hard benches or pews, and dominated by the raised lectern from which Mather delivered his remarks.[1]

Looking down from his perch, Mather faced an audience dressed in the "sadd colors" favored by Puritan laypeople and seated in separate sections for men and women.[2] Members of that audience beheld a thin, long-nosed young man wearing a clerical ruff and "peculiarly apostolical" expression.[3] Only twenty-six years old, Mather had already served for two years as "teacher"—essentially, chief doctrinal officer—of the growing Second Church in the North End.[4] So his listeners would not have been shocked that his serene visage emitted a voice so powerful, if occasionally shrill, that "Hearers would be struck with an Awe, like what would be Produced by the fall of Thunderbolts."[5]

Mather's topic complemented his awe-inspiring manner. Addressing an issue that was something of an obsession among Puritans, he reflected upon the fate of the Jews. Once they had been God's beloved people and dwelled in the land that He had selected for them. Because of their sins, they were expelled from their divinely appointed home and subjected to centuries of degradation. Yet rumors were swirling around Boston's port that the Jews were once again on the move. Encouraged by a man who claimed to be the Messiah, they were said to be selling their goods, abandoning their homes, and setting out for Jerusalem.[6]

Not many years before these stories reached Boston, Puritans in England as well as New England hoped to witness the establishment of God's kingdom in their own lifetimes. The war of Parliament against the king, the execution of the monarch, and the establishment of a Protestant commonwealth were read as signs that the Lord was taking charge of human affairs and leading history toward its conclusion. With memories of these events still lively, rumors of great doings among the Jews must have rekindled visions of millennial glory. Could the Jews' reported migration mean that the end of days was approaching? Could their instigator be Christ himself?

Throwing a damper over the millennial fever smoldering in New England, Mather insisted that the time was not yet ripe for Christ's return. Even so, he affirmed that events involving the people and the Land of Israel were powerful signs of the "great and terrible day of the Lord."[7] Sooner or later, the Jews would go back to the country that God had promised to Abraham. At that moment, they would "recover the Possession of their Promised Land, and have a Glorious *Kingdom* of GOD erected among them, and through them Extended unto the *Gentiles*."[8]

Mather developed his arguments in monthly lectures delivered in the spring and summer of 1666. The following year, he dispatched his notes to London, where they were published in 1669 as *The Mystery of Israel's Salvation, Explained and Applyed*. Over the next four decades, Mather published two book-length sequels—the *Diatriba de Signo Filii Hominis et de Secundo Messiae Adventu* (Discourse on the sign of the son of man and the Second Coming of the Messiah) and the *Dissertation Concerning the Future Conversion of the Jewish Nation*—and preached the same doctrine in sermons. Throughout his long career as New England's leading divine, Increase Mather never wavered in his conviction that God's promise to restore the Jews to their ancient home would one day be fulfilled.

It is important to begin the story of Christian Zionism in America with Increase Mather for two reasons. The first is that doing so challenges the assumption that Christian Zionism is derived from premillennial dispensationalism, which developed centuries later. In fact, the idea that the Jews were destined to go home was common, if not universal, in Puritan New England. As Mather was careful to point out in his lectures, it also has precedents going back to the origins of Christianity.

Second, Mather's teaching complicates an influential interpretation of the Puritans' so-called errand into the wilderness. According to this account, the Puritans saw themselves as successors to the people of Israel, called across the oceans in a latter-day exodus from persecution. Because Israel rejected its promised savior, it was no longer David's capital that would serve as God's beacon to the world. Instead, the "city upon a hill" in North America was the proving ground for man's relationship with his Creator.[9]

But to Mather and many other Puritan divines, the matter was not so simple. Although they invoked the "new Israel" trope to inspire or chastise New England, these ministers and theologians insisted in different contexts on the unconditional nature of God's promises to the original chosen people. At the end of days, they argued, God would reign over a nation of Hebrews from His eternal capital in Jerusalem. As Mather scholar Reinier Smolinski puts it, Puritan thought "pointed toward an entirely different country, and an entirely different people, when identifying who would exercise dominion over the millennial world, a rulership later generations claimed for America."[10]

Belief that the Abrahamic covenant remained incomplete did not mean that Puritans placed themselves on the same footing as Christians elsewhere or that they saw their American settlements as just another British colony. New England *was* a city on a hill with a providential purpose.[11] But part of New England's vocation was to promote the fulfillment of God's promises to the Jews. In his tract *The Gospel Covenant*, the Concord minister Peter Bulkeley encouraged New Englanders to "stirre up everyone to help forward this glorious work."[12]

The "sacred history" that linked the destinies of American Christians and the Jewish people was initially more theological than political.[13] For Mather and Bulkeley, the best way Christians could promote the restoration of Israel was earnest prayer. Subsequent generations of Americans were more inclined to believe that God's will is made effective through acts of state. In

1816, Elias Boudinot, a former president of the Continental Congress and aide to George Washington, wondered whether "God has raised up these United States in these latter days, for the very purpose of accomplishing his will in bringing his beloved people to their own land."[14] In Boudinot's hands, Puritan ideas about Jewish restoration became a source of American exceptionalism, justifying not a retreat into the wilderness but rather a mission to assert power out into the world.

1 All Israel Shall Be Saved: The Calling of the Jews and the Errand into the Wilderness

> For I would not, brethren, that yee should be ignorant of this
> secret (lest ye should be arrogant in your selues) that partly
> obstinacie is come to Israel, vntill the fulnesse of the Gentiles
> be come in. And so all Israel shall be saued, as it is written,
> The deliuerer shall come out of Sion, and shall turne away the
> ungodlinesse from Iacob. And this is my couenant with them,
> when I shall take away their sinnes.
>
> —Rom. 11:25–27, Geneva version

It is often said that the Puritans of New England regarded themselves as the new Israel. According to the familiar story, the devout Calvinists who accompanied John Winthrop on the *Arbella* and its sister ships believed themselves to be chosen by God for an arduous journey to a new Promised Land. Just as the Hebrews concluded a covenant under Moses at Sinai, so the Puritans established an agreement among themselves to establish a community devoted to the service of God. Just as the Hebrews struggled and fought for possession of Canaan, so would the Puritans conquer their American Zion.

John Winthrop's famous sermon, "A Modell of Christian Charitie," did not exactly launch a thousand ships. The text was written at sea, and we do not know if it was actually delivered.[1] Nevertheless, it has been cited many times to explain the Puritans' understanding of their mission. According to social theorist Robert Bellah, the "Modell" was "Winthrop's way of summing up the meaning of the hopes and fears of the colonists in the face of the unknown land that lay ahead. He turned the ocean-crossing into a crossing of the Red Sea and the Jordan River, and he held out hope that Massachusetts Bay would be a Promised Land."[2]

Winthrop was not the only Puritan leader to assert a parallel between New England and Israel. In "Gods Promise to His Plantation," a sermon delivered in 1630 on the departure of Winthrop's fleet, the leading minister John Cotton presented the analogy between the people and the Land of Israel as an important justification for the expedition. Quoting God's promise that "I will appoint a place for my people Israel, and I will plant them, that they may dwell in a place of their owne, and move no more" (2 Sam. 7:10), Cotton argued that the Puritans possessed their own "speciall appointment" in North America.[3]

Referring to statements like this, historian Conor Cruise O'Brien described the Puritans as believing that New England was a "God Land" in which they would become successors to the biblical Israel.[4] Cotton was more cautious. Cotton called his brethren to be *like* Israel. At the same time, he reminded them that God's relationship with the original chosen people remained in effect. The Puritans had their place in North America, but Israel retained territorial rights in the biblical land of promise. Although it emerged from the Protestant Reformation, this understanding of God's promises reflects theological and hermeneutic trends that derive from the first centuries of Christianity. Saint Paul's insistence that "all Israel shall be saved" pointed toward a glorious future in which the Jews would play the pivotal role.

The Mystery of Israel's Salvation

When Jesus walked the earth, Palestine was inhabited largely by Jews, but their position was not untroubled. Jews never controlled all the territory promised to Abraham, they exercised unified sovereignty only for fleeting periods, and they experienced a series of dispersals both forced and voluntary. Despite these challenges, Jews of the first century AD could think of themselves as enjoying at least part of their inheritance. They were descendants of Abraham, Isaac, and Jacob, living in the land given to the patriarchs.

Attachment to Jerusalem amplified Jews' identification with the land. Jerusalem is not mentioned in texts describing the covenant with Abraham or its renewal by Moses. After its conquest by David, however, the city became the center of Israelite worship and a symbol of national identity. The Jewish philosopher Philo testified to the importance of Jerusalem at the dawn of the Common Era. Although born in Egypt and skeptical of traditional conceptions of divinity, Philo reported that Jews everywhere held "the Holy City where stands the sacred Temple of the most high God to be their mother city."[5]

Jesus' disciples assumed that the Land of Israel and city of Jerusalem belonged to them. In the Gospels, they express hope that Jesus would reassume David's throne, asking, "Lord, is this the time when you will restore the kingdom to Israel?" (Acts 1:6).[6] The disciples inquire about the kingdom as a political institution because the occupation of territory was not in dispute. The question was not whether Jews would inhabit their ancestral and holy places; it was whether they would govern them.

The status of the land became more doubtful after the rebellions against Roman rule that began in 66 AD. Over the following decades, the temple was destroyed, Jerusalem devastated, and thousands of Jews killed or driven into exile. Contrary to an enduring myth, Jews were never totally removed from Roman Palestine. But the focal points of Jewish life gradually shifted into the Diaspora.

These shocking developments raised questions about the link between people and land. Had the Lord revoked His promises to the patriarchs and the kings? Or were the upheavals of the first and second centuries just another twist in Israel's tumultuous relationship with God? Some Jews answered by recalling the prophets who spoke God's word during a previous time of trial. During the so-called Babylonian captivity of the sixth century BC, Isaiah, Ezekiel, and others foretold the return of the exiles and the rebuilding of the temple. It is mostly to them, in fact, that we owe the enchanting vision of Jerusalem as a holy city. The Bible reports that prophecies of return were first realized when the Persian king Cyrus granted permission to rebuild the temple (Ezra 6:3–5). Perhaps another, greater king would effect a second restoration in days to come.

Christians were not sure what to make of these prophecies. Most expected Christ's return in glory, but it was not clear whether his promised sovereignty would take political or geographic form. After all, his kingdom was "not from this world" (John 18:36). And when Christ did come back to establish his reign, who would be included among its subjects? Only the descendants of Abraham, Isaac, and Jacob? Or believers in Jesus' divinity, regardless of their ethnic or religious origin?

The tension between particularist and universalist aspects of Christ's message is among the great themes of Saint Paul. A Jew who appointed himself an "apostle to the Gentiles," Paul made it his purpose to assure Christians of non-Jewish descent that they had a place in the church (Rom. 11:13, Eph. 3:8). In one of his most celebrated statements, he asserted: "There is no longer Jew or Greek . . . for all of you are one in Christ Jesus" (Gal. 3:28). In this respect, Paul can be seen as denying that Jews or Judaism had any privileged status.

On the other hand, Paul insisted that God was not finished with the nation of Israel. In his Epistle to the Romans, he answered with a decisive "By no means!" the question of whether God had rejected His people. Paul noted explicitly: "I myself am an Israelite, a descendant of Abraham, a member of the tribe of Benjamin" (Rom. 11:1). According to Paul, his brethren remained "beloved, for the sake of their ancestors" even though most had failed to recognize Jesus as the Messiah. Despite their blindness, "the gifts and the calling of God are irrevocable" (Rom. 11:29).

Did God's gifts include the land? Although he insists that the covenant remains to be fulfilled, Paul does not say. A school of thought known as chiliasm attempted to resolve this confusion. The term is derived from the Book of Revelation. Presented as a vision received by a certain John on the island of Patmos, the text describes the rise and fall of a second empire called Babylon. In the last days of Babylon, Christ returns to resurrect the dead and set up the kingdom of God. This kingdom lasts for a thousand years (in Greek, a *chiliad*) before it is disrupted by Satan, leading to the establishment of "a new heaven and a new earth" and a "new Jerusalem" in which God dwells with His people (Rev. 21:1–4).

The meaning of these words is deeply obscure and has fascinated readers for centuries.[7] Interpreters in the chiliastic tradition treat them as extensions of the prophecies of restoration issued when Israel was subject to the original Babylon. The idea is that the prophets were right in expecting the Messiah to vindicate God's promises by rebuilding the holy city and returning the people to the land. But chiliasts offer an important correction: the Messiah was Jesus, who will accomplish this feat on his second visit rather than the first.

Justin Martyr, who lived in the second century AD and whose name indicates his fate, is among the early spokesmen for this view. In his apologetic *Dialogue with Trypho*, the fictional rabbi Trypho asks Justin whether he expects the kingdom of God and the rebuilding of Jerusalem. Justin answers: "I and every other completely orthodox Christian feel certain that there will be a resurrection of the flesh, followed by a thousand years in the rebuilt, embellished, and enlarged city of Jerusalem, as was announced by the Prophets Ezechiel [*sic*], Isaias [*sic*] and the others."[8] Justin does not limit himself to asserting the future realization of Babylonian-era prophecies. He also discusses the future of the "holy land"—the first appearance of the phrase in Christian literature. Identifying Joshua as a prefiguration or "type" of Jesus, Justin writes that "just as he, not Moses, conducted the people into the Holy Land and distributed it by lot among those who entered, so also will Jesus the Christ gather together the dispersed people and distribute the good land to each, though not in the same manner."[9]

As the phrase "not in the same manner" suggests, Justin put a distinctive spin on promises related to the land. In his Epistle to the Romans, Paul asserted that "not all Israelites truly belong to Israel, and not all of Abraham's children are his true descendants. . . . [N]ot the children of the flesh but the children of the promise are counted as descendants" (Rom. 9:6–8). Of Gentile background himself, Justin echoed Paul, contending that the redeemed Holy Land would be inhabited by Christians of all nations.[10] Justin's chiliasm thus represents an adaptation of Jewish traditions to Christian assumptions. Divine commitments involving the land and Jerusalem were preserved. At the same time, they were modified in a way that made Jews subordinate players in their fulfillment.[11]

Justin's younger contemporary Irenaeus, bishop of Lyon, reiterated these arguments. Dismissing claims that the city and land were metaphors for the spiritual rewards of faith, Irenaeus insisted that promises of restoration "cannot be understood in reference to super-celestial matters."[12] "In the times of the kingdom," Irenaeus predicted, "the earth has been called again by Christ [to its pristine condition], and Jerusalem rebuilt after the pattern of the

Jerusalem above."[13] Despite his insistence on the geographic aspect of the kingdom of God, Irenaeus followed Justin's expansive conception of the people of Israel. According to Irenaeus, "the church is the seed of Abraham."[14] The restored land and new Jerusalem would not be reserved for ethnic Jews, then, even if they converted. Instead, they were the common property of believers in Christ.

Justin probably exaggerated when he claimed that all orthodox Christians held chiliastic views. Even in his day, Christian opinions about the nature of the Second Coming were unsettled.[15] By the second century AD, chiliasm came under sustained attack. Perhaps the greatest Christian Bible interpreter of the period, Origen, contended that the chiliasts projected into the future prophecies that had already been fulfilled. In doing so, he argued, they transformed the completed mission of the Jewish people into a prediction of further glory, belying Christ's gift of salvation to all.[16]

Origen's critique of chiliasm was further developed by Eusebius, a Bible scholar of Gentile origin who became bishop of Caesarea in the early fourth century AD. According to Eusebius, the Roman conquest of the Promised Land was the judgment of an angry God on a disobedient people. Conflating the Empire with the millennial kingdom, Eusebius suggested that imperial building projects in Roman Palestine satisfied the prophecies. This possibility was symbolized by the construction of a church over the site of Jesus' tomb.[17]

Christian expectations for a territorial restoration of Israel were dealt another blow by Saint Augustine. Augustine rejected Eusebius's divinization of the Roman Empire, but maintained that God's promises to Israel were achieved by the establishment of the Christian church. If God preserved the Jews as a distinct people after their rejection of the Messiah, Augustine argued, it was to demonstrate His power. Again, Jews became supporting characters in someone else's story.

This doctrine of collective "witness" provided an indirect justification for the survival of the Jewish people.[18] By arguing that God was using Jews to instruct Christians, Augustine helped rebut Saint John Chrysostom's terrifying encouragements to murder them. But Augustine's account of deserved suffering provided no justification for Jews to return to the Land of Israel or resume their sovereignty. On the contrary, he argued that if Jews had not sinned, "they would have continued in possession of the same realm. . . . If today they are dispersed over almost all the world, amongst all the nations, this is part of the providence of the one true God."[19]

Despite Augustine's enormous influence, the idea of Jewish restoration never disappeared from Western Christianity. Particularly after the Crusades stimulated interest in the Holy Land, the future of the Jews became a recurring theme of speculation by mystics.[20] In the twelfth century, Joachim of Fiore taught that the impending third stage of history would include the return of the Jews to their land. There, they would convert to Christianity and live in brotherhood with a revitalized church.[21] Joachim himself enjoyed a good reputation, but his teachings were condemned as heretical. In the centuries that followed, hopes for Jewish restoration were increasingly confined to the margins of Christian thought. Historian Robert Lerner states that Joachite "exaltation" of the Jews ended with the death sentence imposed on the messianic visionary Nicholas of Buldesdorf on July 8, 1446.[22]

Nicholas's demise provides a reminder that questions about the future of the Jews were not merely scholastic disputes. Catholic theologians grounded the church's legitimacy on its status as the successor to biblical Israel. Teachings of Jewish restoration threatened that claim by suggesting that God's plans were still in motion and would eventually shift their focus to a different community. That is one reason chiliastic ideas proved attractive during the Reformation. By emphasizing the indefeasible character of God's commitments, they gave Protestants hope that He would overthrow false prophets and guide His people through all travails to their appointed destination.

Calling and Covenant

Martin Luther instigated the Reformation by insisting that the Bible, not the church hierarchy, was the ultimate authority on religious questions. On this basis, he contended that scripture taught that salvation could be achieved only through faith. Paul's Epistle to the Romans was crucial to Luther's case. In his view, the Epistle "is really the chief part of the New Testament and the very purest Gospel."[23]

Luther's emphasis on Paul forced him to revisit the issue of God's relationship to Israel. Discussing Paul's insistence that "all Israel shall be saved," he wrote that "this passage is so obscure that hardly anyone will be persuaded with absolute clarity."[24] Luther concluded that the best interpretation was that "Jews who are now fallen will be converted and saved, after the heathen according to the fulness of the elect are come in [to the church]."[25] For Luther, Jewish conversion in the last days fulfilled the prophecies without requiring any return to the Holy Land or Jerusalem.[26]

Luther hoped that greater attention to the Bible would lead to a more devout and unified church. Contrary to his expectation, the principle of *sola scriptura* opened God's word to a remarkable diversity of interpretations. Among these was the teaching of John Calvin, the seminal theologian for Anglo-American Protestantism. While Calvin also doubted any return to the Holy Land, the people of Israel had a more important place in Calvin's thought than in Luther's. Its significance was based on his signature conceptions of election and covenant.

For Calvin, election referred to God's unfathomable and irrevocable decision to have mercy on some sinners and abandon others to damnation. Those whom God destined for salvation could not change His decision by committing any transgression. Those whom He rejected could not hope for any reconsideration.

Because it presents God's decisions as inexplicable and unalterable, the doctrine of election might seem to imply an antinomian rejection of man's responsibility for salvation. But Calvin insisted that election implied expectations about behavior toward God and other human beings. Covenants were the statements through which God explained His commitments to the elect and their obligations to Him and their fellow men. The elect were thus bound to act in the way God demanded of them.[27]

Biblical Israel was Calvin's model for the complicated relationship between election and covenant. The Old Testament showed how God singled out the people of Israel for election and established covenants that laid out their responsibilities. Like nearly all Christians of his day, Calvin believed that people of Israel defied its covenant by rejecting the promised Messiah. So did its election continue after the advent of Christ and establishment of a new covenant between God and the human race?

Calvin turned to Paul with this question in mind. In his *Commentaries on Paul's Epistles*, he affirmed that "God has by no means cast away the whole race of Abraham, contrary to the tenor of his own covenant."[28] Calvin agreed with Paul that the original arrangement with Israel persisted despite the people's obstinacy. Because the Lord did not change His mind, the drama of Israel's election was still in process and would culminate in its reconciliation with God.

Calvin emphasized that being of Jewish descent did not, by itself, imply election. But he believed that it would be contrary to the basic narrative of scripture to deny the physical descendants of the patriarchs any role in God's plan. Continuing his discussion, Calvin explained: "Though in this prophecy deliverance to the spiritual people of God is promised, among whom even Gentiles are included; yet as the Jews are the first-born, what the Prophet declares must be fulfilled, especially in them: for that Scripture calls all the people of God Israelites, is to be ascribed to the preeminence of that nation, whom God had preferred to all other nations. And then, from a regard to the ancient covenant, he says expressly, that a Redeemer shall come to Sion. . . . By these words God distinctly claims for himself a certain seed, so that his redemption may be effectual in his elect and peculiar nation."[29] By insisting that Christ's mission would not be completed until the Jews entered the church, Calvin gave them a vocation for the future. Rather than merely ancestors of the Messiah, they were part of God's still-unfolding plan.

Even though he returned God's original chosen people to a leading position in sacred history, Calvin left existing Jewry mostly out of the picture. His "Israel" was more of a theological construct than a religious, political, or demographic reality. The abstraction that characterized early Protestant ideas about Jewish return is among the reasons some scholars describe them as "restorationist" instead of Zionist. Rather than encouraging the Jewish people to take political responsibility for its destiny, restorationist tropes that emerged from Calvinism emphasized dependence on God and the eventual conversion of the Jewish people.[30]

Efforts to make scripture available to ordinary people were among the signature elements of the Reformation. Among the vernacular translations that reformers produced was the Geneva Bible, published in a series of editions under the editorial guidance of Calvin's colleague Theodore Beza. The Geneva Bible of 1560 was not the earliest rendering of God's word into English, having been preceded by William Tyndale's partial translations and the so-called Great Bible of 1539. But it was the first mass-produced edition to include both the Old and the New Testaments. As a result of its accessibility and outstanding scholarship, the Geneva Bible became a favorite of English-speaking Protestants until well into the seventeenth century. It was what Peter Bulkeley called "our Geneva" that the Puritans carried with them to America.[31]

The impact of the Geneva Bible was not only due to the quality of the translation. To promote understanding, the editors developed a novel apparatus, including placement of the "most profitable annotations vpon all the hard places" right in the margins of the text.[32] Even more than Calvin, these annotations emphasize God's continuing relationship with the Jewish people. Indeed, they make no systematic distinction between Jews and Hebrews or Israelites. Beginning with the commentaries on Exodus, the notes refer to the followers of Moses as Jews. They later describe temple worship and associated rituals as Jewish practices. The implication is that adherents of modern Judaism stand in a lineal relationship with the people of the Bible.

The Geneva notes sometimes offer allegorical readings of God's promises to the Jews. In several discussions, "Israel" is read as a reference to the church. For example, the note to Gen. 13:15, in which God promises Abraham that "the land which thou seest, will I give vnto thee, and to thy seed forever," distinguishes between "the true children of Abram [sic], born according to the promise, and not according to the flesh."[33] Yet the Geneva Bible combines these allegorizing interpretations with affirmations that God's promises had territorial significance. The note to Isa. 63:18 states that the Abrahamic covenant is "perpetual" and includes a title to the land.[34] A bit earlier, at Isa. 58:12, the note explains that Israel under the leadership of the Messiah "shuld buylde again the ruines of Jerusalem and Judea."[35] The note on Ezek. 26:20 foretells the glory of "Judea, when it shall be restored."[36]

The Geneva Bible was not the only source of interest in the restoration of Israel during the Protestant Reformation. It was also encouraged by a reemergence of chiliasm. In his *City of God*, Saint Augustine identified the "millennium"—Latin for the thousand years foreseen by John of Patmos—as the period that began with the foundation of the church. For Augustine, in other words, the reign of Christ included the then-present age.[37] During the wars of religion, however, Protestants began to place this period in the future. Only after the fall of the second Babylon, which Protestants identified with the papacy, would the kingdom of God commence, with all that implied for Israel.

The Millennium and the Politics of Reformation

In addition to Old Testament prophecies of liberation and return, Christian chiliasm draws heavily on the Revelation of John. This profoundly allusive text describes a series of events leading to the defeat of a mystical Babylon by an army of saints led by Christ himself.

The place of Revelation in the Christian canon is controversial. Luther doubted its authority. Calvin repudiated belief in a literal, future millennium as a "fiction . . . too childish either to need or to be worth a refutation."[38] In the scholarly literature, Calvin's position is described as amillennialism. According to philosopher of religion Jerry L. Walls, "[T]he essence of this view is that Christ's millennial reign has already been inaugurated through his death and resurrection and the coming of the Holy Spirit. The millennial reign is thus an invisible one that is presently manifested in the Church."[39] Despite Calvin's warnings, however, many Protestants found chiliastic or "millenarian" ideas irresistible. One reason for their popularity was that they helped Protestants make sense of their own struggles. Revelation assures believers that they will triumph over an overwhelming adversary. This vision must have been deeply appealing to embattled Protestants.

The most influential statement of millenarianism for English speakers was John Foxe's *Actes and Monuments*, popularly known as *Foxe's Book of Martyrs*. A history of persecutions suffered by Christians, the *Book of Martyrs* placed the reformers' struggle in an eschatological perspective. In Foxe's presentation, Babylon was the Roman Catholic Church and the pope was the "beast" fated to be destroyed by the Lord. The implication was that the kingdom of God would not commence until after the reformers' victory. Hope for a future millennium intersected with ideas about God's relationship with Israel. Dire as the situation might appear, Paul's insistence that all Israel shall be saved provided reassurance that history was proceeding according to plan. If the Jews could expect to be rescued from their suffering, so could

Protestants. Thus Foxe was confident that "God will vouchsafe to reduce you [Jews] again into his owne familie, with his elect Saints, and make you partakers of his gladsome gospel."[40]

Reformation millenarianism did not necessarily involve Jews' return to the Land of Israel. Writers like Thomas Draxe, who published a tract called *The Worldes Resurrection or the General Calling of the Iewes*, were primarily concerned with Jewish conversion.[41] But it did not take long before Protestant writers integrated territorial and spiritual predictions. In the early seventeenth century, Thomas Brightman and Joseph Mede published books that connected the dots between the restoration foretold by the prophets, the salvation of all Israel promised by Paul, and the fall of the second Babylon described in Revelation. Along with studies by the German Calvinist Johann Heinrich Alsted, these works would achieve considerable influence among readers becoming known as Puritans.

Brightman's contribution was groundbreaking. In his *Revelation of the Revelation*, posthumously published in 1611, Brightman assumed that the apocalyptic timeline was well advanced. The war against the beast had been initiated by Luther and pursued by Protestant sovereigns. The next step would involve the destruction of Babylon—that is to say, Rome.[42] Just before that great event, John describes the drying up of the river Euphrates "in order to prepare the way for the kings from the east" (Rev. 16:12). According to Brightman, these mysterious kings were none other than the Jews. In a striking passage, Brightman described how Israel would be restored as a nation and reclaim its land as sacred history approached its climax:

> What shall they returne to Ierusalem againe? There is nothing more certaine, the Prophets doe euery where directly confirme it and beate vppon it. Yet they shall not come thether to haue their ceremoniall worship restored; but to make the goodnes of God shine forth to all the world, when they shall see him geue to that nation (which is nowe and hath been for many Ages scattered thorough out the whole world, and inhabiteth no where but by leaue and entreaty) there own habitations where their Fathers dwelt, wherein they shall worship Christ purely, and sincerely according to his will, and commandment alone. Which is a matter that was commonly spoken of by the auncient Iewes, which they vnder-

stood out of the Prophets, but yet lightly and as it were thorough a lat-
tice glauncingly, whence it came to passe that it hath bene defiled with
many old wiues fables, among the auncient Iewes, as it is also nowe at
this daye.[43]

By identifying the Jews as the kings of the East, Brightman offered a neat
solution to the tensions between national and spiritual conceptions of Israel
or between literal and allegorical approaches to interpreting prophecy. God
had a continuing arrangement with the Jews and would make good His promise of the land. But that promise would not be fulfilled until the Jews recognized that Jesus had been the promised Messiah and penitently embraced
him as their king and savior. Turning to Paul to tie these strands together,
Brightman continued: "Seeing then it is certaine that this nation shall come
at last with speed, and earnestness to receive the Gospell, and that in the
last times, as Paul teacheth in Rom. 11.25 . . . it is not likelie, that all mention of so wonderfull a matter, that shall astonish men with beholding
it, should be let passe in this most euident Prophecy of the newe Testament,
too all which we may adde the proper Marke to knowe this Nation by, which
is sett downe in this place, as who are the onely People of the world, for
whose sake we reade both the Sea and the Riuer to haue bene dried vp."[44]

Many Christian Zionists today reject the idea that the church assumed
the status of Israel, superseding the covenant with Abraham.[45] Brightman's interpretation of the apocalypse shows that their intellectual predecessors did not necessarily agree. To be sure, he insisted that Jews as a
people remained dear to God despite their misunderstanding concerning
the identity of the Messiah. But he denied that Judaism had any future as
a *religion*. In order to recover their place at God's right hand, the Jews had
to convert.

Conversion was the condition of political success. Brightman foresaw the
establishment of a mighty state, such that "the whole East shall be in obedi-
ence and subiection unto them, so that this people are not called Kings un-
worthily, in regard of their large and wide Iurisdiction and Empire." By means
of this "full restoring of the Iewes," prophecies that "the Lord of hosts shall
raigne in mount Sion, and in Jerusalem, and shall be glorious before his
Auncient men" would finally be accomplished.[46]

Brightman contended that the Second Coming would occur at the end of the thousand-year kingdom—a view known as *post*millennial. The Cambridge University Hebrew scholar Joseph Mede, by contrast, contended that Christ would appear at the *beginning* of the thousand years. Mede based his *pre*millennial theory on an innovative argument that the Book of Revelation contained a "Synchronisme of prophecies."[47] This meant that the narrative described a course of religious events followed by a parallel series of political developments, rather than a unified chronological sequence.

Applying his novel interpretive method, Mede concluded that the Jews would convert before recovering their land. In his account of Revelation, the crossing of the kings of the East signified an army of Jewish converts destroying the Ottoman Empire. Mede expected that this maneuver would open the way for an attack against the beast's soft underbelly by Protestant armies. After the fall of Babylon, power would be divided between the Protestants of the West and the Christian-Israelites of the East, under the universal authority of Christ.[48]

Sir Henry Finch, a member of Parliament and lawyer rather than a theologian, advanced a perhaps more accessible argument for Jewish restoration. In his 1621 book *The Calling of the Iewes or the World's Great Restauration*, he simply insisted: "Where Israel, Iudah, Tsion, Ierusalem, &c. are named . . . the Holy Ghost meant not the spirituall Israel, or Church of God collected of the Gentiles, no nor of the Iewes and Gentiles both (For each of these haue their promises seuerally and apart) but Israel properly descended out of Iacob's loynes."[49] To Finch, complicated theological or textual analysis were unnecessary. Readers had only to take God at His word.

Finch's literalist interpretation led him to conclude that Jewish restoration would be not only territorial but also political. As he put it, "[T]he same judgement is to bee made of their returning to their land and ancient seates, the conquest of their foes, the fruitfulnes of their soile, the glorious Church they shall reer in the land it selfe of Judah, their bearing rule farre and neere. These and such like are not Allegories . . . but meant really and literally of the Iewes."[50] Despite centuries of controversy about the right interpretation, the evidence of scripture was clear. According to Finch, "[W]ee need not be afraid to averre and mainteyne, that one day they shall come to

Jerusalem againe, be Kings and chiefe Monarches of the earth, sway and govern all, for the glory of Christ that shall shine among them."[51]

Finch's vision of the millennial "bodie politicke" attracted the unfavorable attention of the authorities.[52] In a sermon preached in the presence of King James I, William Laud—later an archbishop of Canterbury famous for hostility to Puritanism—accused restorationist writers of a kind of lèse-majesté. To claim that the Jews would be "chiefe Monarches" of the earth was tantamount to saying that Gentile kings lacked a divine right to rule. According to Laud, the Christian-Israelite empire described by Finch was "a strange *Jerusalem.* Not the old one, which is litterall in my Text. For which Dauid would haue prayers: nor that which succeeded it, *Ierusalem of Jew* and *Gentile* conuerted: for which wee must pray. *But a Jerusalem of gold and precious stones . . . which shall be built for them again upon earth in greater glory than ever was.*"[53] In Laud's opinion, Finch's interpretation of the millennium revived fantasies of political sovereignty that Jesus rejected. He concluded: "[S]o it is not now sufficient that the Iewes shall be (in Gods good time) converted to the faith of Christ, as the Apostle delayers it, Rom. 11. *But these conuerted Jewes must meet out of all Nations: the ten Tribes, as well as the rest, and become a distinct, and a most flourishing Nation againe in Jerusalem. And all the Kings of the Gentiles shall doe homage to their King. Good God, what a fine people haue we here? Men in the Moone.*"[54]

Laud's derision was aimed not only at restorationism; it was also a challenge to the Puritan movement, which used the terms of God's covenant with Israel to challenge the authority of the crown. Tensions between radical Protestants and the Church of England led to the establishment of colonies at Plymouth in 1620 and Salem in 1626. In 1630, they would prompt a modern exodus.

American Zion

What did the Puritans think that they were doing in America? Historian Conrad Cherry expresses a popular view:

> They were on an "errand into the wilderness"; their purpose was to build a holy commonwealth in which the people were covenanted together by

their public profession of religious faith and were covenanted with God by their pledge to erect a Christian society. . . . The original errand, however, was more than a mission for the Puritans themselves. They believed that, like Israel of old, they had been singled out by God to be an example for the nations (especially for England). . . . If they succeeded in their errand, they would mark a turning point in history. If they failed, they would fail not only themselves but their God and the very course of history.[55]

Cherry's description captures the importance that the Puritans attached to their project. Rather than a random sequence of events, they understood history as an enactment of God's intentions. At one time, Israel had been the vehicle of those intentions. By asserting their own role in the fulfillment of God's plan, the Puritans claimed the mantle of the biblical Hebrews.

Puritan identification with Israel was encouraged by an approach to biblical interpretation known as typology. Essentially, typology was the idea that figures and events at earlier stages of the scriptural narrative foreshadow subsequent ones. Often, this principle was used to explain how Christ fulfilled promises that were only incompletely realized in the Old Testament. It was in this sense that Justin Martyr described Joshua, who distributed the Land of Canaan among the Israelite tribes, as a prefiguration of the returned Christ, who would redistribute the Holy Land in the millennial kingdom.[56]

As Justin's example shows, typology has a long history in Christian thought. But Puritan interpreters sometimes went beyond traditional restraints by extending the realization of Old Testament hints from the New Testament into their own time. Arguing that God was still guiding history toward its conclusion, Puritan divines suggested that the fulfillment or "antitype" of biblical Israel was not simply the church; it was the Puritans themselves.

The unofficial title of Edward Johnson's history of early New England, *Wonder-Working Providence of Sion's Saviour*, reflects the intensity of this typological identification. In Johnson's florid words: "As the Lord surrounded his chosen Israel with dangers deepe to make his miraculous deliverance famous throughout, and to the end of the world, so here behold the Lord Christ, having egged a small handfull of his people forthe in a forlorne Wildernesse, stripping them naked from all humane helps, plunging them in a gulph of miseries, that they may swing for their lives through the Ocean of his Mercies, and land themselves safe in the armes of his compassion."[57] For Johnson, the story of Israel was proof that God took peoples under His influence and worked through them to accomplish glorious purposes. In choosing the Puritans, He made New England the vehicle for the completion of promises yet unfulfilled.

Puritan typology was not just rhetoric. Many Puritans believed that they could find favor with God by living like the Hebrews. They christened their sons Samuel and Ezekiel. Place names like Sharon were transferred from the Holy Land to North America. John Cotton even suggested the Deuteronomy could be used as a model for civil legislation in New England. In debates surrounding the compilation of a legal code for Massachusetts, Cotton argued for the adoption of elements of Mosaic law.[58]

Yet Puritan divines also kept in mind what Mather scholar Smolinski calls the "eschatological limits" of typology.[59] New England might have been *like* Israel in important ways. But it could not be a replacement for the Jews because the covenant with Abraham remained in effect. Peter Bulkeley made this point explicitly: "By vertue of the Covenant made with their fathers, they shall be delivered out of the bondage in which they are now holden." Since God did not change His mind, sacred history would culminate with the "full and finall accomplishment in the calling home of the *Jewes*."[60]

Like other Puritans, Bulkeley interpreted that "calling home" primarily as a reference to conversion. Paul's dictum that "all Israel shall be saved" meant acknowledging Jesus as the Messiah. Even so, Bulkeley noted as "remaining in that people, a strange affection unto their own Land." Bulkeley acknowledged that "some may say, this that is spoken of building *Jerusalem* againe, may seem to import, that the *Jewes* shall again repossesse their own Land, which is but a vaine conceit." But he considered God's word to be clear: "[L]et those Scriptures be examined, which speake of their conversion, and it will appeare, that they speake as punctually concerning their inhabiting again their owne Land, and their building and dwelling in their own Cities."[61]

If the Jews were destined to be called home geographically, New England could not be a new Zion. At most, it foreshadowed the millennial kingdom centered on Jerusalem. On that sacred ground, Jews and Gentiles would finally be united in faith. Bulkeley wrote: "Many of those dark Prophecies, which now lye hid in obscuritie, shall then be brought to light. . . . *Jerusalem* shall be a throne of glory to him, then shall the Lord be glorified in them, all the house of *Israel* shall glory in the Lord, and shall draw others of the Gentiles unto them."[62]

What could New England's Puritans do to bring that day closer? Bulkeley answered that they could expose Catholic errors and practice Christian virtue. In this way, they would serve as an inspiring model of the purified church that awaited the Jews. John Cotton agreed. In sermons on Revelation, he encouraged his audience to engage in "pouring out Vials of the corruptions that are found in our own hearts; look that there be no corruptions in us." In this way, "stir we up our selves therefore and one another hereunto, and pray that God would stir up other Nations and People hereunto, then shall we see God's ancient people brought home, and the Lord shall be one over all the Earth."[63] In *Wonder-Working Providence*, Johnson gave a similar account of New England's task. He described his fellow Puritans as "a people not onely praying but fighting for you [ancient people of Israel]" by eliminating unbiblical accretions that inhibited their acceptance of the Gospel.[64]

Prayer would not be sufficient. Within the near future, Cotton expected a "willing people among the gentiles, to convey the Jewes into their owne Countrie, with Charets, and horses, and Dromedaries."[65] But old England seemed more likely than New England to serve as the instrument of providence. Constitutional crisis and outbreak of civil war back at home aroused Puritans' hopes that God was guiding history toward its conclusion sooner rather than later. According to historian B. S. Capp, 70 percent of English ministers who published three or more books in the troubled years between 1640 and 1653 expressed millenarian views.[66]

The most dramatic expression of seventeenth-century English millenarianism was the Fifth Monarchy movement, named for the prophet Daniel's description of four empires that would arise and be overthrown before the coming of the Messiah to establish a final, millennial regime. Rejecting arguments that God would inaugurate the millennium through miraculous intervention, the so-called Fifth Monarchy Men argued that it could be brought about by human action. On this basis, they took the lead in the trial and execution of Charles I. Following the removal of England's king, Fifth Monarchists proposed a quasi-Hebraic constitution, involving the replacement of Parliament with a council modeled on the assemblies that Moses set up for the people of Israel.

English millenarians helped pave the way for the readmission of the Jews in 1656. Cromwell's decision to allow Jews to reside legally in England seems to have been motivated by economic concerns. But he was supported by figures like Hugh Peters (or Peter), a New England colonist who returned to the mother country in 1641 to serve as agent for Massachusetts. An ardent millenarian, Peters believed that Cromwell's Commonwealth was a step toward the establishment of the kingdom of God and Christ's return. The restoration of Israel, in his view, was an important part of this process.[67]

It was for such readers that Menasseh Ben Israel, a Portuguese rabbi living in Holland, composed *The Hope of Israel*, published in English translation in 1650.[68] Some millenarians opposed readmission on the grounds that it would delay Jews' return to the Promised Land.[69] Menasseh countered that while Jews would ultimately be restored, states that harbored them in the meantime would be blessed by God. Citing a verse that remains a favorite of Christian Zionists, Menasseh promised that "God will give blessings upon them who favour us. And those are the trees of the field which then shall rejoyce. So God saith to Abraham, in Gen. 12:3, I will blesse them who blesse thee, and curse them that curse thee."[70]

Despite his encouragement to readmit Jews to England, Menasseh did not think that the road to restoration led only through Europe. Advancing a theory also promoted by the Puritan John Eliot, Menasseh suggested that the so-called Lost Tribes of Israel had made their way to the Americas, where they became the ancestors of the apparently indigenous peoples. A considerable portion of the people of Israel, in other words, was already in the New World. In addition to Menasseh and Eliot, the Lost Tribes theory was promoted by Thomas Thorowgood in his books *Jews in America,* published in 1650, and *Digitus Dei* (The finger of God), published in 1652. These works were widely circulated and continued to attract interest into the nineteenth century, when the idea that Native Americans have a Hebraic origin resurfaced in the teaching of the Mormon prophet Joseph Smith.

By the late 1650s, however, millenarian hopes were on the ebb in England and its American outposts. Cromwell died in 1658. Attempts to extend the commonwealth beyond his life were abortive, disappointing the Fifth Monarchists and other radicals. Increase Mather's writings on Jewish restoration, the most extensive in New England literature, reflected these changed circumstances. In his son Cotton's description, Mather offered a "sober chiliasm" for chastened circumstances.[71]

Sober Chiliasm

Increase Mather's biography illustrates the shifting fortunes of New England. A son of the eminent minister Richard Mather, Increase was a member of its second generation—those actually born in North America. After completing his bachelor of arts degree at Harvard in 1656, Increase sailed for Ireland, where he earned a master of arts degree at Dublin's Trinity College. After graduating in 1659, he entered military service, acting as chaplain to a garrison on the Channel Island of Guernsey.

But conditions were growing insecure for Puritans in old England. With Cromwell dead, restoration of the monarchy was only a matter of time. Charles II appeared publicly in London for the first time on May 29, 1660. The following January, Cromwell's body was exhumed and posthumously executed. By March, Increase had determined that he was in danger. He resigned his military post and embarked for Boston on June 29, 1661. Mather thrived back at home. Marriage to John Cotton's daughter Maria, vast erudition, and a forceful preaching style earned him prominent academic and political roles. Until his death in 1723, Increase was the most prominent divine in New England.[72]

Mather's statements on the restoration of Israel date back to the early years of his Boston ministry. Cotton Mather, named for his famous grandfather, recalled the circumstances:

About the year 1665, the World was Alarmed with Rumours of Motions among the *Jews* in several parts of the World, that made some who were *Waiting for the Consolation of Israel,* to hope, that the *Lord was going to set his Hand again the second time, to recover the Remnant of His People, and assemble the Outcasts of Israel and gather together the Dispersed of Judah.* Mr. Mather Preached a Monthly Lecture, And he took this occasion, to give his Auditory some Elaborate & Judicious Lectures on that Mystery; Rom. xi. 26. *All Israel Shall be Saved,* In those Lectures, he Declared, That he verily believed the Motions then talk'd of *would come to nothing*; and that *the Time for Favour,* the *set Time,* would not yet come on. But he maintained, That *a Time would come,* when the *Israelitish Nations* should be *Converted* from their Infidelity, and *Restored* unto the Possession of their Promised Land, and have a Glorious *Kingdom* of GOD erected among them, and through them Extended unto the *Gentiles*.[73]

Cotton's summary conveys the main points of Mather's position. Although the time was not yet ripe, in the last days the Jews would convert to Christianity and be restored to the Holy Land. As their nominal king, Christ would reign over the rest of the world for a thousand years.

Prophecy played an important role in Mather's account of Jewish restoration. But it is important to note that he took Saint Paul's Epistle to the Romans as his point of departure. By grounding his arguments about Jewish restoration in covenant, Mather staked out a claim to historical orthodoxy. At the same time, he distanced himself from extreme millenarianism associated with the political disaster in England.

In *The Mystery of Israel's Salvation,* Mather described Paul's statement that all Israel shall be saved as "the most pregnant and illustrious testimony and demonstration of the Israelites future vocation" found anywhere in scripture.[74] The purpose of *The Mystery* was to provide the systematic analysis of that vocation that Mather believed still to be lacking. Using a rigorous structure of argument that characterized the Puritan sermon, Mather contended that such an analysis involved answers to three questions: "Who are meant by *Israel.* 2. What [is meant] by all *Israel.* 3. What [is meant] by being saved."[75] Turning to the first question, Mather noted: "We must know there is a double Israel spoken of in Scripture; 1. There is spiritual *Israel, i.e.*—such as in respect of faith and Religion, are the Lord's peculiar ones. . . . 2. There is carnal or natural *Israel, i.e.* those that are by generation of the seed of Jacob, who was afterwards called *Israel.* Hence we read of *Israel after the flesh,* as well as *Israel after the spirit*."[76] Which did the apostle have in mind when he spoke of Israel's calling?

Mather opted for the "carnal" interpretation on grounds of internal consistency. In his view, there was nothing inherently mysterious in the salvation of believers in Christ. After all, that was the central item of Christian faith. The puzzle was that the Jews had been the elect of God but rejected Christ and persecuted Christians. It defied understanding that they should continue to enjoy God's favor. Yet this was apparently what Paul promised.

To be sure, Mather did not claim that literally every descendant of Jacob would be saved. Even with divine encouragement, at least some Jews would persist in their bad old ways. Nevertheless, "when it is said *All Israel shall be saved, i.e.* very many *Israelites* shall be saved. Yea, *all* here noteth, not only many, but most; it signifieth not only a *Majority*, but a very full and large *Generality*."[77] For Mather, the calling of the Jews was collective and national, not merely individual.

Mather confessed that he "was exceeding backward to entertain such a notion, and did long oppose it, as conceiving it might be at best an innocent errour of some that wished well unto the kingdom of Christ."[78] But his reading of Beza, Brightman, and Mede convinced him that the restoration of Israel "is a truth which in some measure hath been known, and believed . . . since the Apostles days."[79] For Mather, the antiquity of the doctrine was a warrant of its veracity. Indeed, he insisted that "in the Primitive times, we read of none but Hereticks that questioned the truth of it."[80]

Increase Mather's "sober chiliasm," as Cotton called it, served dual purposes. In the first place, it was an act of historical recovery. By establishing links between himself and the apostles, Mather reaffirmed the Puritans' claim to be heirs of the early church.[81] At the same time, Increase's interpretation checked hopes for the immediate establishment of the millennium. Responsible Christians could pray for that outcome but should not attempt to accelerate it, as the Fifth Monarchists had done. John Davenport, the minister of New Haven and an ally of John Cotton, made this point directly in his preface to *The Mystery*. According to Davenport, there would eventually be a "political kingdom of Christ." But he cautioned that it would be established only *after* the Second Coming, an event that no man could hasten.[82]

In the meantime, Increase encouraged efforts to convert Jews. By speaking "after the manner of the Jewish religion," he hoped to "draw the Jews to the study of the mystery contained in this Book, and to shew them, that God hath a respect to them as well as to the Gentiles."[83] According to Mather: "It is not as some have thought the best way to deal with the Jews, when they urge, that in the days of Messias [*sic*], they must have such glory bestowed upon them, as the like never was in the world, to tell them that all those things must be understood spiritually, and not literally, which in the Prophets look that way."[84] Instead, "it were better to yield to them, that they shall have such glory as the like never was, only that this must not be at Messias first appearing."[85]

So New England could promote the salvation of Israel by making Christian religion more attractive, by prayer, and by deploying missions. It might be especially suitable for these tasks by reason of its own covenant with the Lord. But that covenant did not render the Puritans' North American refuge the new Jerusalem or the kingdom of God. In fact, Mather explicitly warned against mistaking America for the Promised Land.

From Wilderness to Promised Land?

Christians had wondered about the religious significance of the New World and its inhabitants since the beginning of European exploration. Columbus believed that the Garden of Eden might have been located in South America. Catholic theologians debated whether the Native Americans possessed souls. For Protestants inspired by chiliasm and millenarianism, the Western Hemisphere held additional interest. Since the new continents were not mentioned in scripture, they seemed to be blank spots on the eschatological map. Yet students of prophecy could not believe that God would leave such a vast portion of the world out of the apocalyptic drama. Surely America (in the broadest sense) had to play some role.

One possibility came from William Twisse, an eminent theologian and the author of a preface to Joseph Mede's *Clavis Apocalyptica*. In a letter written in 1634, four years after John Winthrop and his fleet sailed from England, Twisse begged Mede to "let me know *what your opinion is* of our *English plantations in the New World*."[86] For his own part, Twisse suggested that the New World might be the location of the new Jerusalem described in Revelation.

Mede offered good wishes for the colonies, but he considered that the New World was more likely the kingdom of the devil than the new Jerusalem. Struggling to place the unknown country in the Book of Revelation, he argued that the Indians' forefathers had been planted there by Satan around the time of Christ. Alluding to enemies of the restored Israel mentioned in the prophecy of Ezekiel as well as Revelation, Mede wondered whether the natives might serve in the "Army of Gog and Magog."[87]

One might expect New England writers to protest against this dismal account of their venture. Yet Increase Mather endorsed Mede's denial that New England or the Americas were holy lands. In his *Dissertation Concerning the Future Conversion of the Jewish Nation*, he declared: *"Mr. Mede's* conjecture is ingenious, and may probably prove true."[88] For Mather, New England was a wilderness in which believers could prepare themselves for glory, but it was not God's country. Furthermore, its rival occupants were more likely the spawn of Satan than Lost Tribes.[89]

Some of Mather's contemporaries hoped that America might play a more positive role in the millennium. For example, the Salem minister Nicholas Noyes denied that "America in general & New-England in particular" would be excluded from the kingdom of God. Against Mede and Mather, Noyes contended that "notwithstanding the present bad circumstances of America, I know no reason to conclude this Continent shall not partake of the Goodness of God in the latter days; nor why the Sun of Righteousness may not go round the Earth, as the Sun in the Firmament doth go round Heaven."[90] At the end of days, America would enjoy a place in the sun.

Yet Noyes did not think that New England would be the seat of the millennial kingdom, either. Like Mede and Mather, he insisted that God's rule would be established in Jerusalem, which was to be repopulated by converted Jews. Indeed, Noyes based his hope for America on faith that God would fulfill that promise. "If God can do such things, may do such things, hath done such things already, and will do such things again for his Ancient People the Jews; and there be prophesies and promises, that God will do such things; not only, for the Jews, but for Christian places that are in ruines, over-run with sin & misery. Why should we not hope and pray for the accomplishment of them?"[91]

The judge and diarist Samuel Sewall saw closer connections between the old and the new Israel. In his 1697 *Phaenomena quaedam Apocalyptica*, Sewall "endeavoured to prove that *America's* Name is to be seen fairly Recorded in the Scriptures." In his opinion, the New World "stands fair for being made the seat of the Divine Metropolis."[92] Unlike more conventional restoration theorists, Sewall contended that there would be a new Jerusalem in the New World. The millennial kingdom would be based in North America—most likely, somewhere in Mexico.[93] Yet it would be inhabited by converted Jews, just as the prophets had promised. As Sewall put it: "This City of God is especially made up of Jews, and from thence it hath its Name."[94] For Sewall, a Gentile Jerusalem was a contradiction in terms.

Settlement of this new city of God would be easy, Sewall suggested, because the ten tribes were already in North America. Citing Menasseh, among other authorities, he claimed that the Lost Tribes had traveled there through Siberia, where their descendants had become apparently indigenous peoples. Rather than traveling east to the Holy Land, Sewall proposed, the Jews of Europe would travel *west*, joining their long-lost brethren in the new Jerusalem. He believed that they were already doing so, citing a tiny Jewish population in North America, including several families in New York and at least two Jews in Boston.[95]

Although it had prominent advocates, belief in Jewish restoration was never universal among New England Puritans. In the 1660s, church authorities were concerned that Increase Mather's comparatively restrained account of Israel's salvation was provocative and untimely.[96] Objections to Increase's account of Jewish restoration even came from within the Mather family. In his study *Figures and Types of the Old Testament*, Increase's brother Samuel contended that the prophets' descriptions of the future of Israel were actually references to the church.[97]

Cotton Mather initially echoed his father's arguments about the salvation of all Israel, but eventually concluded that the Jews had no further part to play in God's design.[98] Instead of a return to Jerusalem, Cotton Mather wrote of the "theopolis Americana"—the *American* city of God.[99] Confronted with this change of opinion, Sewall wrote unhappily that Cotton "seems to me to think that there is no general calling or conversion of the Jews, or that it is already past and gone."[100]

One explanation for Increase and Cotton Mather's diverging views on the relation between New England and old Israel was the shifting fortunes of the Puritans themselves. As New England's place in the British Empire stabilized, there was less reason to look forward to the end of days. In this sense, belief in Jewish restoration might have been a victim of the Puritans' success in transforming a wilderness into a home, if not exactly the Promised Land.

Theological developments also discouraged interest in the fate of the Jews. By the turn of the eighteenth century, the rigorous theology of election and covenant derived from Calvin seemed sterile and disheartening. New religious movements emphasizing experience over predestination were on the horizon. Their influence was disproportionate to their numbers, but the Puritans represented the past of American Christianity. Evangelicals committed to personal witness and less doctrinal approaches to scripture were the future.

Even so, many American Christians continued to hope for the salvation of *all* Israel. In the eighteenth century, they combined this expectation with a new understanding of how God wanted them to live. Puritans' exemplary status as a city upon a hill demanded extraordinary piety that would model a proper relationship with the Lord. For some of their descendants, not so much faith as liberty was the chief advantage that America could offer to the cause of Jewish return.

2 | On Eagles' Wings: Jewish Restoration and the American Republic

And Moses went up unto God, and the Lord called unto him out of the mountain, saying, Thus shalt thou say to the house of Jacob, and tell the children of Israel: Ye have seen what I did unto the Egyptians, and how I bare you on eagles' wings, and brought you unto myself. Now therefore, if ye obey my voice indeed; and keep my covenant, then ye shall be a peculiar treasure unto me above all people: for all the earth is mine.

—Exod. 19:3–5, King James Version

The Great Seal of the United States is not an obvious reflection of a relationship between America and the Jewish people. A depiction of a fierce eagle clutching arrows and an olive branch, it more obviously evokes ancient Rome, whose legions carried standards bearing a similar device. The motto *e pluribus unum* contributes to the neo-republican aura.[1] All in all, the Great Seal appears to be the product of a society in the grips of an obsession with classical antiquity.[2]

Yet classical sources were not the only frame of reference for the seal. The educated elite of the Revolutionary period and early republic were steeped in Roman history and the Latin language. But many Americans relied on the Bible as a repository of political models and rhetoric.[3] In a survey of documents from 1760 to 1805, political scientist Donald Lutz found that the Old Testament was the most quoted text.[4]

It should not be surprising, then, that the Great Seal had religious as well as civic republican resonances. Whether or not they knew much about ancient Rome, Americans were aware that the seal's central image was present in scripture.[5] At Mount Sinai, God describes the Israelites' deliverance from Egypt as a passage on "eagles' wings" (Exod. 19:4). He goes on to remind the Israelites of their covenant: so long as they were obedient to God, they would remain "my treasured possession out of all the peoples" (19:5). The eagle appears in the Book of Revelation, as well. In John's vision, it spirits away from persecution the mother of a child destined to rule nations (Rev. 12:14). The mother is traditionally identified with the church—an image that the Puritans used to represent their errand into the wilderness.

A biblical interpretation of the seal was not just an abstract possibility. It was explicitly asserted by patriotic clergy. Presbyterian minister David Austin reminded his Elizabeth, New Jersey, congregation that God's eagle "has taken her station on the broad seal of the United States."[6] For Austin, the seal was a reminder of Americans' dependence on the same God who led Israel through the wilderness to the Promised Land.

Historian Eran Shalev has documented the popularity of the "American Zion" trope in the revolutionary and early republican periods.[7] For many Americans, the emergence of the new nation was a replay of the history of biblical Israel on a grander scale. Nicholas Street, Austin's uncle, offers one example. According to Street, the United States was "acting over the part of the children of Israel."[8] Timothy Dwight, who later served as president of Yale, extended Street's comparison. His epic poem *The Conquest of Canäan* compared the liberation of America to Joshua's war for the Promised Land.[9] Some claimed that Americans were closer to God than Israel had ever been. According to the Massachusetts divine Abiel Abbot, Americans were "raised even above the people of ISRAEL in their best days."[10]

But appropriation of Israel's place in God's favor was not the only way of putting America into sacred history. While some writers identified Americans as the eagle's passengers, rescued by the Lord from oppression, others argued that the United States was the eagle, providing safe passage to the still-chosen Jews. The latter interpretation claimed a providential role for America but subordinated it to a different understanding of God's purpose. The prosperity and power that Americans might enjoy were not for their sake alone. They were a sacred trust held for the old Israel.

A vision of the United States as fated partner of the once and future chosen people had advocates among politicians as well as members of the clergy.

Among them was Elias Boudinot, a sometime parishioner of Austin's and a member of the committee of the Continental Congress that commissioned the Great Seal. According to Boudinot, the eagle reflected the fact that "America has been greatly favoured by God, in all her concerns, both civil and religious, and she has much to hope, . . . according as she shall attentively improve her relative situation among the nations of the earth, for the glory of God, and the protection of his people."[11] By "his people," Boudinot meant not Americans but the first bearers of the ark. "Who knows," he asked, "but God has raised up these United States in these latter days, for the very purpose of accomplishing his will in bringing his beloved people to their own land."[12]

The Millennium and National Purpose

Comparisons between the English-speaking inhabitants of North America and the people of Israel had been features of American culture since the beginning of British settlement. In New England, the story of the biblical Hebrews provided both a justification for undertaking the errand into the wilderness and a reason to hope for its favorable result. God led the first chosen people out of the desert and into Canaan, where they enjoyed peace and prosperity under a divinely appointed constitution. So might He lead the Puritan elect into their appointed plantation.

An analogy with Israel did not make New England or North America a substitute for the Promised Land of the Bible, however. Leading Puritans insisted that Jerusalem would be the capital of the millennial kingdom—and that it would be populated by religiously converted but nationally distinct Jews. For a group of divines that includes John Cotton and Increase Mather, the saints of New England were following the pattern of the people of Israel. But they did not supplant the Jews in God's favor.

These assumptions about the restoration of Israel remained intact in the thought of Jonathan Edwards. Called America's "greatest artist of the apocalypse" by historian Perry Miller, Edwards devoted attention to millenarian issues throughout his career.[13] In one of his most famous statements, dating from the height of the Great Awakening, Edwards even suggested: "'Tis not unlikely that this work of God's Spirit, that is so extraordinary and wonderful, is the dawning, or at least a prelude, of that glorious work of God, so often foretold in scripture, which in the progress and issue of it, shall renew the world of mankind. . . . And there are many things that make it probable that this work will begin in America."[14]

Edwards's remark has been interpreted as a claim that the millennial kingdom would be established in America. This is a serious misreading, according to theologians Gerald R. McDermott and Michael J. McClymond, who argue: "Neither New England nor America was a significant factor in Edwards's description of the millennium."[15] Edwards did identify America as a possible starting point for the glorious work of God. But he "almost always situated the focal point of the millennium in Canaan and described the millennium itself in international terms."[16]

For Edwards, David's citadel remained the true city on the hill. It would be from Jerusalem that "the truth should shine forth, and true religion spread into all parts of the world."[17] This could not occur until the original inhabitants returned. Edwards reasoned that "it is the more evident, that the Jews will return to their own land again, because they never have yet possessed one quarter of that land, which was so often promised them, from the Red Sea to the river Euphrates."[18] In his personal copy of the Bible, he wrote that the restoration of Israel would involve an "external state as a nation in their own land."[19]

Edwards's belief in the territorial restoration of Israel did not mean that he had much regard for Judaism. Like his predecessors, he assumed that Jews' return would be accompanied by conversion and repentance for their rejection of Christ. In 1747, British writer Samuel Collet published a *Treatise of the Future Restoration of the Jews and Israelites to Their Own Land*, in which he suggested that geographic return might precede conversion.[20] Edwards rejected this idea as "strange and unaccountable."[21] God was not finished with the Jewish people, but He had no more use for their outmoded religion.[22]

Edwards was more interested in the religious than the political significance of Jewish restoration. It was in the 1750s and 1760s, during the war between British and French forces in North America, that invocations of Israel by New England clergy acquired a distinct civic dimension. Biblical Israel was the prototype of a pious nation guided by God to victory. By emulating its politics, New England and British America as a whole might hope to secure divine aid in their struggles.[23]

The Lord Is a Man of War

The conflict known as the French and Indian War or the Seven Years' War was a key moment in the development of British colonists' identification with Israel. Sermons of the period compared the war to a crusade, with Catholic France standing in for the infidel enemy. Their rhetoric drew heavily on the Book of Revelation. According to historian Nathan Hatch: "In the years of the French wars the ministers' constant use of such highly charged images as 'the Man of Sin,' 'the North American Babylon,' 'the Mother of Harlots,' and 'the Romish Antichristian Power' expressed their sense of the cosmic significance of the conflict and showed that the traditional apocalyptic view of history retained great power."[24]

The influence of classic Calvinism had waned by the middle of the eighteenth century, but Americans continued to regard the Hebrews as the exemplary covenant people. Especially in New England, it was almost habitual to compare English-speaking Protestants to biblical Israel. In a sermon delivered in the presence of the governor and other dignitaries of Massachusetts, Samuel Dunbar preached:

> God often gives his people direction, as to their present duty and safety, by an uncommon coincidence of things in providence; so that whoso is wise, and observes them, may understand the loving-kindness of the Lord. . . . So God defended Jerusalem from the numerous army, and proud threatenings of the Assyrian monarch. So God saved England in former days from the formidable Armada of the Spanish, and the last year from the threatened, and perhaps really intended, invasion of the French: and, but a few years ago, he saved New-England from the powerful armament of their French enemies, who came into these American seas. The ancient famous cloud, the symbol of God's presence, served to Israel for protection, as well as direction. God's presence is to his people, a sun and a shield; a shield to defend them, as well as a sun to comfort and direct them.[25]

Dunbar's reference to the cloud that led the Israelites through the desert reasserts the typological parallel. As in the biblical exodus, God had helped the people of New England evade their enemies and find a way home. Once in that home, the Lord would defend them—provided that they held up their end of the bargain.

Dunbar did not suggest that this arrangement—unlike the seal designed several decades later—involved a republican form of government. His reference to the unsuccessful siege of Jerusalem honors the good king Hezekiah. Puritans had a conflicted relationship with a royal family they suspected of pro-Catholic inclinations. But the replacement of the Stuarts with a Protestant dynasty and the pressures of war against an indubitably Catholic power encouraged a more positive attitude toward the Crown.[26] According to Charles Chauncy, the verse from 2 Sam. 13:3—"The God of Israel said, the Rock of Israel spake to me; he that ruleth of Men must be just, ruling the Fear of God"—was "designed for the instruction and benefit of Solomon, David's son and appointed successor to the throne of Israel."[27] Chauncy went on to argue that this divine wisdom was exemplified in modern times by the British constitution.

The justification of rebellion through identification with the people of Israel became popular years later, during the crisis of the 1770s. It received a classic presentation in Thomas Paine's *Common Sense*, which includes a discussion of God's warning, delivered through the prophet Samuel, that the kings of Israel would inevitably become tyrants.[28] Paine's religious views were unorthodox, but Boston minister Samuel Cooper, whose congregation included John Adams, provided a more pious version of the same reasoning. Cooper declared: "The form of government established in the Hebrew nation by a charter from heaven, was that of a free republic, over which God himself, in peculiar favor to that people, was pleased to preside."[29]

In addition to a shift in its constitutional implications, the war of independence saw a nationalization of the analogy with biblical Israel. Previously focused on New England, membership in "Israel" was extended to all the colonies. For Cooper, Massachusetts corresponded to only one of the tribes into which God's people were divided. Historian Shalev shows how this trope was deployed as an argument for unity among the states. Like the Hebrews, whom Joshua brought together into the army that conquered Canaan, the American tribes were urged to establish a union under a righteous leader.[30] For Justin Martyr, Joshua's role as conqueror and distributor of the land made him a type of Christ. For American patriots, he was a forerunner of George Washington.

The idea that the destinies of Israel and America were analogous sometimes led to rhetorical obscurity. In a sermon of thanksgiving for peace with Great Britain in 1783, the chaplain to the Continental Congress, George Duffield, reviewed the sorrows and triumphs of the war. By describing the thirteen states as "chosen American tribes," he suggested that the United States had assumed Israel's status.[31] Just a few pages later, though, Duffield clarified that God's favor toward America did not involve any change in the original covenant. Echoing Edwards, Duffield contended that the process leading to the millennium might begin in America but would end in God's real country. In Duffield's words, "here shall the various ancient promises of rich and glorious grace begin their compleat divine fulfillment; and the light of divine revelation diffuse it's [*sic*] beneficent rays, till the gospel of Jesus have [*sic*] accomplished it's [*sic*] day, from east to west around our world. A day, whose evening shall not terminate in night; but introduce that joyful period, when the outcasts of Israel, and the dispersed of Judah, shall be restored; and with them, the fulness of the gentile world shall flow to the standard of redeeming love: And the nations of the earth, become the kingdom of our Lord and Saviour."[32] The independence of "our American Zion" was just one step toward the new Jerusalem in the original land of promise.

Ezra Stiles made a similar case in "The United States Elevated to Glory and Honor," a sermon delivered in the same year. According to Stiles, "the future prosperity and splendor of the United States" was a harbinger of the time when "the words of Moses, hitherto accomplished but in part, will be literally fulfilled; when this branch of the posterity of Abraham shall be nationally collected, and become a very distinguished and glorious people, under the great Messiah the Prince of Peace."[33] Even as he sketched a tantalizing picture of America as God's most favored nation, Stiles reminded his audience that America was not, strictly speaking, a new Zion. Instead, it was a refuge for true religion and righteous politics—the wilderness where the eagle had landed.

According to his biographer and son-in-law Abiel Holmes (grandfather of the Supreme Court justice Oliver Wendell Holmes, Jr.), Stiles calculated that the restoration of Israel would occur around 2370.[34] That gave the United States plenty of time to enjoy glory and honor without usurping God's relationship with the true Israel. Civic millenarian visions like Duffield's and Stiles's placed the United States in the main current of sacred history. Only if we ignore their references to the Jews, however, can they be understood as arguments that the Americans had become the chosen people.

The Millennium and the Age of Revolution

The prophetic books of the Old Testament and the Book of Revelation are filled with descriptions of the revolts of peoples, the depredations of tyrants, and the fall of kingdoms. It is not surprising that the occurrence of such phenomena in modern times have led students of prophecy to consider whether the events they observed pointed toward a greater purpose. The Age of Revolution in Europe inspired arguments that the world was entering the last stages of God's plan.

In 1788, the Philadelphia minister Elhanan Winchester reflected on the century that had elapsed since England's Glorious Revolution and asked: "[W]ho can tell what wonders are about to take place in the world?" His answer recapitulated the scenario developed by Brightman:

> The Turkish empire is to be weakened, and by some means the way will be opened, and the Jews will return to their own land. . . . Christ shall appear to all the inhabitants of the world, who shall tremble at his presence: the Jews shall look upon him whom they have pierced, knowing him by the sears of his wounds, they shall mourn bitterly, and this event shall issue in their long promised conversion. . . . [A]ll the twelve tribes being returned and settled anew in their own land, shall become the people of God; the Lord shall reign over them in his holy mount. . . . Then comes that glorious period of a thousand years, when peace, harmony, prosperity, love, and the knowledge and glory of God shall fill the earth as the waters cover the sea.[35]

Unlike Stiles, Winchester did not venture to set a date for these events. Nevertheless, he proposed that they might be accomplished within the next hundred years. In addition to American independence, Winchester noted among hopeful signs the revival of "the spirit of liberty" in France. He observed: "If the establishment of civil and religious liberty there should take its date from this year, it would be a great and glorious wonder of God, and would cause this season to be long remembered with pleasure."[36]

The outbreak of revolution the following year encouraged belief that God's plans were on fast-forward. As thrones were toppled and Europe moved toward general war, Americans became increasingly disposed to think that the end was coming. In her seminal study of millenarian themes in American political thought, historian Ruth Bloch found: "Between 1793 and 1796 the number of works on eschatology printed in America multiplied, averaging between five and ten times more per year than during the period 1765 to 1792."[37] When Americans' thoughts turned toward the end of days, they also became more interested in the fate of the Jews.

The career of David Austin exemplifies the boom in apocalyptic speculation. The scion of a prominent Connecticut family that included Nicholas Street, Austin was also a spiritual descendant of Jonathan Edwards: Edwards's son Jonathan, Jr. was the local minister in Austin's youth; and after graduating from Yale in 1779, Austin continued his education with Joseph Bellamy, one of Jonathan Edwards's most celebrated students.[38] After completing his studies, Austin was ordained as minister of the Presbyterian church in Elizabeth, New Jersey. In 1794, he published a volume combining his own sermons on millenarian issues with reprints of Edwards's *An Humble Attempt To Promote Explicit Agreement and Visible Union of God's People* and Bellamy's 1758 volume *The Millennium*.[39] Austin's contribution was titled "The Downfall of Mystical Babylon," a reference to the Book of Revelation.

According to Austin, the American Revolution had moved the apocalyptic timeline forward, but the struggle was not over. Across the Atlantic, God's hand could be discerned in the course of a second and more violent revolution. True, the revolutionary government in Paris represented an "infidel power, now waging war against all revealed religion."[40] Even so, the Jacobins were doing the Lord's work by suppressing the Catholic Church:

"What though you call the instruments of this successful attack upon Rome a lawless banditti—a race of infidels—men who profess to 'know no God but Liberty, and no gospel but their Constitution.'—What then! are they not, in the hand of God, as well chosen instruments for the execution of threatened vengeance upon mystical Babylon, as the heathenish kings of the east were, for the same design, upon the Babylon of the Chaldees?"[41]

By the "Babylon of the Chaldees," Austin meant the neo-Babylonian empire that sacked Jerusalem and took as hostages the aristocracy of Judah. The instrument of God's vengeance, in that case, was Cyrus of Persia, who defeated Babylon and restored the Israelites. For Austin, modern events were following the type or pattern set by the biblical Hebrews. It followed that God would again raise up a champion to do His work by destroying Babylon.

Because of its atheism, revolutionary France could not act as the modern Cyrus. That role was reserved for the United States, which Austin personified as the "man-child" born into safety by the eagle in the Book of Revelation. Austin explained: "Let them read the predictions—of heaven respecting the increase of his dominion—that he was to rule all nations with a rod of iron; that is, bring them into complete and absolute subjection; and that the young hero might be equal to this mighty conquest, he is supported by an omnipotent arm; he is caught up unto God and to his throne. Behold, then, this hero of America wielding the standard of civil and religious liberty over these United States!"[42]

Austin's statement could be read as a claim that the United States was the Christian nation par excellence, called to a new kind of world leadership. Yet the reference to Cyrus suggests a specific purpose for that leadership. The prophet Isaiah describes Cyrus as anointed by God to liberate Israel from the captivity of physical Babylon. If the parallel held, the American would play its part by restoring the Jews from the mystical Babylon. In this way, America could act as the man-child of liberty without assuming covenantal prerogatives that God had reserved for the people of Israel.

Austin hinted at this interpretation by concluding "The Downfall of Mystical Babylon" with a long quotation from Theodore Hinsdale, a fellow Yale graduate and a minister in Windsor, Connecticut. In "The Christian Religion Attested by the Spirit of Prophecy," Hinsdale argued that the survival of the Jews despite so much suffering proved that God was reserving them for a future task. He then looked forward to the conquest and rebuilding of Judaea and Jerusalem by a politically revived, albeit religiously converted, Jewish people. Austin reproduced Hinsdale's remark without comment or correction. Apparently, he regarded it as continuous with his vision of America's millennial destiny.[43]

Austin was certainly an eccentric and perhaps a madman. Following a dispute with his New Jersey congregation, he moved in 1797 to New Haven, where he began preparations for the restoration of the Jews, buying ships and warehouses to convey them and their goods to Palestine. These activities elicited bemused recollection decades later.[44] Despite his quirks, though, Austin's conviction that a special bond existed between the American republic and the seed of Abraham made an impression on more balanced minds. Among them was Elias Boudinot, a venerable patriot who attended Austin's church in Elizabeth and became a leader of an organization that welcomed Jews to America—as a haven from which they might one day be restored.

Elias Boudinot and the Appointed Refuge

Elias Boudinot is among the least familiar members of the founding generation. Born in Philadelphia to a family of Huguenot extraction, he served as member and president of the Continental Congress, commissioner of prisoners for Washington's army, member of the first two U.S. Congresses, director of the U.S. Mint, and president of the American Bible Society.[45] Although he worked primarily as an administrator, Boudinot was also a prolific author of theological-political reflections. He was motivated to take up the pen around 1790, when he determined that "the important events of that day . . . were an exact fulfillment of the predictions of the Sacred record."[46]

Among the confirmations of prophecy that Boudinot observed was a rising tide of religious skepticism. His first extended work aimed to arrest this development by demonstrating the salutary influence of Christianity on politics. Dubbed *The Age of Revelation*, it answered *The Age of Reason*, Paine's provocative critique of revealed religion.[47] In Boudinot's judgment, only a pious people could have won independence.[48] The decline of faith would therefore be "introductive of the dissolution of government and the bonds of civil society."[49] The fate of the French showed what happened when a nation rejected God. For inspiring this apostasy, Boudinot blamed "the famous Rousseau . . . champion of the enemies of Christ crucified."[50]

Boudinot's hatred of Paine and Rousseau did not mean that he rejected reason. The most prominent nonbiblical source in *The Age of Revelation* was John Locke, whose natural rights theory helped inspire the Declaration of Independence. For Locke, however, there was no contradiction between philosophy and prophecy. In his commentary on Saint Paul's epistles, which was also cited by Jonathan Edwards, he argued that "the jews shall be a flourishing nation again, professing christianity, in the land of promise, for that is to be re-instated again, in the promise made to Abraham, Isaac, and Jacob."[51] Boudinot agreed. In his opinion, the survival of the Jewish people when so many of their persecutors had been overthrown proved that history followed a divine plan.[52] The nature of that plan is the subject of Boudinot's book *The Second Advent*, begun in 1790 but mostly written in 1798.

Boudinot's central argument is that prophetic texts like Isa. 11:12, which promises that God will "assemble the outcasts of Israel and gather the dispersed of Judah from the four corners of the earth," cannot be understood as metaphors. Instead, they are literal descriptions of things to come. Boudinot supported this conclusion by quoting passages from Revelation that describe the glorified Jerusalem: "The reason is clearly given, for this wonderful change in the state and circumstances of God's people, so unlike what they are at present, scattered over the earth, with scarcely a spot to place their feet. . . . God having declared most expressly by his prophet, 'that he will create new heavens and a new earth, and that the former shall not be remembered or come into mind any more'; by which it is to be understood throughout the Scriptures, the political forms of government in the world, with the grandeur and lustre of their dominions, their political heights and glory."[53] The restoration of Israel, in other words, was not merely a spiritual transformation, but also a geo-political event.

To be sure, the Jews would not recover their state before they converted. The condition of their geographic and political reestablishment was a reconciliation with the Messiah they had once spurned. But Boudinot denied that Jewish conversion would involve a seamless merger with the Gentile church. God said that the people rescued on eagles' wings would be a "priestly kingdom and a holy nation" (Exod. 19:6). It followed that the Jews "are to be named priests of Jehovah—ministers of God shall be their title. They shall eat the riches of the nations, and in their glory they are to boast—Their seed shall be illustrious among the nations, and their offspring in the midst of the people.—All who see them shall acknowledge that they are the seed, which the Lord hath blessed."[54] Boudinot thus expected that the people of Israel would remain nationally distinct even after they adopted Christianity.

All this Boudinot concluded from the prophets' explicit statements. He found in their penumbras references to the United States.[55] On his account, "Jehovah will call from the East the Eagle . . . to bring to pass the design has formed and execute it."[56] Reasoning that North America might appear to be the East if one took Jerusalem as a point of orientation, Boudinot proposed that the winged executor of God's plan "may come from that far distant land."[57] More generally: "America has been greatly favoured by God, in all her concerns, both civil and religious, and she has much to hope, and much to fear, according as she shall attentively improve her relative situation among the nations of the earth, for the glory of God, and the protection of his people.—She has been raised up in the course of divine Providence, at a very important crisis, and for no very inconsiderable purposes. She stands on a pinnacle—She cannot act a trifling or undecided part."[58] Boudinot's description of America evokes the city upon a hill, but subordinated any role that America might play in the millennium to this one as an agent of Jewish redemption. America was a providential nation, but its mission lay outside itself.

America was suited for the task partly because it bore the imprint of biblical Israel more strongly than any other nation. Broadening the Puritan errand to include the whole country, Boudinot urged his readers to recall their own exodus story: "[T]he first settlers of this wilderness, were the sons and daughters of banishment, flight, and persecution. This desart [*sic*] proved an asylum for the Church of Christ, when the enemy came in as a flood; then she flew into the wilderness, as on the wings of an eagle."[59] Having been rescued by God's eagle, Americans were poised to offer the same service to the Jews—*if* they remained faithful to the Lord. As Boudinot put it, "Let not our unbelief, or other irreligious conduct, with a want of a lively, active faith in our Almighty Redeemer, become a stumbling block to these outcasts of Israel, wherever they may be. They will naturally look to the practice and example of those calling themselves Christians for encouragement. Who knows but God has raised up these United States, in these latter days, for the very purpose of accomplishing his will in bringing his beloved people to their own land."[60]

How could Americans fulfill their commission when they had contact with so few Jews—just a few thousand around the turn of the nineteenth century? Boudinot answered in a manner pioneered by John Eliot, Menasseh ben Israel, and Thomas Thorowgood: millions of Jews were already in America in the guise of Native Americans. Boudinot does not seem to have been familiar with the complete history of this idea. Instead, he relied on Austin's boyhood pastor Jonathan Edwards, Jr., who promoted the Lost Tribes theory in his study *Observations on the Language of the Muhhekaneew Indians*.[61] Whatever his authorities, Boudinot's argument for the Hebraic origin of the Native Americans is a blend of scriptural reasoning and ethnographic speculation. Based on his readings of 2 Kings and the apocryphal Book of Esdras (a Greek version of the Book of Ezra), Boudinot argued that members of the ten Lost Tribes had made their way to Scythia—central Asia—following their expulsion from Canaan by the Assyrians. Adopting nomadic habits, the Lost Tribes could then have wandered toward the Northeast, where they would eventually have encountered the Bering Strait. Crossing the strait would have led them into North America.[62]

Boudinot acknowledged this idea would be merely hypothetical if there were no modern evidence to link the American aborigines with ancient Israel. Drawing on philological work by Edwards, Jr., however, he claimed that there were cultural similarities between the Native Americans and the biblical Hebrews. Boudinot paid special attention to the ostensibly theocratic structure of Native American society, quoting Locke's argument in the *Letter Concerning Toleration* "that the commonwealth of the Jews, differed from all others, being an absolute theocracy." In Boudinot's opinion, "the Indians profess the same thing precisely. This is the exact form of their government."[63]

Boudinot's insistence on the devout character of the Native Americans/ Lost Tribes was part of his broader exhortation to national piety. In order to appeal successfully to a faithful people, he argued, Americans would have to remain so themselves. Boudinot was not recommending the establishment of a Christian theocracy, which he regarded as a contradiction in terms. But he contended that Americans had to acknowledge the centrality of faith to the fulfillment of their collective vocation.

With a proper understanding of the destination, Americans did not have to wait for divine intervention. Boudinot encouraged missions that would help Native Americans recall their past. If "wonderfully brought to the knowledge of their fellow men," he proposed, "they may be miraculously prepared for instruction, and stand ready, at the appointed time . . . to be restored to the land and country of their fathers, and to Mount Zion the city of David, their great king and head, and this in direct, positive and literal fulfillment of the numerous promises of the God of Abraham, Isaac and Jacob, their pious progenitors and founders, near four thousand years ago."[64] Despite his fascination with the Lost Tribes, Boudinot did not neglect the Jews of Europe. He encouraged them to emigrate to America, where, "[b]y this glorious and important revolution, an asylum for all the oppressed of the earth, of every nation, and every party, was not only secured in this free and fertile region, but the principles of rational liberty were established and made known to the world, and the inestimable fact (till now scarcely credited) of a people governing themselves, strictly speaking, verified by actual experiment."[65]

Boudinot even hinted that America might offer practical assistance in restoring the Jews to their rightful home. Invoking the eagle, he speculated that "the land spreading wide the shadow of her wings, may be some maritime nation, the sails of whose ships, and the protection given by them, are here prophesied of."[66] By coincidence, it happened that Americans "are a maritime people—a nation of seafaring men. Our trade and commerce have greatly encreased for years past . . ." Boudinot concluded that "We may, under God, be called to act a great part in this wonderful and interesting drama."[67]

Boudinot devoted more pages to these arguments than most other writers but he was not alone in his basic sentiments. In the early republic, many Americans sought a purpose for their country in prophecies about the people and Land of Israel. America, they thought, was too important to be left out of God's plan. But its significance was contingent on the fulfilment of His ongoing covenant with the Jews.

From Boudinot to the Book of Mormon

Drawing on existing discourses of restorationism and republicanism, Boudinot wove together strands that would have been familiar to many readers. In 1797, the *Theological Magazine* reported as widely accepted the belief "that in the millennium the Jews will literally be gathered from their present dispersion, be re-settled in Palestine, and kept a distinct nation as they formerly were."[68] The *Theological Magazine* was based in New York, but the fascination with Israel that it described still retained something of a New England flavor. Harriet Beecher Stowe, the author of *Uncle Tom's Cabin*, described New Englanders of the period as "Hebraistic in their form; they spoke of Zion and Jerusalem, of the God of Israel, the God of Jacob, as much as if my grandfather had been a veritable Jew."[69]

Theories of Jewish restoration acquired an increasingly national and ecumenical tinge as New England exported population and culture to other regions.[70] In 1814, Albany minister John McDonald urged the recruitment of missionaries not only from "New-England, cradle and nurse of American churches," but from all over the country, to enlighten the Jews about their future glory.[71] According to McDonald, this hopeful purpose distinguished the American eagle from other national insignia. The Roman and Persian armies also carried eagles into battle. "But their eagles represented that winged bird in hostile attitude. . . . The American eagle, without one unfriendly feature, extends her wings for the protection of her own nation, and offers a shelter for the persecuted of all the nations of the earth."[72]

As McDonald hoped, attempts to synthesize biblical prophecy, the Puritan origin myth, and American national purpose circulated beyond his own congregation. In 1823, the Revolutionary War veteran and Poultney, Vermont, minister Ethan Smith published *A View of the Hebrews*, a study of prophecies relating to Jewish restoration. Citing Boudinot and McDonald, among other authorities, Smith concluded that "the prophetic writings do clearly decide, that both Israel and the Jews shall, in the last days, before the

Millennium, be literally restored to their own land of Palestine; and be converted to the Christian faith."[73] There was no obvious place for America in
this sequence of events, but Smith judged that "[i]t would be strange if so
great a section of Christendom as our United States, could claim no appropriate address in the prophetic writings."[74] The image of the eagle was again
crucial. According to Smith,

> those two great wings shall prove but an emblem of a great nation then
> on that continent; far sequestered from the seat of [the] antichrist, and
> of tyranny and blood; and whose asylum for equal rights, liberty, and
> religion, shall be well represented by such a national coat of arms,—the
> protecting wings of a great Eagle; which nation in yonder setting of the
> sun, (when in the last days, judgments shall be thundering through
> the nations of the eastern continent,) shall be found a realm of peaceful
> protection to all, who fly from the abodes of despotism to its peaceful
> retreat; even as an eagle protects her nest from all harm. Yea, a land
> that, when all other lands shall be found to have trampled on the Jews,
> shall be found to have protecting wings for them; free from such cru-
> elty, and ready to aid them.[75]

More explicitly than his predecessors, Smith tied America's providential task
to religious liberty. Only a land of "freedom and religion" could provide
the necessary refuge for the Jews.[76] But toleration was strategic: the task of
American churches was to use their freedom to encourage conversions. Smith
thus urged his readers: "By prayer, contributions, and your influence, be prepared to aid every attempt for the conversion of the Jews and Israel; and God
will be his own interpreter, and will make the duty plain."[77] Smith hoped to
start by evangelizing the descendants of the Lost Tribes.

Smith might be little more than a curiosity if not for his association with
a more influential figure. A line can be drawn from *The View of the Hebrews*
to one of the most extraordinary documents of American culture: the Book
of Mormon. The existence of the Book of Mormon became known to Joseph
Smith of Manchester, New York, on September 21, 1823. While praying in
the woods, he was visited by an angel who informed him of the existence of
golden plates, inscribed with a long-forgotten language. Smith attempted to

exhume the plates the following day, but the angel prevented him from doing so on that day and for four more years. On September 2, 1827, Smith was finally allowed to remove the plates and instructed to translate them. He accomplished the task with the assistance of a pair of mystical eyeglasses that the angel told him to find near his home. Over the next few years, Smith undertook the work with the help of scribes who committed his oral translation to paper. After his first assistant, Martin Harris, absconded with the manuscript, Smith hired a local schoolteacher named Oliver Cowdery. Cowdery had been brought up in Vermont, where his family lived for a time in Poultney. The Congregational minister there was none other than Ethan Smith.[78]

Historian Richard Bushman points out that Lost Tribes theories were so widespread that there is little in the Book of Mormon that could have been found only in the work of Ethan Smith.[79] As Smith admitted, *The View of the Hebrews* compiled evidence for a common belief. What is clear is that the Book of Mormon surfaced in a society and a period in which claims about Jewish restoration and the biblical lineage of Native Americans were already in wide circulation. Setting aside the circumstances of its authorship, that may help explain why many Americans found the narrative presented in the Book of Mormon to be appealing.

But the version of Jewish restoration that the Book of Mormon presents was not entirely familiar. Beginning immediately before the sack of Jerusalem by the Babylonians, the narrative describes a company of Israelites who flee the kingdom of Judah for a new land of promise in North America. There they divide into two groups, the Nephites and Lamanites, and spend centuries at war. This war is interrupted by the appearance of Christ, who reminds them that they are Lost Tribes of Israel; they establish peace.

The truce does not hold. Eventually, the Nephites are wiped out, leaving the Lamanites in possession of the continent. The victorious Lamanites then forget Christ's reminder of their origin and sink into barbarism. Their descendants become Native Americans, whose habits are but a faint echo of their ancestors'. It is a stark contrast to Boudinot's belief that the Native Americans were upstanding Hebrews in all but name.

Despite the degraded condition in which it presents the descendants of the Lost Tribes, the Book of Mormon points toward their ultimate redemption. During his visit to America, Christ reiterates the promises of Isaiah and Ezekiel: "I would gather them together in mine own due time, that I would give unto them again the land of their fathers for their inheritance, which is the land of Jerusalem, which is the Promised Land unto them forever." Restoration will be followed by conversion: "And it shall pass when the time cometh, when the fulness of my gospel shall be preached unto them; and they shall believe in me, that I am Jesus Christ, the Son of God, and shall pray unto the Father in my name."[80]

The Book of Mormon's description of Christ's visit to the New World was a novelty in itself. Another distinctive feature of Joseph Smith's teaching was the claim that the restoration of the old Israel would be preceded by the construction of a new Jerusalem in America.[81] In a revelation received in September 1832, Smith informed his followers that the new Jerusalem "shall be built, beginning at the temple lot, which is appointed by the finger of the Lord, in the western boundaries of the State of Missouri, and dedicated by the hand of Joseph Smith . . . and others with whom the Lord was well pleased."[82] As the Articles of Faith of the Church of Jesus Christ of Latter-Day Saints puts it: "We believe in the literal gathering of Israel and in the restoration of the Ten Tribes; that Zion with be built upon this continent; that Christ will reign personally upon the earth; and, that the earth will be renewed and receive its paradisiacal glory."[83]

Smith's promise of a literal American Zion was not unprecedented. More than a century earlier, Samuel Sewall had proposed that the new Jerusalem would be built in the Western Hemisphere. The difference was that Joseph Smith did not claim that the construction of the millennial kingdom in Missouri replaced or excluded the restoration of the Jews to Palestine. Instead, he suggested that there would be *two* Zions, one in America and another in the Holy Land. Smith's apostle Orson Pratt attempted to clarify the matter in a pamphlet response to a puzzled Mormon. Without denying the location of the new Jerusalem in Missouri, Pratt explained that the American Zion would supplement the old. "Because Zion, in ancient times existed at Jerusalem," Pratt wrote, "many have supposed that the Zion of the last days, so frequently the subject of prophecy, will also exist at Jerusalem. But when we compare the events which are to transpire at Jerusalem, with those which will take place in Zion, we are constrained to believe them to be two different places and cities, separated from each other, and inhabited by people in circumstances quite different from each other."[84]

This doctrine of a double Israel demanded revision of the timeline developed by seventeenth-century millenarians. In the new order of events, the American elect and the converted descendants of the Lamanites first gather in North America to build a holy city. At a later point, the Jews assemble in Jerusalem, reestablishing sovereignty there. This Jewish community or state attracts the enmity of surrounding nations, leading to a disastrous war. At the last moment, Christ returns in person, defeating the enemies and converting the penitent Jews, whose numbers are augmented by the return of their long lost brethren. Pratt explained that when the "ten tribes are redeemed from their afflictions before the Jews, consequently they first come to Zion among the redeemed saints, and partake with them in all the glory of Zion, until the Jews and Jerusalem shall also be redeemed, when they shall return to Jerusalem, and receive their inheritance in the land of Palestine, according to the divisions of that land in Ezekiel's prophecy, and become one nation with the Jews."[85]

Following the salvation of all Israel, the American Zion and Hebrew Jerusalem coexist. According to Pratt: "Both Zion and Jerusalem will remain on the earth during the Millennial reign of Christ; both will be preserved when the present heaven and earth pass away; both will come down out of heaven upon the new earth; and both will have a place upon the new earth for ever and ever—the eternal abode of the righteous."[86] For Pratt, America was not merely a contributor to the restoration of the Jews. It was an equal partner in the story of redemption.

Jewish Restoration and American Destiny

The Mormon account of the millennium offers an ingenious resolution of the tension between conceptions of America as the new Israel and expectations of Jewish restoration. Sidestepping the vexed question of whether American Christians were successors to the biblical Hebrews, it suggested that there were actually two Israels, both necessary to the fulfillment of God's plan. The righteous would be at home in the American Zion and the old Jerusalem.

This reassessment of the connection between the new and the old Israel had long been regarded as a weird innovation. But it involves only slight modification of claims that were less controversial. Consider again the words of George Duffield, who argued that in the United States "shall the various ancient promises of rich and glorious grace *begin* their compleat divine fulfillment; and the light of divine revelation diffuse it's [*sic*] beneficent rays, till the gospel of Jesus have accomplished it's [*sic*] day, from east to west around our world. A day, whose evening shall not terminate in night, but *introduce that joyful period, when the outcasts of Israel, and the dispersed of Judah, shall be restored*; and with them, the fullness of the gentile world shall flow to the standard of redeeming love: And the nations of the earth, become the kingdom of our Lord and Saviour."[87] Like Jonathan Edwards, Duffield proposed that the work of redemption was beginning in America but never claimed that it would end there. While God selected the New World for settlement by a purified church, the flight of the eagle was not one-way. After depositing the church in America, it might depart for a second journey to bear Israel home. God's finger pointed from the West back to the East, retracing the journey of the Puritan fathers.

In his novel *White-Jacket*, Herman Melville famously claimed: "We Americans are the peculiar, chosen people—the Israel of our time; we bear the ark of the liberties of the world."[88] The intricacy of the biblical tropes of chosenness and exile described in this part and chapter makes Melville's language more ambiguous than is usually recognized. Rather than indicating that Americans are unconditionally chosen, the image might depict them as engaged in a kind of historical torch race in which the divine flame that sheds light onto the nations is passed from hand to hand over the centuries. Such a race would not be complete until the ark and the covenant that it represented were restored to the Israel of all time and returned to their rightful place.

PART II
American Cyrus

On Thursday, March 5, 1891, William Eugene Blackstone arrived at the White House to do the Lord's work. With his sparse hair and large ears, Blackstone may have suffered from the chill that lingered over Washington. But he had reason to be optimistic about the appointment before him. Accompanied by Secretary of State James G. Blaine, Blackstone was escorted to his meeting with President Benjamin Harrison. After exchanging the appropriate courtesies, Blackstone presented Harrison with a petition that he had drafted and circulated over the previous months. It asked the president to use his influence to realize goals nearly two millennia in the making: the repopulation of the Holy Land by Jews and the reestablishment of their sovereignty there. The petition, known as the Blackstone Memorial, began by observing that the Jews of Eastern Europe, particularly Russia, were subject to grievous persecution. In addition to a wave of pogroms, Russian Jews suffered from the so-called May Laws of 1882, which restricted their rights of residence and their ability to transact business.[1] Conceding that Russia could not be compelled to tolerate Jews, Blackstone concluded that, "like the Sephardim of Spain, these Ashkenazim must emigrate."[2]

Where could millions of refugees go? According to Blackstone, Western Europe had no room for them, while America was too distant to offer refuge. The biblical homeland presented the ideal solution: "Why shall not the powers which under the treaty of Berlin, in 1878, gave Bulgaria to the Bulgarians and Servia to the Servians [sic] now give Palestine back to the Jews? These provinces, as well as Roumania, Montenegro, and Greece, were wrested from the Turks and given to their natural owners. Does not Palestine as rightfully belong to the Jews?"[3] Blackstone's references to Bulgaria and Serbia reflected the growing influence of nationalism in the late nineteenth century. Throughout Europe, colonized and dispersed nations were staking claims to their own states. It was paradoxical, Blackstone suggested, that the great powers supported the national ambitions of Balkan peoples against the Ottoman Empire but showed little interest in doing the same for the Jews.

In addition to asserting their right to the land, Blackstone argued that the Jews could pay for the satisfaction of that right. Russia's Jews were poor, but international Jewry was rich. The romance of the cause would lead to an outpouring of generosity. As the petition described it: "If they could have autonomy in government the Jews of the world would rally to transport and establish their suffering brethren in their time-honored habitation. For over seventeen centuries they have patiently waited for such a privileged opportunity."[4]

The petition's arguments were political and economic, but Blackstone's motives were religious. In his best-selling tract *Jesus Is Coming*, Blackstone argued that the restoration of the Jews to Palestine was part of a series of extraordinary events that would culminate with the end of days. First, the Jews would begin to go home. Their return to the Promised Land would be followed by the Rapture of faithful Christians, leaving the Antichrist to wreak havoc on an unsuspecting world. In the midst of the climactic battle of Armageddon, Christ himself would return to lead the forces of God to victory. The whole process would conclude with the establishment of a divine kingdom centered in Jerusalem.[5]

Blackstone considered that meteorological developments offered evidence that God was preparing the Holy Land for this outcome. Drawing on his observations as a pilgrim a few years earlier, he claimed that the "rains are increasing, and there are many evidences that the land is recovering its ancient fertility."[6] Perhaps because he paid so much attention to the weather and the soil, Blackstone hardly noticed that the land was already inhabited. According to him, Palestine under Ottoman rule represented an "astonishing anomaly—a land without a people for a people without a land!"[7] Although the controversial phrase is generally attributed to the British

Christian Zionist Lord Shaftesbury, this may be its first use in print by an American.[8]

Blackstone knew that his eschatological beliefs were not universally accepted. To demonstrate the broad appeal of his proposed solution to the Jewish problem, he appended to the memorial the names of 413 "representative" Americans who endorsed his conclusions.[9] The signatories included Chief Justice of the Supreme Court Melville Fuller; Speaker of the House Thomas Reed; Representative Robert R. Hitt, chairman of the House Committee on Foreign Relations; congressman and future president William McKinley; business tycoons J. P. Morgan, John D. Rockefeller, and Cyrus McCormick; assorted Protestant and Jewish clergymen; and the editors of ninety-three major newspapers.

Blackstone was able to attract such impressive endorsements because the main tropes of his argument were already embedded in American thought. It was not only believers in the imminent, personal return of Christ who expected the territorial and political restoration of the Jews. American Christians of a variety of denominational and theological orientations were convinced that the Jews were destined to go home—and that the United States could help them do so.

Despite the prominence of its signatories, the White House did not pursue Blackstone's plan. In the annual message he sent to Congress in December 1891, President Harrison protested against "the harsh measures now being enforced against the Hebrews in Russia" but did not make any reference to Palestine.[10] Nor did the president welcome Jews to the United States. Although Harrison acknowledged that Jews had prospered in America, he maintained that "the sudden transfer of such a multitude under conditions that tend to strip them of their small accumulations and to depress their energies and courage is neither good for them nor for us."[11]

One reason that Blackstone's efforts met little immediate success was the opposition of the diplomatic establishment. In his response to the memorial, the U.S. consul in Jerusalem described Blackstone's proposal as "one of the wildest schemes ever brought before the public."[12] In Selah Merrill's judgement, "[t]he Jew needs to learn that his place in the world will be determined by what he can do for himself, and not so much by what Abraham did for himself four thousand years ago."[13] Although he was trained as a Congregational minister and had taught Hebrew at a theological seminary, Merrill believed that it would be folly to base America's foreign policy on biblical covenant.[14]

American Jews also criticized the petition. While they shared Blackstone's concern for Jews in Russia, many Jewish leaders rejected the suggestion that they were "mere sojourners in the various nations" where they currently lived.[15] Orthodox Jews mostly believed that only the Messiah could redeem the land and people of Israel. Adherents of the Reform movement, on the other hand, were attracted to the idea that America was the modern Zion.[16]

What Blackstone described as a "privileged opportunity" looks more like a failed encounter, then.[17] But he considered himself vindicated when Theodor Herzl convened the first Zionist Congress in Switzerland in 1897. Less than a decade after Blackstone presented the memorial, it appeared that the prophecies were nearing completion. Blackstone spent much of the next twenty-five years promoting that goal by means of preaching, writing, and lobbying activities. For these services, Louis Brandeis, America's most prominent Jewish public figure and the figurehead of its Zionist movement, credited him as the real "father of Zionism."[18]

Whether or not this description is accurate, Blackstone's emphasis on politics distinguishes his Christian Zionism from Puritan restorationism or the patriotic millenarianism of the early republic. While they hoped fervently for the return of Israel to its land, advocates of these views had little interest in practical measures to bring it about. For Blackstone, by contrast, Jewish restoration was a diplomatic and logistical problem that could be resolved by acts of state. While continuing to trust in God, he argued that the Lord works through men. The Bible identified a precursor for the role that Blackstone urged the United States to assume. In his cover letter to President Harrison, Blackstone urged him to become the successor to the Jews' ancient liberator, Cyrus of Persia.[19]

Blackstone slipped into obscurity after his death in 1935. The State of Israel recognized him in 1956, when a stand of trees in the Jerusalem National Forest was dedicated to his memory.[20] But the only physical monuments to his life and work in the United States are a grave in Glendale, California and a residence hall at Biola University, a Christian school near Los Angeles, where Blackstone served as dean.[21] Yet Blackstone's dream of American intercession in the Middle East on behalf of the Jewish people did not disappear. Soon after leaving office in 1952, Harry Truman was introduced to an audience at the Jewish Theological Seminary as the man who helped create the State of Israel. The former president objected: "What do you mean, 'helped create'? I am Cyrus!"[22]

3 Gather Yourselves Together: From Restorationism to Zionism

> Gather yourselves together, yea, gather together, O nation that
> hath no shame; before the decree bring forth, before the day
> pass as the chaff, before the fierce anger of the Lord come
> upon you, before the day of the Lord's anger come upon you.
> —Zeph. 2:1–2, Revised Version

Before the nineteenth century, few Americans regarded the restoration of the Jews as a political project. It might be the object of hope and prayer, but was unlikely to be achieved without divine intervention. Reflecting on the phrase "all Israel shall be saved" in Romans 11, Increase Mather noted that Saint Paul was converted by a vision that he received while on the road to Damascus. Perhaps modern Jews would enjoy a similar experience *en masse*.[1]

The assumption that conversion would precede territorial restoration was opened for revision by the turmoil that followed the French Revolution. With nations on the march throughout the world—including clashes between French and British forces in the Holy Land itself—it seemed possible that God might attend to geographical and political issues before addressing spiritual ones. Responding to the volatile international circumstances, British prophecy writers including James Bicheno, George Stanley Faber, and Edward Bickersteth modified the traditional timeline, proposing that the Jews' recovery of their land and state would come first, with conversion occurring at a later point.[2] According to Bicheno: "The gathering of the dispersed Jews, preparatory to their conversion, is their political resurrection."[3]

The priority of "political resurrection" did not mean that Jewish conversion was unnecessary. Most Christian writers agreed that the final reconciliation between Israel and God required a collective turn to Christ. Unlike miraculous conversion on the Pauline model, though, the new understanding of Israel's destiny shifted the emphasis from divine intervention to human activity. As one American advocate for Jewish return put it, "God accomplishes his great purposes through the agency of nations, and of individuals in their political capacity."[4] This assumption became the basis for the emergence of Christian Zionism.

Revival and Restoration

Americans' interest in Jewish restoration was encouraged by the religious revival that swept the United States in the first half of the nineteenth century. Inspired by evangelists such as Charles Finney, countless Americans examined their consciences and affirmed their faith in Christ. Recalling the previous century's revival led by figures including Jonathan Edwards, the movement has been dubbed the Second Great Awakening. It was among the definitive events of American history before the Civil War.[5]

Although it shared an emphasis on personal spiritual renewal with its predecessor, the Second Great Awakening was distinguished by a more optimistic evaluation of human agency. According to historian Daniel Walker Howe, "Edwards had regarded religious revivals as ultimately mysterious, the action of divine grace. By contrast Finney boldly proclaimed, 'A revival of religion is not a miracle' but a human work, a 'result of the right use of the constituted means.'"[6] For Edwards, God's will was irresistibly transformative. For nineteenth-century evangelists, it was realized through intentional action by pious men and women.

Differing assessments of the connection between human activity and God's plans extended to the future of the Jews. Theologians in the Puritan tradition had long affirmed that Jewish restoration was inevitable. On the whole, though, they assumed that the salvation of "all Israel" would occur at a stroke and in miraculous fashion. In Edwards's opinion, the main thing that American Christians could do to bring that about was to pray for God to turn Jewish hearts to Jesus.

This relatively hands-off attitude began to change in the nineteenth century. Encouraged by prophecy interpretations developing in Britain and the growth of Jewish communities in the United States, more Americans concluded that restoration was a goal toward which they could make practical contributions. By 1820, societies had been established for developing a proactive relationship between Christians and Jews. The Female Society of Boston and Vicinity for Promoting Christianity Among the Jews was led by pioneering historian of religion Hannah Adams, whose works devoted extensive attention to chiliastic and millenarian themes.[7] The New York–based American Society for Meliorating the Condition of the Jews (ASMCJ) recruited prominent sponsors, including John Quincy Adams, the presidents of Yale and Princeton, and the statesman and prophecy writer Elias Boudinot, who served as its first president.[8]

As their names indicate, the Female Society of Boston and the ASMCJ had missionary intentions. Their efforts to convert the sons of Abraham, Isaac, and Jacob were modeled on the London Society for Promoting Christianity Amongst the Jews, better known as the London Jews' Society, whose leaders included the wealthy laymen Thomas Baring, Henry Drummond, and Lewis Way. By means of their financial contributions and social influence, the status of Jews became the major issue in British religious debates in the 1820s.[9]

Yet the patrons of these societies did not regard Jewish conversion as an end in itself. Desirable though it might be, the salvation of individual Jews was understood as a contribution to a process that would culminate in national restoration to the Promised Land. In his inaugural address to the ASMCJ, Boudinot explained: "We Christians are assured, by unerring truth . . . that in all these severe and unheard of sufferings of this unfortunate nation, that they will see their error; they will repent, and turn unto the Lord their God: that he will have mercy upon them, and restore them to their ancient city, and set them chief among the nations of the earth."[10] Conversion was essential, but in Boudinot's understanding, the ASMCJ's goal was also to help the people of Israel return physically to God's country.

British writers assumed that their own government, with vast resources at its disposal, would provide logistical support for Jewish restoration. Reflecting on the image of the eagle in Isaiah, Faber argued that Britain was the "mighty maritime nation of faithful worshippers" to which the prophet alluded.[11] The Royal Navy, after all, was the most powerful in the world.

Boudinot endorsed Faber's practical reading of the prophecy but disputed his identification of the protecting eagle. Britain had diplomatic influence and military power. Yet America possessed the political virtue that the Jews would need to learn in order to make proper use of their home. Merely transporting Jews to Palestine would not be enough to recover their national preeminence. Because they would also need experience in self-government, he proposed that Jewish immigrants be welcomed to the United States, where they could be trained in the arts of citizenship.

Boudinot's hope that America would play a leading role in the restoration of the Jews may seem quixotic. But it reflected contemporary thinking about a different problem: slavery. In 1817, the American Colonization Society (ACS) was founded with the goal of returning free blacks to Africa. As with the Jews, the idea was that an abused race could be uplifted during its American sojourn and subsequently returned to its natural home. Boudinot was connected to the ACS through his son-in-law Robert Finley, who enjoyed Boudinot's financial and political patronage.[12] In these circles, there was nothing strange about the idea that America should promote the social improvement and geographic repatriation of a far-flung and, as it was believed, degraded, people.[13]

Like most previous restoration theorists, Boudinot believed that the Jews would be converted *before* they returned to Palestine. Indeed, this was the basis of his approval of Jewish immigration to the United States. The ASMCJ's star missionary, the Jewish convert to Christianity Joseph Samuel C. F. Frey, suggested a different theory. Frey acknowledged that a few Jews might convert in Britain or America—an outcome for which he worked at the London Jews' Society and New York's Free Presbyterian Church.[14] Finding little success, however, he concluded that the majority of the world's Jews would return to Palestine *before* they accepted Christ. Reviewing the prophecies, Frey affirmed "the future restoration of my nation to the literal land of Canaan; that they will rebuild the city Jerusalem; that they will afterward be besieged by many nations, who shall be destroyed by God himself: and *in that day* Judah and Israel shall be converted unto God."[15] For Frey, land and political autonomy were preconditions rather than consequences of salvation.

Jewish converts to Christianity—Hebrew Christians, as they were known in the nineteenth century—have historically enjoyed disproportionate attention in Christian Zionist thought. Despite their small numbers, they were seen as living proof of the leading role that God had in store for their people. The habit of deferring to these harbingers of the millennial church persisted into more recent times. After World War II, Jewish converts such as Charles L. Feinberg were leaders in promoting Christian Zionist ideas to American audiences.

Yet Jews have not always had to convert in order to cultivate Christian support for the restoration of Israel. While Christian Zionists counted Orthodox Jews as natural allies, they more often found collaborators among relatively secular Jews who found it easier to ignore theological differences that separated them from Christians. The efforts of Boudinot's and Frey's contemporary and sometime critic Mordecai Manuel Noah are an early example of this somewhat improbable alliance.

American Ararat

Mordecai Manuel Noah is among the most colorful figures in American political history. Born in 1785 in Philadelphia, he worked as a diplomat, journalist, dramatist, and party operative in a period stretching from the James Madison administration to the beginning of the crisis that tore apart the Union. Something of a huckster, Noah talked himself into a position as U.S. consul in Tunis on the grounds that a Jew would find it easier to conduct diplomacy with a Muslim power. When he was fired, he blamed anti-Semitism. Actually, Noah botched negotiations for the return of American hostages and was suspected of financial improprieties.[16]

After returning from North Africa, Noah began a campaign for the restoration of the Jewish people to the Promised Land. Aware of the London Jews' Society as well as proposals for African repatriation, Noah managed to combine sincere reverence for America with an insistence that Jews' residence there was only temporary.[17] In an 1818 address delivered at the consecration of Synagogue Shearith Israel in New York City, Noah asserted: "Until the Jews can recover their ancient rights and dominions, and take their rank among the governments of the earth, this is their chosen country; here they can rest with the persecuted from every clime, secure in person and property, protected from tyranny and oppression, and participating of equal rights and immunities."[18] The qualifier "until" was crucial. While Noah did not venture to set a date for the return to Jerusalem, he reassured the Jews of New York: "God will never break his covenant with his people Israel. . . . Never were prospects for the restoration of the Jewish nation to their ancient rights and dominion more brilliant than they are at present."[19]

Noah knew that many Christians shared similar hopes. In his address to Shearith Israel, he praised the "numerous bible societies established in this country, . . . doing good to Jews and christians [*sic*], by teaching each other the benefits and blessings of toleration, and keeping constantly in view our common origin."[20] Yet Noah's approval could be only partial because he believed that these Christians were pursuing the wrong goal. Instead of trying to convert Jews in America, Noah argued, the Bible societies and missionaries should help them achieve their country in Palestine.

Noah's delicate relationship with Christian missionaries played a role in the formation of the ASMCJ. Under the laws of the time, the charter of the society required approval by the state legislature. Noah happened to be in Albany when the matter came up for debate in 1820. Apparently due to his informal lobbying, the legislature insisted that the society change its name, dropping a proposal that it be called the Society for Evangelizing the Jews. In order to secure approval for its existence, the ASMCJ had to express concern for Jews' welfare in this world as well as their fate in the next.[21]

This issue was not just semantic. The founders of the ASMCJ saw Jews' dispersion as punishment for their rejection of Christ. This punishment was not expected to be permanent, since they would eventually be rescued by a loving God. But the missionaries' premise was that Jews had much to atone for. Noah rejected this doctrine as humiliating and counterproductive. Rather than a matter of divine grace, he proposed that Jewish possession of the Promised Land was a question of "just and unalienable rights."[22] These rights had been trampled by foreign conquerors. To restore Palestine to the people of Israel was merely to recover what had been stolen from them.

The echoes of the Declaration of Independence in Noah's rhetoric were not a coincidence. Inverting the idea that the United States was reliving a sacred history initiated by the biblical Hebrews, Noah suggested that the people of Israel could imitate American history by asserting its own right to self-government and assuming a separate and equal station among the powers of the earth. This was, needless to say, a long-term project. Until it achieved success, America could live up to its own principles by practicing religious toleration. For the likes of Boudinot, John McDonald, and Ethan Smith, freedom of religion was something of a lure designed to draw Jews into encounters with the Gospel. For Noah, it was proof of America's superiority to the tyrannies condemned by the Bible and the Declaration alike.

Jefferson himself indicated approval for Noah's Americanization of the Jewish story. In response to a copy of the *Discourse* that Noah sent to him, he wrote: "Your sect, by its sufferings, has furnished a remarkable proof of the universal spirit of religious intolerance. . . . Our laws have applied the only antidote to this vice, protecting our religions, as they do our civil rights, by putting all on an equal footing."[23] John Adams went further. In response to Noah's address, the ex-president wrote: "I could find it in my heart to wish that you had been at the head of a hundred thousand Israelites . . . & marching with them into Judea & making a conquest of that country & restoring your nation to the dominion of it. For I really wish the Jews again in Judea an independent nation."[24] Although increasingly heterodox in his old age, Adams had been reared in a New England still in the grips of fascination with Israel. In what some might consider a portentous coincidence, Adams's diary for July 4, 1771, reports his attendance at a dinner where "[c]onversation turns upon Revelations, Prophecies, Jews, &c."[25]

Noah offered two plans for fulfilling the intertwined destinies of Israel and America. The first was the Ararat project, which involved a sort of Jewish reservation in the United States. Noah agreed with Boudinot that Jews would benefit from the opportunity to learn the art of republican government. As a location for this educational experience, Noah proposed Grand Island, near Buffalo, New York. In negotiations conducted through the early 1820s, Noah arranged to purchase the island and give it the resonant name of Ararat.[26]

Noah laid the cornerstone for a settlement on September 15, 1825, amid an elaborate procession of "masonic and military companies."[27] In the name of the God who led the Israelites through the wilderness, he proposed to "revive, renew, and reestablish the Government of the Jewish Nation under the auspices and protection of the constitution and laws of the United States of America."[28] Evoking the Hebraism of the Revolutionary era as well as the

Puritans, Noah turned to the Old Testament in designing institutions of government. Since the Hebrews enjoyed their greatest success before they adopted monarchy, Noah announced that he would assume the office of judge of the Jewish people.

In addition to religious obstacles—Noah had no right to make himself judge—there were constitutional problems with the proposed arrangement. How could the Ararat community be governed both by Jewish and by American law? Noah ignored this question, partly because he was not much interested in details, but also because he regarded the Jewish colony as a temporary arrangement. Ararat was the biblical Noah's refuge, not his permanent home. The American Noah suggested that the settlement in upstate New York would play a similar role for Jews suffering dislocation and persecution. Reassuring Americans who might fear admitting a religiously alien community into their midst, Noah explained that in "calling the Jews together under the protection of the American Constitution and laws and governed by our happy and salutary institutions, it is proper for me to state that this asylum is temporary and previsionary."[29] While they might find sanctuary in America, "Jews never should and never will relinquish the just hope of regaining possession of their ancient heritage, and events in the neighborhood of Palestine indicate an extraordinary change of affairs."[30]

Much of the press mocked Ararat as an absurd solution to a nonexistent problem. Reflecting the generally favorable attitude toward Jews among Americans at this time, journalists affirmed Jews were welcome to live as equal citizens until such time as the Lord chose to restore them. Jewish leaders, for their part, accused Noah of claiming an illegitimate authority to speak on behalf of the Jewish people. Historian Adam Rovner has found that the rabbis whom Noah appointed "commissioners of emigration" without their consent denounced his scheme.[31] In the event, Ararat failed to attract even a single resident.

But Noah did not give up his dream of enlisting America in the cause of Jewish restoration. In 1844, he offered a second proposal in a lecture delivered to capacity crowds in New York City and revised for publication the following year. This time, his speech featured a crucial change of audience. In the consecration address and Ararat proclamation, Noah spoke primarily to Jews. In "Discourse on the Restoration of the Jews," he placed his hopes in the cooperation of Christians.[32] Noah had reason to think such cooperation might be forthcoming. By the 1840s, the idea that restoration might precede conversion had become mainstream. Joining British writers like Bicheno, Faber, and Bickersteth, Americans added their voices to the conversation about the future of the Jews. Among them was George Bush, a professor of Hebrew at New York University and ancestor of the presidents who share his name.[33]

The same year that Noah delivered his "Discourse," Bush published a commentary on chapter 37 of the Book of Ezekiel. That chapter recounts the prophet's vision of a desert valley filled with desiccated bones. At God's command, Ezekiel orders the bones to recover their flesh. After they miraculously do so, God explains that "these bones are the whole house of Israel." The Lord then instructs Ezekiel to inform Israel that, as He restored life to the dry bones, "I am going to open your graves, and bring you up from your graves . . . and I will bring you back to the Land of Israel" (Ezek. 37:11–12). Eminent scholars, including the seventeenth-century Bible commentator and political theorist Grotius, argued that the passage referred to the restoration of Jews from the Babylonian captivity. It followed that the prophecy involved no prediction of future events. Professor Bush rejected this view. He contended that Ezekiel foretold a second "recall of the Jewish race from their prolonged dispersion among the nations, and their reinstatement in the land of covenanted heritage."[34] According to Bush, the "obvious purport of several of the clauses goes to ascertain the time of the accomplishment as utterly incompatible with that of the literal return from Babylon under the decree of Cyrus. The announcements bear nothing more unequivocally on their face, than that this re-establishment in the land of Canaan shall be final and permanent."[35]

The prophecy of the dry bones was a favorite item of textual support for Christian arguments for Jewish restoration. More distinctive was Bush's insistence that the territorial and political aspects of this event would occur prior to conversion. Bush had no doubt that the Jews would eventually join the church. In the meantime, "the return to Palestine will, as to the bulk of the nation, precede their ingrafting into Christ."[36] The reason, Bush contended, was that the Jews were not heathens but a "covenant people."[37] Their salvation thus involved the completion of an existing relationship with God rather than the establishment of a new one.

Because conversion would be a consequence rather than a cause of restoration, Bush urged Christians to adopt a different strategy for realizing God's will. Rather than waiting for a miracle, they should concentrate on creating the political conditions for a Jewish return to the land. Implicitly criticizing the missionaries, Bush insisted:

> It is ever to be borne in mind that the fulfillment of prophecy is effected by the ordinary course of Providence, in which the agents act from appropriate motives, and without the express design of accomplishing the purposes of Heaven. When the Most High accordingly declares that he will bring the house of Israel into their own land, it does not follow that this will be effected by any miraculous interposition which will be recognized as such. . . . It does not appear, therefore, that any special duty of Christians is involved in this predicted lot of Israel, except so far as governmental action may be requisite in removing the political obstacles that stand in the way of the event.[38]

Like many of his contemporaries, Bush was reverent of Jews' past and certain of their glorious future. Even so, he had mixed feelings about Jews in the present. In Bush's opinion, Jews had come to America in pursuit of wealth. They were likely to leave for the same reason: "[T]he affairs of the nations . . . may take such a turn as to offer to the Jews the same carnal inducements to remove to Syria, as now prompt them to migrate to this country."[39]

A self-appointed champion of his people, Noah rejected such aspersions on Jewish motives. Even if the Jews lacked their ancient virtue, they would respond to appeals to liberty and self-determination. Perhaps no nation displayed a greater contrast between its noble past and decadent present than the Greeks. Against the odds, however, they had overthrown foreign domination. There was no reason the Jews could not do the same. In Noah's judgement, the two struggles were actually connected. Because the Ottoman Empire had been weakened by the Greek war of independence, it might also be willing to relinquish its hold on Palestine.[40]

Noah had to step more delicately when it came to missionaries. Although he characterized missions as contrary to "the manifest predictions of the prophets," he acknowledged that increased contact between Christians and Jews might promote "charity and good feelings, which cannot fail to be reciprocally beneficial."[41] But Noah insisted that most Jews were not interested in converting. Therefore, missionary societies "should unite in efforts to promote the restoration of the Jews in their unconverted state, relying on the fulfillment of the prophesies [*sic*] and the will of God for attaining the objects they have in view after that great advent shall have arrived."[42]

The settlement of the religious issue could wait for a miracle, in other words. The political one could not. Appealing to the assumption that God works through men rather than merely upon them, Noah suggested the when "we do no more when he disposes events to correspond with the fulfillment of his promises and the prediction of his prophets, we leave undone that which he entails upon us as a duty to perform. . . . He has spoken—he has promised. It is our duty, if the fulfillment of that Divine promise can be secured by mortal means and human agency, to see it executed. Will the dews of heaven produce a harvest without the labour of a husbandman?"[43] Like his invocation of natural rights, the agricultural trope in Noah's rhetoric was Christians was part of a familiar tradition. Charles Finney also used the image of the fertile field—derived from Jesus' parable of the sower—to explain why Christians could not simply wait for God to awaken their fellowmen.[44] Rather than merely predicting Jewish restoration, Noah challenged his audience to do something to make it happen. God had prepared the ground, but men would have to plant the seeds and reap the harvest.

Noah presented Jewish restoration as a distinctively American task. Evoking the Puritan errand into the wilderness, he enthused: "Let the first movement for the emancipation of the Jewish nation come from this free and liberal country. Call to mind that Moses was the first founder of a republican form of government, and that first settlers on this continent adopted the Mosaic laws as their code and strictly enforced them."[45] However dubious as history, these claims express a coherent set of ideas. Synthesizing American origin myths, millenarian theology, and republican politics, Noah not only argued that Christians had a responsibility to promote Jewish restoration, but also that they were upholding their own national calling by doing so.

Critics derided him as a buffoon and con man, but Noah made a deep impression on some Christians who were attempting to make sense of their relation to Jews—and their own place in the course of Providence. In 1845, John Price Durbin, who served as chaplain of the U.S. Senate and president of Dickinson College, insisted on "the undoubted fact of the restoration of the Jewish state in Palestine . . . by the operation of political and social causes working gradually until the result shall be concluded and established by political combinations."[46] He credited Noah with demonstrating that conversion was not a "necessary condition" for restoration but would instead "follow rapidly."[47]

Beyond his political and academic standing, Durbin had unusual experience in these matters. Unlike previous writers on Jewish restoration, he had actually visited the place in question. For Puritans and revolutionary patriots, Zion was as much a symbol as it was a geographic location. For Durbin and a growing number of nineteenth-century Americans, it was a real place that might soon be the location of extraordinary events.[48]

Where Vulture unto Vulture Calls

The so-called Holy Land occupies an outsize place in the American imagination. From the Hebraic place names of New England to Revolutionary-era depictions of George Washington as a modern Joshua uniting the tribes, Americans have played out their history on a mental map derived from the Old Testament. Scholar Hilton Obenzinger describes this imaginative transposition as "sacred geography"—a territorial counterpart to the sacred history that justified Americans' understanding of themselves as a covenant nation.[49]

Yet the symbolic importance of the Holy Land was not supported by extensive firsthand knowledge. Palestine was far from North America, and its condition under Ottoman rule offered few political or economic incentives to make the grueling trip. Religion was travelers' primary motive. In addition to acquiring a better understanding of scripture through direct observation of its setting, American Protestants saw it as their responsibility to preach the Gospel as they understood it to the Muslims, the mostly Eastern Orthodox Christians, and the handful of Jews who inhabited the biblical landscape.[50]

An early expedition for this purpose departed Boston in 1819. In a sermon delivered immediately before its departure, the missionary leader Levi Parsons outlined his plan. Prefiguring Professor George Bush, Parsons argued that only a miracle would *prevent* Jews from going home. With Ottoman power declining, it seemed that the doors to Palestine were already opening. Parsons proposed to beat the Jews to their goal by establishing a mission in Jerusalem. In this way, he and his colleagues would be prepared to convert them at the very moment that the prophecies were realized.[51]

Parsons died in Egypt without reaching his destination. But his dream of a Christian welcoming committee for repatriated Jews was realized in 1841, when a joint Anglican-Lutheran bishopric in Jerusalem was established under Michael Solomon Alexander, a Jewish convert to Christianity affiliated with the London Jews' Society. According to Durbin, who visited Bishop Alexander and toured his operation, this was "doubtless the most important religious event that has happened in Palestine since its reconquest by the Mohammedans."[52] Reversing the outcome of the Crusades, the "Hebrew diocese of St. James" convinced Durbin that English-speaking Protestants were central to the future of Palestine and the Jewish people.[53]

English-speaking, perhaps. But would Britons or Americans take precedence? With its mastery of the seas, Britain seemed the more plausible answer. In 1842, New York minister Stephen Higginson Tyng attended an anniversary gala of the London Jews' Society, where he met prophecy commentators and their political backers.[54] They convinced him that "Britain is the chosen instrument, in the hand of God, for the accomplishment of this great object."[55] Yet other Americans were reluctant to give up the possibility that God nominated the United States to be a second Cyrus. In the wake of Levi Parsons's abortive expedition, Americans launched a series of voyages to Palestine.[56]

In 1840, the Mormon prophet Joseph Smith directed his apostle Orson Hyde to travel east. One of his tasks was to dedicate the Holy Land for the return of the Jewish people—a perplexing but crucial element of the double Zion theory. After his arrival in Jerusalem, Hyde ascended the Mount of Olives. There he prayed to God to move the powers of the earth "to look with a friendly eye towards this place, and . . . to restore the kingdom unto Israel—raise up Jerusalem as its capital, and constitute her people a distinct nation and government, with David Thy servant, even a descendant from the loins of ancient David to be their king."[57] The scholar Steven Ricks points out that Hyde's prayer did not ask God's aid to missions aimed at Jews. In keeping with Mormon eschatology, this task was reserved for Christ himself.[58]

Warder Cresson made another attempt to connect America with the Holy Land. A Quaker and an associate of Mordecai Noah who got himself appointed U.S. consul in Jerusalem, Cresson astonished his superiors by converting to Judaism.[59] In response, Cresson's family made an unsuccessful attempt to have him declared legally insane. Cleared of madness, Cresson returned to Palestine.[60] He then founded a colony near Jerusalem, where he enlisted the ASMCJ in a scheme to provide agricultural training to an anticipated wave of Jewish emigrants.[61]

Cresson was fictionalized by Herman Melville, who toured Palestine in the 1850s after the critical and commercial failure of *Moby-Dick*. *Clarel*, Melville's epic poem inspired by his journey, returns to questions about the future of Israel that he had also raised in *White-Jacket*. The plot revolves around an American student who visits Palestine in an attempt to shore up his waning faith. There he meets Nathan, a convert to Judaism of Puritan descent who sees life in the Holy Land as an antidote to religious doubt. Echoing Cresson, Nathan emphasizes that Jewish restoration is a goal to be secured by human efforts. Nathan describes his motive as follows:

> The Hebrew seers announce in time
> The return of Judah to her prime;
> Here was an object; Up and Do!
> With seed and tillage help renew—
> Help reinstate the Holy Land.[62]

Inspired to by this maxim, Nathan establishes a settlement on the plain of Sharon. Unfortunately, his effort goes unappreciated by the local population. Surrounded by enemies, Nathan develops a paranoia that evokes his ancestors' fear of Native Americans. His settlement becomes a fortress and ultimately a self-made prison.

In the guise of Nathan, Melville presented Cresson as a strange and tragic figure. Other American travelers, such as the pioneering archaeologist Edward Robinson, were more respectable. Boasting of Americans' piety, Robinson contended that his countrymen were "providentially led" to the Holy Land on the grounds that "in no country are the Scriptures better known or more highly prized."[63] By conducting scientific research, Americans could confirm their relationship to the Land of Israel without making Cresson's extraordinary commitment to the God of Israel.

Americans looking for a political role in the future of the Holy Land could point to the dispatch of a U.S. Navy surveying party to Palestine in 1847. The Philadelphia minister and prophecy commentator Joseph A. Seiss noted as "a singular fact, in this connection, that the United States government, without any assignable cause for it, did, only a few years ago, send out Lieut. Lynch and his party, to explore the Jordan and obtain detailed and authentic descriptions of the condition and topography of Israel's land. England has done the same, as if these countries, so closely allied in so many particulars, were already laying the foundations for their work and mission in bringing back the dispersed children of Abraham."[64] Like Tyng, Seiss acknowledged that America could, at that moment, be only a junior partner in this special relationship. But he expected that its potential to contribute would grow as Providence worked its influence.

Although they disputed the Holy Land's precise relation to the United States, most writers agreed that Ottoman Palestine was a wasteland, in need of physical as well as spiritual restoration. In *Clarel*, Melville described it as a place "[w]here vulture unto vulture calls, And only ill things find a friend."[65] The pilgrim William Prime, who published a popular narrative of his travels, concurred. Contrary to his expectations, he found that the "general aspect of Jerusalem is very melancholy. . . . There is no such thing as cheerfulness about it," he reported.[66]

Paradoxically, the degraded conditions that travelers described showed them that God was preparing the land for the return of His people. According to Durbin: "The present state of Palestine is another sign indicating the restoration of the Jews, and their conversion to Christianity. The facts to be particularly remarked are the emptiness of the land with respect to population, indicating that Providence is making room for the sons of Israel. The land is comparatively 'desolate' without inhabitant."[67] Although it includes the qualifier "comparatively," indicating that Durbin did not completely ignore the existing inhabitants, his description evokes Lord Shaftesbury's notorious characterization of Ottoman Palestine as "a land without a people for a people without a land."[68]

The idea that Palestine was a ravaged wilderness played an important role in the development of Christian Zionism. If the land was not populated or properly used, it was thought to be because God was preserving it for its rightful occupants. In addition to justifying Jewish return, providential emptiness linked the future of Israel to European settlement projects elsewhere in the world. Historian Beshara Doumani notes that not only Palestine but also "the Americas and Africa were portrayed as virgin territories ready for a wave of pioneers."[69]

Such perceptions of a vacant Promised Land may have been convenient but were not cynical. Rather than evasions of a moral dilemma, they were part of an optimistic attitude that infused American religious life in the period. This view, which can be traced back to Brightman's interpretation of the Book of Revelation, is known as postmillennialism. Postmillennialism posits that Christ will appear *after* the faithful establish the kingdom of God through their own efforts. In the words of historian James Moorhead: "Postmillennialism was the moral government of God stretched out on the frame of time. . . . In order to vindicate the government of God, the temporal process *as a whole* had to yield far more happiness than woe."[70]

But postmillennialism was not the only current in American religion during the nineteenth century. In the wake of the Civil War, a different attitude toward sacred history gained influence. Advocates of this more pessimistic tendency contended that the world was, in effect, getting worse. Echoing Joseph Mede, premillennialists argued that the millennium would commence only after the Second Coming and would be preceded by a period of unprecedented turmoil.

Come, O Lord

For much of the nineteenth century, postmillennialism was the dominant strand in the Protestantism that claimed a large majority of Americans among its adherents. Inflamed by the Second Great Awakening, American Protestants anticipated Christ's return after they had prepared his kingdom through vigorous labor. This eschatology matched Americans' image of themselves as a progressive people, destined to spread the blessings of (Protestant) Christianity, modern technology, and republican government through the continent and even the globe.[71] The repatriation of the Jews could fit neatly into this vision. By helping to bring the Jews home and working for their conversion, postmillennialists believed that they were building up the kingdom of God.[72] Thus the writer Hollis Read promised that the people of Israel "shall return *before* the Millennium and their restoration and conversion to Christianity shall be so important and efficient means of the conversion of the world to Christ and the establishment of the Messiah's kingdom, that it [is] said to be as '*life from the dead.*'"[73]

Affirmations of belief in Jewish return by postmillennialists going back to Edwards and Brightman challenge the argument that Christian Zionism emerged from eschatological innovations by John Nelson Darby. In practice, Christian Zionism could be justified on postmillennial as well as premillennial grounds. The debate had less to do with the timing of the Second Coming than with the nature of the millennium. Would Christ's regime be primarily spiritual? Or should believers expect an "earthly and physical" kingdom of God?[74]

Premillennialism was not simply a British import. In his *Dissertation on the Prophecies Relative to the Second Coming of Jesus Christ*, Detroit minister George Duffield, a grandson of the George Duffield who served as chaplain to the Continental Congress, pointed out that Americans such as Boudinot and Increase Mather taught that Christ's return would inaugurate a literal millennium including the restoration of the Jews.[75] The revival of interest in premillennialism among British Christians was a transatlantic phenomenon, as well. Among the most influential authorities was the Scottish theologian John Cumming, who cited the activities of Mordecai Noah as evidence that the divine plan was accelerating toward its conclusion.[76]

Premillennial ideas were encouraged by political events as well as theological arguments. The outbreak of the Civil War made hopes for progressive improvement harder to sustain. In 1863, Seiss observed that critics had once mocked his argument that peace could be expected only under the government of Christ. With conflict raging, he responded: "Seven years of additional study and observation . . . have only deepened the writer's belief in the truthfulness of the representations he has given."[77] For many postmillennialists, the war seemed like a terrible detour in God's plan. For many premillennialists, increases in disorder and suffering were signs of the impending apocalypse. These signs included the immense buildup of military resources. In his 1866 study *Christ's Second Coming: Is It Pre-Millennial or Post-Millennial?*, Robert Cunningham Shimeall suggested that the growth of U.S. forces was the result of a divine intention to accomplish an American-led restoration of the Jews before the Second Coming.

Seiss and Shimeall were just two of the premillennial teachers who addressed the American public in the years surrounding the Civil War. This group also included members of sects inspired by the failure of Christ to return on October 22, 1844, as predicted by the popular preacher William Miller. Miller had denied that the Jews would be restored in the millennium. But some followers concluded that his failure to pay attention to this aspect of prophecy explained his erroneous prediction.[78] Among those whose disappointment led to the conclusion that the Jews would go home before Christ returned was Clorinda Minor, an ex-Millerite who established a colony near Jaffa.[79]

In terms of enduring influence, though, these premillennialists were overshadowed by John Nelson Darby, a former Anglican who helped found the evangelical Plymouth Brethren. In 1862, Darby made the first of seven trips to North America to promote his beliefs. Over the next few decades, his eschatology became almost synonymous with premillennialism, eventually displacing rival doctrines.

Premillennial dispensationalism derives part of its name from the idea that history is divided into distinct periods. Known as dispensations, each period is constituted by a specific relationship between God and mankind. Darby, his followers, and his critics argued about the precise number of dispensations, with seven becoming a popular solution because it corresponded to the days of creation. The minutiae of that debate are less important than the underlying principle: that time has an order that corresponds to the narrative structure of Scripture.[80]

A second pillar of Darby's teaching was a sharp distinction between Israel and the church. According to him, references to Israel in the Bible are never metaphors for the community of believers in Christ. Instead, they refer to the covenanted descendants of Abraham. Where does that leave the church? To answer this question, Darby turned to the Book of Daniel. In chapter 9, the angel Gabriel informs the prophet that the Messiah will appear sixty-nine weeks after the order is given to restore and rebuild Jerusalem. But rather than being recognized for what he is, the Messiah will be rejected, leading to a turbulent period in which the city and temple are again destroyed. After the passage of an additional week, the Messiah will return and bring about an end to troubles by establishing the kingdom of God (Dan. 9:24–27).

An old tradition of interpretation holds that Daniel's "weeks" refer to periods of seven years. Starting the calculation from Cyrus's order to rebuild the temple, this interpretation places the advent of the Messiah in the first century BC. That was the wrong answer for Christians who identified Jesus as the fulfillment of Daniel's prophecy. By counting from the rebuilding of the city as a whole on orders from Cyrus's successor Artaxerxes, however, it was possible to extend the reckoning so that the Crucifixion occurred sixty-nine "weeks"—483 years—after the decree. Holding to the prophetic schedule, it followed that the Second Coming should have occurred one week—or seven years—after that.[81]

That was not what happened, of course. Christians continue to wait for the Lord's promised return. Darby explained this anticlimax by proposing that the seventieth week of the prophecy was not the seventieth week in strict chronological order. Since Israel turned away from the Messiah, he argued, God put the timeline on hold, inserting a parenthesis of indeterminate length *between* the sixty-ninth and seventieth week. According to Darby, the dispensation focused on the church, which included all of history since the Crucifixion, was a kind of intermission in the story of God's relationship with Israel. In order to complete the sequence described by Daniel, God would eventually turn His attention back to Israel.

Yet it did not make sense that God would simply abandon the church at the critical moment. Darby resolved the conundrum with the help of Saint Paul. In his first Epistle to the Thessalonians, Paul promised believers that they would "meet the Lord in [the] air; and thus we shall be always with [the] Lord" (1 Thess. 4:17, Darby translation). Darby taught that this obscure statement meant that God would remove Christians to heaven at the beginning of

Daniel's seventieth week. With the church literally vanished, the events determined for the last seven years before Christ's return would proceed in rapid succession. These included the territorial restoration of Israel, the establishment of a covenant between Israel and the Antichrist, the Antichrist's betrayal of that agreement and ensuing persecution of Israel, and finally the rescue of a pious remnant by the visibly returned Christ.[82]

Darby did not invent any of these claims. The division of sacred history into eras, the emphasis on promises to Israel, and the insistence on the earthly nature of the millennium were recurring themes in Anglo-Protestant thought going back to the Reformation. The doctrine of the Rapture is more distinctive. Even so, it has precedents in the work of Increase Mather.[83] What was novel in premillennial dispensationalism was the way in which Darby made an articulated system of these elements. His synthesis of covenantal and prophetic themes connected past, present, and future, allowing believers to see history from God's perspective.

The very complexity of Darby's eschatology probably aided its popularization. On one level, the exposition of premillennial dispensationalism required massive knowledge of scripture. Those who acquired this knowledge were able to "out-Bible" critics, acquiring imposing reputations in the process.[84] But such learning was more effective in polemics than necessary for belief because the main aspects of premillennial dispensationalism were not hard to grasp. God was the lord of history and was coming for His people. This was a message that anyone could understand. Dispensationalism was initially regarded with suspicion, even by other premillennialists. By the 1890s, however, it had become the leading form of premillennialism and one of the country's most vital religious movements.

The Problem of Agency

Premillennial dispensationalism seems flamboyantly irrational to secular eyes—a quality that encourages the sensationalist treatment it often receives in the popular literature on Christian Zionism. Yet it shares an important quality with an avowedly atheist doctrine that emerged around the same time. Like Marx's philosophy of history, premillennial dispensationalism establishes a logic of transformation through catastrophe and suggests that the final stage is about to commence. Such theories of change pose a dilemma. Should those who know what is going to happen wait for irresistible forces to take effect? Or is it necessary for them to act to move the process forward?

American Protestantism in the early nineteenth century was broadly characterized by confidence in man's potential to change the world. With God's help, postmillennialists believed that they could progressively improve religion, morality, and politics. Darby, by contrast, took a nonactivist stand. Since no actions could speed up God's timetable, there was little point in efforts to make the world better. Darby's skepticism regarding human agency was particularly intense when it came to politics. Scholar Robert O. Smith reports that he sternly informed followers: "We do not mix in politics; we are not of this world; we do not vote."[85]

James H. Brookes, Darby's leading American popularizer, reiterated the counsel of distance from politics. In *Israel and the Church*, his summary of dispensationalism, Brookes mourned: "Even to this day the error exists, as seen in the State-Church establishments of Europe, and in the habitual tendency of the churches in America to 'intermeddle with civil affairs with concern for the commonwealth.' . . . All of this confusion arises from the fact that so many under the present dispensation of grace, still occupy Jewish ground."[86] The phrase "Jewish ground" refers to Darby's idea that God's covenant with Israel was earthly, while His relationship with the church was spiritual. To engage in politics was to usurp God's covenant with the Jews, ignoring Christians' otherworldly vocation.

Brookes did predict the eventual return of the Jews to Palestine, emphasizing the indefeasible character of God's covenant with Abraham. But he suggested that this would be accomplished by Jews acting independently of Christian participation. Brookes was also scornful of the idea that references to the United States could be found in scripture. Austin, Boudinot, John McDonald, and Ethan Smith read prophecies of the eagle as foreshadowing American power. Brookes insisted that "the vast American Republic" was nowhere to be found in the God's word.[87]

Warnings against politicizing eschatology cut against the grain of Americans' inclination to view themselves as agents of Providence. Despite

Darby's and Brookes's insistence on the distance between Israel and the church, politics and religion, more flexible premillennialists suggested that these categories were not absolutely separate. Treated as an interpretive strategy rather than a fixed doctrine, dispensationalism could be fused with more positive conceptions of American destiny. William Eugene Blackstone was a leading exponent of this fusion.

The Blackstone Memorial

Blackstone described himself as God's "errand boy."[88] Born in upstate New York in 1841, he was raised as a Methodist in Jefferson County, just a few counties away from the "burned-over district" that Charles Finney identified as the most evangelized in the country. Likely exposed to millenarian ideas in childhood, Blackstone adopted premillennialism while living in Chicago in the 1870s.[89] Among his mentors was the evangelist Dwight L. Moody, who pioneered what historian Matthew Avery Sutton calls an "engaged premillennialism" that combined deterministic eschatology with a disposition toward practical activity.[90]

Blackstone made his own contribution toward this synthesis in *Jesus Is Coming*, a tract published in several editions beginning in 1878. Reportedly among the best-sellers of the period, *Jesus Is Coming* summarizes and simplifies dispensational doctrine. It is a faithful report, for the most part, but also includes intriguing variations. More explicitly than Darby and Brookes, for example, Blackstone placed the status of the Jews at the center of God's plan. According to Blackstone: "If we want to know our place in chronology, our position in the march of events, look at Israel. Like the red thread in the British rigging, it runs through the whole Bible. Prophecies to the people like Ezek. 37, and prophecies to the land like Ezek. 36. Israel shall be restored to Palestine and no more be pulled up out of their land. Hundreds of prophecies affirm this dispensational truth. . . . [The] title deed to Palestine is recorded, not in the Mohammedan Serai of Jerusalem nor the Seraglio of Constantinople, but in hundreds of millions of Bibles now extant in more than three hundred languages of the earth."[91]

Blackstone's confidence in Jewish restoration was bolstered by the pilgrimage to the Holy Land that he undertook in 1888–89. After touring

Jerusalem and other holy places, he returned to the United States convinced that God was making the land ready for its rightful owners. All signs pointed in this direction, including the fact that "rains are increasing, and there are many evidences that the land is recovering its ancient fertility."[92] The agricultural image that Blackstone invoked recalls the Second Great Awakening more than it does rigorous dispensationalism. God prepared the soil for extraordinary events, but men had to plant and nourish the seeds.

As a first step, Blackstone organized a Conference of Israelites and Christians Regarding Their Mutual Relations and Welfare. A rare example of interfaith dialogue before the twentieth century, the conference met in Chicago during Thanksgiving week of 1890 and attracted participation by local rabbis as well as Christian clergymen. One thing the participants agreed about was that their conversation vindicated American traditions of religious liberty and civil equality. Yet they found themselves at odds when it came to the future of the people and Land of Israel. Blackstone and his fellow Methodist J. M. Caldwell argued for restoration. Rabbi Emil Hirsch of the Chicago Sinai Congregation rejected their proposals. In what must have been stentorian tones, Hirsch explained: "WE, THE MODERN JEWS, say that we do not wish to be restored to Palestine. We have given up the hope in the coming of a political, personal Messiah. We say 'the country wherein we live is our Palestine, and the city wherein we dwell is our Jerusalem.' [Applause.] We will not go back. We do not expect to go back to Palestine to again form a nationality of our own."[93]

Hirsch was not only speaking for himself. His statement reprised the official stance of Reform Judaism in the United States. According to the so-called Pittsburgh Platform adopted in 1885, Reform Jews "consider ourselves no longer a nation but a religious community and therefore we expect neither a return to Palestine nor any of the laws concerning a Jewish state."[94] In their eagerness to secure a place in American life, the Reform movement came close to asserting that the United States was the Promised Land.

Unusually for an early dispensationalist, Blackstone had warm personal relationships with Jews. But Jewish opposition to restoration made little sense to him. In his view, Jews had two coherent options. If they were dissatisfied with the burdens of Judaism, on the one hand, they could convert to Christianity and take their place in the church. A passionate missionary despite his belief that the bulk of Israel would be restored in unbelief, Blackstone devoted considerable effort toward evangelism.[95] On the other hand, Blackstone respected the consistency of Jews who remained faithful to the law and prophets. He reasoned that this faith should make them eager to go home. Blackstone did not seem to be aware that Orthodox Judaism generally opposed the establishment of a Jewish commonwealth before the messianic age. With some exceptions (mostly in Europe), Orthodox Jews were waiting for the Messiah to act first.[96]

Blackstone considered these complications in the months that followed the Chicago conference. By late winter 1891, he was collecting endorsements of a petition to the president of the United States. The document was ready for presentation in March. Although its claims are broadly consistent with premillennialism, the memorial includes no explicitly dispensationalist arguments. Instead, it appealed to humanitarian considerations and the exciting idea that the United States was an instrument for the achievement of God's purposes.[97] Reviving an image that also appeared in David Austin's writings, the cover letter urged President Harrison to become a successor to Cyrus of Persia.[98]

What distinguishes the Blackstone Memorial from the effusions of an Austin is its measured tone, formal presentation, and the way that it responded to events thousands of miles away. Rumors of increasing Jewish immigration to the Holy Land had circulated from time to time since Increase Mather's day. But Blackstone presented his scheme as European Jews were organizing functional movements to reclaim and resettle Palestine. Just six years after Blackstone presented his memorial, Theodor Herzl convened the first Zionist conference in Basel. With the foundation of political Zionism, restoration ceased to be a theological abstraction and became a live option.

From Restorationism to Zionism

The puzzle of Jewish participation had challenged restorationist thinkers for centuries. In order for the prophecies to be fulfilled, Jews were expected to begin the journey home under their own power. Reports that this process was under way gathered force through the nineteenth century. Restorationists in Britain and the United States paid close attention to projects including Warder Cresson's agricultural colony and settlements around Jerusalem funded by Jewish philanthropists including Judah Touro, Sir Moses Montefiore, and Nathan Rothschild. The Hoveve Zion (or Hibbat Zion) movement, founded in response to the persecution of Jews in the Russian Empire, was another promising sign. Its role in the first *aliyah*, or modern emigration to Palestine, was among the developments that convinced Blackstone that the time was right for his memorial.

Yet Hoveve Zion did not have the religious basis that Christians expected. Although not necessarily secular, many members embraced a form of Judaism that diverged from traditional orthodoxy.[99] The somewhat relaxed character of the emigrants' observance disturbed Jews as well as Christians. When Hoveve Zion established its first settlement, Rishon l'Zion, the rabbis of Jerusalem complained that the residents did not possess phylacteries and that men and women danced together.[100]

The relationship between messianic redemption and nationalist activism in the future of the Promised Land was made even more complicated by the emergence of political Zionism. Hoveve Zion at least gestured toward the biblical narrative. The name of their first settlement, Rishon l'Zion, near what is now Tel Aviv, was a reference to Isaiah's vision of restoration. Theodor Herzl, on the other hand, counted on Machiavellian diplomacy rather than to divine assistance. How could this be the miracle that students of prophecy awaited?

Blackstone answered by returning to scripture. He found the clarification he needed in Zephaniah, a minor prophet who wrote around the same time as Jeremiah. Through Zephaniah, the Lord commanded Israel to gather before facing punishment for its sins. Blackstone used these verses to justify political Zionism despite its infidelity. He explained:

Zephaniah 2:1–2 is being fulfilled in the present Zionist movement, in which the Jews are making a purely secular effort to regain Palestine. "Gather yourselves," says the Almighty, as though He stepped aside and let them exhibit the foolishness and calamitous results of their purely national movement. Dr. Herzl, their leader, is reported to have said, at the first congress in Basel, in 1897, "We must buy our way back to Palestine, salvation is to be by money." And one of the first speakers at that same congress said of the Sultan, "If his majesty will now receive us, we will accept him as our Messiah." It is a godless movement and the prophet tells us that it will bring upon them the "day of Jehovah's anger."[101]

Blackstone's interpretation of Zephaniah sheds light on the apparently instrumental attitude of some Christian Zionists toward Jews and Zionism. To dispensationalists like Blackstone, Jewish return to the Land of Israel was immensely important but not the end of the story. Once in Palestine, they expected the Jews to suffer a terrible tribulation before finally accepting Christ. In that respect, it was appropriate and perhaps essential that Jews should return to Palestine in a condition of unbelief. Even as He drew His people closer to Himself, God was creating the conditions for their chastisement and ultimate redemption.

It might be thought that these expectations would make evangelism unnecessary, yet Blackstone did not abandon his missionary efforts. In fact, he continued to evangelize Jews, even at official Zionist gatherings. The willingness of audiences to sit through these sermons indicates the high esteem in which he was held.[102] But Blackstone could excuse Zionists who rejected religious practice just as he maintained a grudging respect for Jews who continued to keep the commandments while rejecting Zionism. Both groups were unwitting servants of the Lord.

From Blackstone's perspective, Jews who considered themselves Americans first were the real apostates. Abandoning both the people and the God of Israel, they made an idol of their temporary refuge. Blackstone insisted that Christians should never discriminate against or persecute Jews—a grave sin that would bring punishment on their own heads. But neither should they fail to remind Jews of their real home.

4   I Will Not Utterly Destroy the House of Jacob: Liberal Protestantism and the Partition of Palestine

> Are ye not as the children of the Ethiopians unto me, O
> children of Israel? saith Jehovah. Have not I brought up Israel
> out of the land of Egypt, and the Philistines from Caphtor,
> and the Syrians from Kir? Behold, the eyes of the Lord
> Jehovah are upon the sinful kingdom, and I will destroy it
> from off the face of the earth; save that I will not utterly
> destroy the house of Jacob, saith Jehovah.
> —Amos 9:7–9, American Standard Version

The spring of 1916 was a pivotal moment for Palestine. Following torturous negotiations that had begun the previous year, Great Britain, France, and Russia signed the secret Sykes-Picot agreement, which defined the spheres of influence that they planned to claim after the collapse of the Ottoman Empire. Dividing most of the territory between Britain and France, the agreement left unclear the status of Jerusalem and its environs. An international regime of some kind was foreseen, but its nature and its relation to the growing Jewish population were not determined.[1]

Thousands of miles away, another document concerning the future of Palestine was being completed. At the encouragement of the leaders of the American Zionist movement, including Louis Brandeis and the Reform rabbi Stephen S. Wise, William E. Blackstone composed a second version of his memorial for submission to President Woodrow Wilson. The revised petition differed in some details, such as emphasizing the worldwide nature of the Jewish problem rather than its specifically Russian dimensions. But the thrust of the text was the same as the one that Blackstone had delivered to Benjamin Harrison a quarter-century earlier: the United States should use its influence to convene an international conference to address the fate of the Jews; land should be secured for them in their biblical homeland; and a more or less autonomous political entity should be established there.

The petition was ready in May, just as the Sykes-Picot agreement was being concluded.[2] Bearing the signatures of eighty-one prominent figures, it was also endorsed by the General Assembly of the Presbyterian Church and associations of ministers in Southern California, where Blackstone had moved to serve as dean of the Bible Institute of Los Angeles (later Biola University).[3] The ecumenical character of the signatories reflects the fact that Christian Zionism was not then associated with apocalyptic expectations or conservative politics. The committee of clergymen that Blackstone organized to present the petition to Wilson included theological and political liberals such as the Methodist bishop J. W. Bashford; F. M. North, president of the Federal Council of Churches of Christ; and YMCA leader John R. Mott.[4]

Due to strategic concerns in the American Zionist leadership, the petition was not officially presented to the president. It appears, however, that it was unofficially shown to him. In later years, Wise reported that Wilson was excited by the prospect "that I, a son of the manse, should be able to help restore the Holy Land to its people!"[5] Brought up in a devout Presbyterian household, Wilson was familiar with the religious background of Jewish restoration long before Blackstone came onto the scene.

Wilson's affinity for Zionism had diplomatic consequences. By October 1917, he was prepared to assure the British government that the United States would endorse a Jewish homeland in Palestine. The Balfour Declaration followed in November. The following month, on December 11, 1917, the British general Edmund Allenby entered Jerusalem.

American Christians greeted the capture of Jerusalem as a potentially epochal event. In late December, a writer for the *Christian Century* observed that "the achievement of Allenby takes the Holy City from out of the hands of the Turk for administration at the hands of Christians. And the dreams of Israel's scattered hosts, without a fatherland since Calvary, flame up anew and give fresh glory to the Zionist movement."[6] A few weeks later, the editors answered the question "Shall We Have a Republic of Judea?" in the affirmative, reasoning that the "setting up of a Jewish republic would have meaning for all the religionists of the world."[7]

The views expressed in the *Century* are of particular interest because of the magazine's role as a forum for liberal Protestantism. According to historian Gary Dorrien: "Liberal theology seeks to reinterpret the symbols of traditional Christianity in a way that creates a progressive religious alternative to atheistic rationalism and to theologies based on external authority."[8] Liberal denominations have become associated with criticism of Israel since the 1967 war. For much of the twentieth century, however, they provided Zionism's most vocal Christian advocates.[9]

Yet liberal Protestants' attitudes toward Zionism were qualified by some distinctive concerns. One obstacle was the universalism that characterized liberal Protestant thought. Although they expressed this commitment in different ways, liberal Protestants sought moral and political principles that could be applied to all peoples. Judaism in general and Zionism in particular could be seen as demanding special treatment for one nation and territory.

Liberal Protestants also rejected the ostensibly literal approach to the Bible applied by the theological conservatives beginning to be called fundamentalists. Rather than forecasts of things to come, argued University of Chicago professor Shirley Jackson Case, the prophecies should be understood as metaphorical addresses to believers at a less advanced stage of civilization.[10] Finally, liberal Protestants were characteristically hesitant about the use of force in politics. Chastened by the horrors of World War I, liberal Protestants tended to argue that coercion exacerbated conflict. Many concluded that war was always immoral.

These concerns made Zionism problematic for liberal Protestants but were not necessarily decisive. They could be overcome if the alternatives to a Jewish state were open to even more serious objections. Historian Caitlin Carenen has documented how a nearly forgotten liberal forerunner to today's so-called Israel lobby combined humanitarian concerns with a profound sense of Christian responsibility for Jewish suffering.[11] To those concerns,

Reinhold Niebuhr added an innovative conception of prophecy as a source of political guidance.

Liberal Theology and Wilson's Crusade

Liberal Protestantism is often traced back to the German theologian Friedrich Schleiermacher. In the early nineteenth century, Schleiermacher sought to reconcile Christianity with the Enlightenment, which cast doubt on traditional tenets of faith. Among other innovations, he encouraged the development of scholarly techniques that treated the Bible as a composite of texts written long after the events that they describe. Schleiermacher's ideas reached the United States through ministers and theologians educated at German universities, then considered the best in world. By the end of the nineteenth century, theological liberals—also known as modernists—dominated academic theology and the most socially prominent churches.

Liberal Protestantism was linked with postmillennialism. Liberal Protestants believed that modern science and morality had liberated religion from obscurantist orthodoxy. Denying the personal return of Christ, many argued that a progressive social order was the only divine kingdom that mankind could expect.[12] The most influential expression of this expectation was the Social Gospel developed by Walter Rauschenbusch. Before World War I, the Social Gospel dealt primarily with economic issues. As the United States moved toward intervention, Rauschenbusch turned to the task of "christianizing . . . international relations." He defined this task as "disarmament and permanent peace, for the rights of the small nations against the imperialistic and colonizing powers . . . for the orderly settlement of grievances,—these are demands for social righteousness and fraternity on the largest scale."[13] These goals are virtually a theological rendering of Wilson's Fourteen Points.[14]

The Social Gospel was an important part of the background to liberal Protestants' responses to the Balfour Declaration and the British Mandate in Palestine. They might have agreed with dispensationalists that mankind was approaching the kingdom of God. But they had a very different notion of what that would involve. For premillennialists and dispensationalists, the restoration of the Jews was a prelude to the Rapture and the Second Coming. For liberals, it was part of establishing a righteous world order.

Adolf A. Berle presented the case in a 1918 pamphlet, "The World Significance of a Jewish State." A professor of applied Christianity at Tufts University, Berle was a Christian socialist and anti-imperialist whose son, A. A. Berle, Jr., would play a prominent role in the New Deal.[15] The pamphlet is dedicated to Brandeis, whom Berle describes as the "exemplar and leader of the liberating influence of the Jew in American life."[16] His admiration was not due simply to Brandeis's pioneering legal career. According to Berle: "The Jew himself is a social factor of such importance to the world that his racial and national interests are world-interests *per se*. . . . [W]hatever tends to unify the Jews, especially religiously, and centre their thought and action in a solidarity, religious and social, in a concrete form representative of the highest and finest aspirations of the race, is a sublime subject for speculation."[17]

The Jews could best discharge this worldwide purpose in their own land. In Berle's judgment, Zionism was "far from being the mere colonization scheme that many persons imagine."[18] By pursuing a national home in Palestine, Jews were promoting a wider transformation of human affairs. "In fact," Berle wrote, "it may be the new Messianic Kingdom itself, appearing on the horizon of world politics and betokening the time when the human race shall indeed beat its swords into ploughshares and spears into pruning hooks and learn war no more!"[19]

Fundamentalists were usually wary of the socialist currents in Zionism.[20] Berle, by contrast, was enthused by experiments with collectivism that could make Jewish Palestine "the political instructor of the entire world."[21] The lesson could be religious as well as socioeconomic. Criticizing the atheism that he associated with Herzl, Berle speculated that settlement in Palestine would promote the renovation of Judaism by eliminating practices that separated Jews from other peoples. Modernized Judaism and Christianity might even be synthesized in years to come. According to Berle, "One of the very first and important results of all this will be, that the religion of Israel will be understood—and what may that not mean both for Israel and for Christendom—and therein lies a possibility of modification of the religion of the whole world!"[22]

Berle's pamphlet echoes Saint Paul's promise that all Israel shall be saved. Even so, it expressed a troubling ambivalence about Jewish character. For

Berle, Israel was once a great nation—and would be one again. In the interim, though, most Jews did not live up to the standards of their heritage. Rather than seeking the kingdom of God, they were seduced by "modern commercialism."[23] Berle's criticism of Jews' ostensible vulgarity allowed him to undertake an extraordinary moral inversion. As workers for progress beyond war and capitalism, Berle suggested, liberal Christians were more faithful to the inner meaning of Judaism than were non-Zionist Jews.

Berle's appropriation of the ethical heritage of Judaism became a recurring feature of liberal Protestant responses to Zionism. Even when liberal Protestants approved of Jewish settlement in Palestine, it was only to the extent that Zionist practices corresponded to their idea of how Jews should behave. Dispensationalists like Blackstone have been accused of drawing an invidious distinction between good Jews, who play their theologically determined role, and bad Jews, who defy God by pursuing selfish interests. But a similar distinction was implicit in liberal Protestant attitudes toward Zionism, even when the terms of approbation were shifted.

Fosdick, Holmes, and Mandatory Palestine

Berle's statements reflected the excitement of the moment in which he wrote. The rapid succession of the Balfour Declaration and military victory made restoration seem within reach—and not only by means of British power. In 1920, the United States asserted a right of consultation concerning Britain's League of Nations mandate for Palestine. Two years later, Congress affirmed its commitment to a "national home for the Jewish people" with a bipartisan resolution sponsored by two pillars of the WASP elite: Representative Hamilton Fish and Senator Henry Cabot Lodge. The resolution proclaimed American support for an "undertaking which will do honor to Christendom and give to the House of Israel its long-denied opportunity to reestablish a fruitful Jewish life and culture in the ancient land."[24]

The situation grew more complicated after Britain actually assumed the mandate in 1924. Confronted with the realities of colonial administration, Americans became more attentive to the practical and moral objections to Jewish immigration, let alone to Jewish autonomy. Liberal Protestants were divided on the question of whether Palestinian Arabs were *a people* who possessed a right to national self-determination. But they were certainly people, whose presence could not be ignored.

As in the previous century, assessments of Zionism were worked out in the pilgrimage literature.[25] In books that combined travelogue and theological reflection with political commentary, the liberal clergymen Harry Emerson Fosdick and John Haynes Holmes attempted to reconcile their observations of life in Mandatory Palestine with arguments for Jewish return. Both pronounced themselves supporters of a limited form of Zionism that emphasized cultural revival in the Promised Land. But they opposed a Jewish state in favor of a binational vision of Palestine's future.

Fosdick was the more prominent of the two figures. Born in upstate New York, he attended Colgate University and was ordained as a Baptist minister in 1903. Shifting denominations, he was called to First Presbyterian Church in New York City, where he won national attention in 1922 with his sermon "Shall the Fundamentalists Win?" So vigorous was his defense of liberal positions that Fosdick was charged with heresy by the Presbyterian Church. John Foster Dulles, later Eisenhower's secretary of state, defended him in the ensuing ecclesiastical trial. Unable to remain with the Presbyterians, Fosdick returned to the Baptists. Under the patronage of John D. Rockefeller, he was appointed to the pulpit of the newly constructed Riverside Church in New York City, an accomplishment of sufficient importance to garner a cover story in *Time* magazine.[26]

Fosdick visited Palestine in the spring of 1926. His account of the journey appeared in installments in the *Ladies' Home Journal* and in full as the book *A Pilgrimage to Palestine*. Despite its traditional title, Fosdick's impressions were colored by his progressive perspective. One reviewer suggested that the book should have been titled the "pilgrimage of a theological liberal to Palestine."[27] Fosdick's liberalism is most evident in his account of what he calls "Hebrew-Christian" religion. Unfolding a historical narrative parallel to the course of his journey, Fosdick traced the development of this religion from the tribal cult of the Hebrews during the conquest of Canaan through the civil religion of the judges, followed by the prophets' transcendent monotheism, and culminating in universal morality of Jesus.[28]

In a chapter called "Palestine Tomorrow," Fosdick considered what this process might mean for the Holy Land. Although he acknowledged its sentimental appeal, he argued that Zionism was misunderstood by most Americans. Fosdick contended that the American, "accustomed to think of Judaism in terms of religion, naturally interprets Zionism in the same terms, and pictures pious colonists for the love of their God endeavoring to repeople and reclaim their Holy Land."[29] According to Fosdick, this interpretation departed from reality in crucial ways. To begin with, the majority of the Zionists were not observant Jews. They were secular socialists who might be considerably less sympathetic to American Christians.

Fosdick went to some lengths to defend "non-theistic" socialism, but rejected religious "monism" as a recipe for disaster.[30] The war had demonstrated that no people was free from moral obligations to others. The danger in the idea of chosenness was that it allowed Zionists to dismiss the rights of the Arab population. "In the early stages of its development," Fosdick recalled, "Zionism was advertised as the movement of a people without a land to a land without a people. Nothing could be more dangerously false than such simplification of the issue."[31] Fosdick also had grave doubts that the land could support further immigration. It was an "absurd pretense that into this poor land . . . millions of persecuted Jews from southeastern Europe can be poured, when the plain fact is that the country can do no more than absorb with difficulty a few thousand each year."[32]

Fosdick, in other words, rejected the neat solution to the Jewish problem that Blackstone envisioned. God was not miraculously preparing the land for its rightful owners. The persecuted Jews of the world could not be transferred to the Levant. Nevertheless, Fosdick regarded Jewish domination as inevitable. Raising the mythic parallel with the settlement of North America, Fosdick equated Arabs to Native Americans: picturesque but primitive. According to Fosdick: "The Jew . . . comes with the very qualities which the Arab notoriously lacks—energy, vitality, aggressiveness, knowledge of the methods of modern science—and the Arab has not the faintest chance in competition."[33] A Jewish Palestine was coming, but it would be conceived in sin rather than a return to paradise.

Fosdick hoped that competition could be transformed into cooperation before any irremediable injustices were committed. After his return to the United States, he denounced "a chauvinistic, arrogant, political Zionism" that pursued autonomy or statehood. As an alternative, Fosdick praised "moderate Zionism" that aimed for a Jewish community under binational or international administration. According to a report in the *New York Times*, Fosdick "singled out the Rev. Judah L. Magnes of the Hebrew University at Jerusalem, as one of the moderate Zionists who were combating the influence of the extreme nationalists. He said that if Zionism could be led by Dr. Magnes or a man like him, there would be hope of success with a program of education and cultural revival instead of political ambition as its motive."[34]

Fosdick's praise of Magnes, who had signed Blackstone's second memorial, calls attention to stress points in liberal Protestant conceptions of Zionism. A cultivated representative of the Reform tradition, Magnes hoped to make Palestine home to a Jewish minority devoted to cultural pursuits. His was a goal that liberal Protestants could endorse because it represented a middle course between universalism and particularism, morality and politics. Magnes's personal refinement also provided a vivid contrast to the uncouth political Zionists whom Fosdick denounced. The distinction between good and bad Jews had been extended to Palestine.

John Haynes Holmes, pastor of New York's Unitarian Community Church, was another admirer of Magnes. Before Magnes emigrated to Palestine in 1922, he and Holmes led interfaith worship services and collaborated on welfare projects inspired by the Social Gospel.[35] When Holmes visited the Holy Land in 1929, the chancellor of Hebrew University acted as his guide, leading him on an adventurous automobile tour. In addition to his relationship with Magnes, Holmes maintained friendly relations with Wise, Magnes's rival as America's leading Zionist after Brandeis became a justice of the Supreme Court. Unlike Fosdick, Holmes maintained connections to the American branch of the Zionist movement.[36]

Yet Holmes's and Fosdick's views in the 1920s were surprisingly similar. Like Fosdick, whose pilgrimage book he reviewed favorably, Holmes contended that Zionism was "fundamentally an ethical and spiritual phenomenon."[37] Autonomy or statehood was unnecessary. Holmes based this conclusion on his interpretation of the prophetic tradition. According to Holmes, the Jew's "one vast achievement in the world, his one unique contribution to humanity, is his prophets' dream of righteousness and peace upon the earth."[38]

Like Fosdick, Holmes could not resist interpreting Palestine through the lens of American history. Zionists were pioneers; Arabs were backward natives. The dilemma was that the natives had to be either conciliated or eliminated. "Zion can never prosper, nor even long survive, in the midst of a hostile population," Holmes wrote. "This population must either be exterminated, as Americans exterminated the North American Indians, or it must be befriended and fostered as partners in an undertaking which is to be regarded as a joint enterprise."[39]

Zionism was thus in danger of repeating American crimes. Holmes wondered whether a better option might be found in American history. Changing the terms of the comparison from relations between Europeans and natives to relations between the states, he asked, "Is it impossible to write a constitution in that land which shall create a political balance of power between the two contending interests, which in turn shall give security to both sides, as the American Constitution gave security to states small as well as large?"[40] In the eighteenth century, biblical Israel offered a precedent for the union of states. Holmes proposed that America return the favor by providing strategies for finding shared interests among rival populations in Mandatory Palestine.

Holmes's suggestion that Palestine follow an American model of political development goes along with his criticism of British administration. He reported: "Nothing of all I saw in Zion so disturbed me . . . as the elevation of 'Bloody Balfour' as one of the patron-saints of Zionism."[41] With the Balfour Declaration, "there intruded, like Satan into Paradise, the consciousness of power. . . . Not to the righteousness of their cause merely, nor to the justice of their principles, nor yet to their own ways of gentleness and peace, need they now look for protection, but to the overshadowing might of British arms."[42] Jewish settlement on these terms would be little more than an armed outpost of the empire—the antithesis of the righteous city of which the prophets spoke.

The course of events in Palestine made his words more ironic than Holmes might have hoped. While he was working on the manuscript in August 1929, riots broke out in Jerusalem and spread to Hebron, Safed, and Jaffa. After a week of violence, several hundred were dead. Most of the Jews were murdered by mobs; most of the Arabs were killed by British troops attempting to restore order. It appeared that the ways of gentleness and peace might not be sufficient to establish peace upon the earth.

In the foreword to *Palestine To-Day and To-morrow*, Holmes admitted that readers could not help interpreting his argument in light of these events.[43] Nevertheless, he claimed that he found nothing in the text that he wished to change. This verdict apparently included the challenge that Holmes posed at the end of the text: "Israel must decide whether she shall be a people, winnowed out of all other peoples a 'suffering servant' of God for his work of justice and peace upon the earth or a nation 'like all the nations.'"[44]

Holmes does not mention the source of the phrase "suffering servant." But readers would have recognized that it comes from Isaiah, whose depiction of a man of sorrows is read by Christians as prefiguring the agonies of Jesus. Holmes was subtly and perhaps unintentionally implying that Israel's duty was to engage in a collective imitation of Christ. The moral legitimacy of the Jewish presence in Palestine depended on Jews turning the other cheek.

The prophets do call the people of Israel to risk suffering pursuit of justice. As Reinhold Niebuhr pointed out, however, they do not seem to envision it being entirely wiped out. The rise of the Third Reich made this prospect terrifyingly real. In Niebuhr's view, making sense of Zionism under these conditions demanded a reevaluation of the relation between covenant and prophecy.

Niebuhr and the Jewish Question

As his friend Arthur Schlesinger, Jr. remarked, Reinhold Niebuhr casts a long shadow.[45] Although it has been nearly seventy years since he appeared on the cover of *Time* and more than forty since his death, Niebuhr remains the only Protestant theologian who is regularly cited in public discourse. During his lifetime, he was also America's most prominent Christian advocate for a Jewish state. In a eulogy delivered at Niebuhr's funeral, Rabbi Abraham Joshua Heschel described Niebuhr as a "lover of Zion and Jerusalem, imbued with the spirit of the Hebrew Bible, . . . a staunch friend of the Jewish people and the state of Israel."[46]

Niebuhr did not arrive at these views all at once. Born in Wright City, Missouri, the son of an immigrant clergyman, Niebuhr was raised in the distinctive culture of the German American Midwest. He received no formal education in English until he began graduate studies at Yale, where he came under the intellectual influence of the Social Gospel and William James.

Niebuhr's favorable attitude toward Judaism was unusual in these milieus. According to historian Egal Feldman, "Jewish rejection of Jesus as the Messiah and its alleged responsibility for the Crucifixion were matters strongly embedded in American Protestant teaching. The conviction that the 'New Israel' had superseded the 'Old' and that 'Judaism' was a religion of 'Laws' which had achieved their fulfillment with the coming of Christ were not debatable matters."[47] Modernists, in particular, used a critique of Judaism to distinguish themselves from their rivals. In a famous polemic, the University of Chicago's Shailer Matthews described dispensationalists' sharp distinction between Israel and the church as an atavistic fixation.[48]

Theological objections to Judaism were not incompatible with progressive political or social views. No less prominent a liberal than Walter Rauschenbusch argued that Judaism was the "most persistent force which pushed Jesus toward death."[49] Rauschenbusch denounced ethnic bigotry and maintained friendships with Jews, including Magnes. Nevertheless, he hoped that they would either reform Judaism in such a way that it would become barely distinguishable from Christianity, or simply convert.[50]

Niebuhr's intellectual formation included elements that would lead him to different conclusions. One was an appreciation for Judaism as a source of genuine theological insight. In the thesis that he submitted for his master of divinity degree, Niebuhr praised the Hebraic conception of body and soul as a unity for countering the dualism that Christianity inherited from Greek philosophy.[51] This conclusion challenged the progressive schema of religious development advanced by the likes of Fosdick.

Niebuhr was also impressed by his interactions with Jews in the social reform movement around Detroit, where he served as pastor of the Bethel Church from 1915 to 1928. In a diary entry published in his pastoral memoir, *Leaves from the Notebook of a Tamed Cynic*, Niebuhr reported: "The more I make contact with the Jews the more I am impressed with the superior sensitiveness of the Jewish conscience in social problems. . . . I do not say that there is not in privileged Jewish groups more complacency than is compatible with their avowed devotion to the Hebrew prophets, but there is at least a considerable appreciation of the genius of prophetic religion and some honest effort to apply the prophetic ideal to life."[52]

Niebuhr's rehabilitation of Judaism within the framework of liberal Protestantism informs his earliest statements on Zionism. In a newspaper column published soon after he left Detroit to take a position at Union Theological Seminary in New York, Niebuhr reported: "I have always regarded Zionism as a legitimate ideal of tremendous significance for which one has all the more sympathy because so many seemingly insuperable obstacles stand between it and its fulfillment."[53] The column praises Magnes as a moral exemplar. But Niebuhr acknowledged that Magnes's "critics contend that his scheme is impossible, that spiritual ideals can only be realized on the basis of political and economic facts, that any cultural venture without a political basis will be too ephemeral to claim the loyalty and the sacrifices of the Jewish people."[54] Despite a "personal pacifistic bias in favor of an end which can be carried out without the use of coercion," Niebuhr was inclined to place himself among these critics. He concluded that "the ideal of a political homeland for the Jews is so intriguing that I am almost willing to sacrifice my convictions for the sake of it."[55]

Yet Niebuhr hesitated to endorse political Zionism. Influenced by the Social Gospel, he still hoped that voluntary cooperation would make coercion unnecessary. Niebuhr soon abandoned this hope. In *Moral Man and Immoral Society*, published in 1932, he argued that "a sharp distinction must be drawn between the moral and social behavior of individuals and social groups, national, racial, and economic; and that this distinction justifies and necessitates political policies which a purely individualistic ethic must always find embarrassing."[56] Niebuhr asserted that liberal Christians falsely assumed that groups could or should practice personal virtues such as charity. But while individuals overcome egoism and act in service to others, he insisted, it is exceptionally difficult for groups to do so.

Niebuhr contended that the nation was the ultimate focus of group allegiance. No bigger group could command the allegiance of individuals, while no smaller one satisfied their desire for power. Contemporary readers associated Niebuhr's account of group conflict with Marx. But his emphasis on the nation rather than class as the relevant unit of analysis is a significant deviation from Marxism—and an important element in his case for Zionism.[57]

Niebuhr's account of group formation led him to reevaluate the possibility of uncoerced progress. Earlier in his career, he believed that moral appeals and education could lead to improvement within and among societies. Now he concluded that "the rational capacity to consider the rights and needs of others in fair competition with our own will never be so fully developed as to create the possibility for the anarchistic millennium which is the social utopia, either explicit or implicit, of all intellectual or religious moralists."[58] Because reason and moral instinct were insufficient, force was indispensable: "[A]dequate political morality . . . will recognise that human society will probably never escape social conflict, even though it extends the areas of social co-operation. It will try to save society from being involved in endless cycles of futile conflict, not by an effort to abolish coercion in the life of collective man, but by reducing it to a minimum by counseling the use of such types of coercion as are more compatible with the moral and rational factors in human society and by discriminating between the purposes and ends for which coercion is used."[59]

Niebuhr credited Judaism with upholding adequate political morality against both secular and religious utopians. While Christians pursued individual salvation, "[i]t was the peculiar genius of Jewish religious thought, that it conceived the millennium in this-worldly terms. The Gospel conception of the kingdom of God represents a highly spiritualized version of this Jewish millennial hope, heavily indebted to the vision of the Second Isaiah."[60] For Niebuhr, prophecy was not a prediction the future, but neither was it naïve moralism. Instead, it was distinct genre of social and political thought.

Niebuhr's ostensibly Hebraic conception of prophecy has complicated implications for the locus of group identity, the nation. On the one hand, appeals to transcendent authority counter man's tendency to regard the nation as the highest object of loyalty. Citing a favorite passage, Niebuhr reminded readers: "The prophet Amos could cry in the name of the Lord, 'Are ye not as the children of the Ethiopians unto me.' But his was a voice in the wilderness among the many who regarded Israel as the special servant of God among the nations of the world."[61] The critical function of the prophet, in other words, is to remind the nation that it is not the sole recipient of divine favor. There is a higher law, which the nation must obey or face judgement.

On the other hand, prophecy is not simply a critique of politics in the name of abstract justice. Since it is impossible for human beings to comply fully with the demands of morality, such a critique could unintentionally license the unconstrained pursuit of power. Prophecy provides an alternative to this cynical response by building "a citadel of hope, which is built on the edge of despair."[62] In promising that God will perfect the world as well as judge it, Niebuhr argued, prophecy encourages human beings to take their fate into their own hands: "Men are inclined to view both individual and social moral facts with complacency until they view them from some absolute perspective. But the same absolutism which drives them to despair, rejuvenates their hope. In the imagination of the truly religious man the God, who condemns history, will yet redeem history."[63]

Niebuhr did not claim that this vision was limited to the biblical Hebrews. Remaining a theological liberal, he credited Judaism with articulating in symbolic language a dilemma faced by *all* human beings. As historical custodians of the prophetic tradition, on the other hand, Jews experienced in especially acute form the tensions between God and nation. For Jews, prophetic religion was both a gift that pointed beyond the people of Israel and an affirmation of its unique status. The prophets—at least in Niebuhr's reading—did not call Israel to accept a permanent condition as the suffering servant. Rather, they appealed to Israel to improve itself within the limits of human capacities and the national form so that it might act as a model for others.

Niebuhr's fear that cultural Zionism was unrealistic seemed to be vindicated by the political situation in the early 1930s. The economic crisis and the rise of antidemocratic regimes in Europe convinced him that man could never build the kingdom of God by persuasion alone. This more pessimistic outlook strengthened Niebuhr's support for Zionism. In a world on the brink of madness, the Jews more than any other people needed a state of their own.

Anti-Semitism and Jewish Survival

Liberal Protestants, like Americans more generally, did not immediately recognize the threat of Adolf Hitler. Although they discussed allegations of anti-Semitic persecution, liberal religious intellectuals expressed doubt about their veracity or hinted that German Jews had brought the unpleasant circumstances on themselves. According to historian Deborah Lipstadt, this attitude was rooted in the old conception of Judaism "as a soulless religion of dry legalisms and national particularism."[64] To the extent that liberal Protestants did protest the Third Reich in its first years, it was in defense of so-called non-Aryan Christians—converts to Christianity or their descendants, who were still considered Jews under Nazi racial laws.[65]

Niebuhr was an early critic of this stance. In the pages of the *Christian Century*, he pointed out that limiting criticism to racial anti-Semitism gave implicit sanction to theological anti-Semitism. Although he had echoed conventional objections to Judaism as a young minister, Niebuhr now found them unacceptable.[66] By ignoring the plight of Jews as Jews, Christians were abandoning their own religious responsibility.[67]

What would be the most effective way of meeting that responsibility? Niebuhr dismissed boycotts of German goods as well-intentioned but unlikely to make much difference. He reasoned that they might even be counterproductive, hurting the Jews whom they were intended to help by cutting off financial support from abroad. Another possibility was opening America's doors to Jewish refugees. This alternative won the support of many liberal Protestants, including Holmes and Fosdick, but found little favor with the public. As a result of strong opposition, the Roosevelt administration dropped its tentative efforts to relax immigration controls.[68] If Niebuhr had once been merely sympathetic to Zionism, persecution in Europe and the restrictive refugee policy at home made supporting it seem imperative. In an address to Hadassah, the women's branch of the Zionist Organization of America, Niebuhr argued that despite the challenges involved, "Palestine must not be abandoned. . . . What is left of a conscience in the western world must be united to stiffen opposition to any policy of abandonment. The Jews have never had so clear a right to support from all decent people as in this case."[69]

Heightened urgency led to new institutions. In 1932, two organizations were set up to organize Gentiles who supported Jewish settlement in Palestine: the American Palestine Committee (APC) and the Pro-Palestine Federation of America (PPFA). Founded at a banquet at the Mayflower Hotel in Washington, the APC was designed to appeal to political figures and included several U.S. senators, Vice President Charles Curtis, and Supreme Court Justice Harlan Stone. The PPFA, based in Chicago, was more religious, counting Holmes and the muckraking journalist and Social Gospeler Charles Edward Russell among its founding members.[70] Despite their prominent membership, neither organization amounted to much. The APC collapsed in the year of its founding. The PPFA held a few lecture events and published occasional pamphlets before it folded.[71]

The British White Paper of 1939, which restricted Jewish immigration to Palestine, provoked a stronger reaction. The Christian Leaders, Clergymen and Laymen, on Behalf of Jewish Immigration into Palestine Federation was formed to oppose the white paper on the basis of "the Christian conscience."[72] Its members included Niebuhr and prominent liberals including the Methodist Bishop Francis J. McConnell. After war broke out, a hasty reorganization of the international Zionist movement led to the establishment of the Emergency Committee for Zionist Affairs (ECZA) to coordinate Zionist activities in the United States. As part of their public relations and lobbying strategy, ECZA decided to sponsor non-Jewish affiliates. The revival of the APC was announced in March 1941. The foundation of the Christian Committee on Palestine (CCP) followed in December 1942.

The division of labor between these organizations was roughly similar to that between the original APC and the PPFA. The revived APC appealed to political figures, including Senator Harry Truman.[73] The CCP membership was weighted toward clergymen.[74] Despite their differences in emphasis, both groups appealed to religious considerations. It was a matter of returning the people of Israel to their Promised Land, not just ameliorating suffering. Historian Carenen reports that the press release announcing the formation of the APC even cited Blackstone as a forerunner of its efforts.[75]

Niebuhr, a charter member of the CCP, was its most prominent spokesman. In "Jews After the War," an essay that the *Nation* ran in two parts in early 1942, Niebuhr argued that Jewish sovereignty in Palestine was a necessary part of any postwar settlement. According to Niebuhr: "The Jews require a homeland, if for no other reason, because even the most generous immigration laws of the Western democracies will not permit all the dispossessed Jews of Europe to find a haven in which they may look forward to a tolerable future. . . . A much weightier justification of Zionism is that every race finally has a right to a homeland where it will not be 'different,' where it will neither be patronized by 'good' people nor subjected to calumny by bad people."[76]

Toleration was desirable, Niebuhr argued, but it was not good enough. Like other nations, Jews had the right to self-determination rather than being compelled to depend on the sufferance of even a generous majority. Only then could they escape invidious distinctions between the right and wrong sorts of Jews. Based on this reasoning, Niebuhr concluded: "Zionist aspirations, it seems to me, deserve a more generous support than they have been accorded by liberal and democratic groups in Western countries. Non-Zionist Jews have erred in being apologetic or even hostile to these aspirations on the ground that their open expression might imperil rights painfully won in the democratic world. Non-Jewish liberals have erred equally in regarding Zionism as nothing but the vestigial remnant of an ancient religious dream, the unfortunate aberration of a hard-pressed people."[77]

Although they were expressed in secular terms in the *Nation* articles, these conclusions rested on religious positions that Niebuhr expressed elsewhere. Some liberal Protestants contrasted nationalism with the prophets' ostensibly universal moral teaching. Niebuhr countered that Zionism was compatible with prophecy, correctly understood. Prophetic criticism of Israel, Niebuhr argued, should never be read as a demand that it act as a suffering servant beyond all endurance:

> The great prophets of Israel, particularly Jeremiah and the second Isaiah, frequently spoke the word of God "against Israel." They did indeed speak this word on the basis of the conviction that God had particularly chosen Israel. Amos, in fact, combines the idea of a special destiny ("you only have I chosen") with the idea of a special punishment ("therefore will I visit you with your iniquities") in a very dialectical way. It is this dialectic of prophetism which cannot fully work itself out in the modern situation. It cannot be fully developed, because the word of God spoken against the nation in all universal monotheism can hardly be entertained when the nation is faced with annihilation.[78]

To be sure, Niebuhr did not appeal to biblical prophecy in the same way as Blackstone. In his view, the prophecies were a way of articulating psychological and political insights, rather than a forecast of events to come. Nevertheless, his argument was based on his theological commitments and aimed to weave contemporary events into the continuing story of God's covenant with Israel. Niebuhr was a Christian Zionist, not just a Christian who supported Zionism.[79]

The risk of annihilation became more difficult to deny as the war continued. Despite official reluctance to acknowledge the extermination program and skepticism in the American press, it was recognized by the end of 1942 that the Nazis were conducting a campaign of genocide.[80] In April of 1943, representatives of Britain and the United States met in Bermuda to discuss possible responses. No serious proposals were forthcoming.[81]

The Social Gospel and cofounder of the CCP Henry Atkinson denounced this silence in an article for *Christianity and Crisis*, a journal that Niebuhr founded in 1941 to challenge pacifist tendencies in the liberal churches. Atkinson insisted that "the failure of the Bermuda Conference to develop a constructive program to help these millions of helpless Jews is a shocking scandal" that was inspired by the "ghost of political expediency and appeasement." As a result of their naïveté and inaction, American Christians had blood on their hands. Echoing Niebuhr's polemic against abstract moralism, Atkinson proclaimed: "The Christian conscience cannot rest content in expressions of goodwill and pious intentions, but must be translated into a definite program of action. It is the conviction, therefore, of an increasing number of Christian leaders, that, in the present crisis, Palestine should be made accessible to Jewish refugees from lands of persecution."[82]

The CCP was formally committed only to the lifting of the 1939 White Paper, which restricted Jewish immigration to Palestine. Much of its leadership was nevertheless favorable to Jewish sovereignty in at least part of the historical Promised Land.[83] In this respect, they followed the line set by ECZA, which resolved that "Palestine be established as a Jewish Commonwealth" at a convention at the Biltmore Hotel in New York in the spring of 1942.[84] Although some Jewish leaders continued to take principled stands against Zionism, especially in its political variants, the Biltmore program made it became harder for Christians to represent assimilationists, pacifists, and cultural Zionists as good Jews, in contradistinction to the bad Jews of Zionism. Changes in the balance of power in the Jewish community authorized a more assertive Christian Zionism.[85]

Immigration, Partition, Independence

Before the 1940s, the Zionist movement in America was not necessarily associated with the pursuit of a Jewish state. Although it included political Zionists who aimed at independence, it also embraced cultural Zionists who would be satisfied with a Jewish community in Palestine under binational or international administration. This ambiguity allowed liberal Protestants who were squeamish about nationalism to consider themselves supporters of Zionism. John Haynes Holmes, for example, served on the executive committee of the CCP.[86]

The Biltmore program made this balancing act more challenging. In 1944, the Federal Council of Churches, the leading liberal umbrella group, produced a study guide called "The Conflict over Palestine" for use by its members. Although it avoided stating a final judgment, the pamphlet highlighted the tension between Zionism, Arab rights, and skepticism about the enterprise among some American Jewish leaders. The implication was that Zionism was morally, theologically, and politically misguided.[87]

The APC and the CCP, by contrast, doubled down on a Jewish state. At a gala attended by Senators Robert Taft and Robert Wagner and Vice President Henry Wallace, a joint committee of the organizations adopted a resolution "that Palestine may be reconstituted by the Jewish people as a free and democratic Jewish Commonwealth."[88] Many speakers appealed to humanitarian and legal concerns in support of this conclusion, including invocations of the Lodge-Fish resolution of 1922. Assistant Attorney General Norman Littell drew a connection between the political and religious arguments, urging the audience to "clearly recognize our responsibility as American citizens, unless we wish to turn our backs on the most sacred heritage of the Christian epoch."[89]

Among Christian intellectuals, Niebuhr provided the most elaborate justification for a Jewish commonwealth. Acknowledging this outcome would be morally problematic, Niebuhr contended that "Zionist leaders are unrealistic in insisting that their demands entail no 'injustice' to the Arab population. . . . It is absurd to expect any people to regard the restriction of their sovereignty as 'just,' no matter how many other benefits accrue from that abridgement."[90] Despite this, he argued that the injustice would be less serious than the consequences of denying a state to Jews.

Niebuhr's conclusion was based on assumptions that run through his responses to Zionism. The first was that territorial sovereignty was a condition of *any* people's existence, even when its members enjoyed favorable conditions in their countries of refuge. For Niebuhr, "the survival of the nation is more or less guaranteed by the security of a 'homeland.'"[91] He was unwilling to extend the same support to Palestinian Arabs' claims due to a second assumption: that they understood themselves as generic Arabs rather than a distinct people attached to a particular place. As such, their rights could be satisfied by a broader territorial adjustment. According to Niebuhr: "The [Zionist] solution must, and can, be made acceptable to the Arabs if it is incorporated into a total settlement of the issues of the Mediterranean and the Near Eastern World; and it need not be unjust to the Arabs in the long run if the same 'imperial' policy which establishes the Jewish homeland also consolidates and unifies the Arab world."[92]

Niebuhr's qualified endorsement of an "imperial" policy points toward a third element of his case for Zionism. He was convinced that the hegemonic powers owed Jews a nation-state not only as security against persecution in the future but also as "a partial expiation" for the vexed history of Jewish-Christian relations.[93] As early as 1938, Niebuhr had spoken of the "sense of shame" he experienced when he reflected on Christian indifference to Jewish suffering.[94] He felt no such debts to Muslims, whose religion he would later characterize as a threat to Western civilization. And Arab Christians hardly figured in his analysis.

Niebuhr synthesized these arguments in testimony before the Anglo-American Committee of Inquiry, which was convened in the winter of 1946 to consider solutions to the Palestine problem. He appeared on behalf of the CCP, along with Daniel Poling, editor of the *Christian Herald*, who represented the fundamentalist position within that organization.[95] In his testimony, Niebuhr endorsed a "Palestinian state with a Jewish majority."

Challenged to explain the consistency of this view with the arguments of *Moral Man*, Niebuhr continued:

> I disagree with my Christian and Jewish friends who take an individu-alistic, liberalistic attitude and say Jewish nationalism is egotistic. This seems to me to be very unrealistic in approach. That is, a group has as much right to live as an individual has. Through its survival impulse, per-haps it is morally neutral, but it gets to be selfish. The will to power develops out of the survival impulse, but I don't think that a group that is established can very well say to a culture which lives in a very pre-carious position, that is, a nation without a base, it is very difficult to say to them, "It is a selfish thing for you to want to be established."[96]

This reasoning did not imply that all or even most Jews had to go to Pales-tine. Niebuhr condemned quotas that limited Jewish entry to the United States and insisted that Jews had the right to disappear into liberal socie-ties by assimilation or conversion if they chose to do so. Yet he argued that Jews faced "an intolerable tension" in making this choice when they had no assurance that Jewish ethnicity and culture would survive in their absence. The establishment of a Jewish state would thus enhance freedom outside Palestine as well as providing a national home for Jews who wanted one: "If the Jews have a homeland, where there is security for the perpetuation of their ethnic group, then the individual Jew in the various nations will not have the collective survival impulse . . . in the same way as now."[97]

The price of this freedom was population transfer. Asked how this could be accomplished, Niebuhr endorsed former president Herbert Hoover's pro-posal for the removal of Palestinian Arabs to Jordan. Niebuhr distanced him-self from forced deportation, suggesting that those who left their homes could be compensated for lost property. Even so, historian Rafael Medoff observes that Niebuhr took "a maximalist approach to the Palestinian Arab issue that went beyond the public position of the Zionist movement itself."[98]

The journalist John Judis argues that Niebuhr's testimony "was another example of how American liberals, in the wake of the Holocaust and the urgency it lent to the Zionist case, simply abandoned their principles when it came to Palestine's Arabs."[99] It would be more accurate to say that those principles were never clear-cut when it came to Zionism. For Niebuhr, religious identity was inextricable from national identity. Jews were entitled to a state because their religion made them outsiders in any other society. He saw Palestinians, by contrast, as part of a larger and more secure Muslim population. In his opinion, its right of self-determination could be satisfied in other ways.

The Federal Council of Churches provided a platform for religious criticism, making it something of an institutional nemesis to the CCP.[100] But outright anti-Zionism was unusual in the immediate aftermath of World War II. When the Anglo-American Committee of Inquiry recommended that Palestine be opened to Jewish immigration, reversing the White Paper, the *Christian Century* editorialized: "If this can be it should be done, for doing it will save the lives of the most exposed Jews in Europe."[101] The extent of Niebuhr's and Atkinson's enthusiasm remained exceptional, but liberal Protestants were more favorable to Zionism in the immediate aftermath of World War II than they had been before it.[102]

American Cyrus

Broad, if not always deep, approval for Zionism among liberal Protestants continued to be a factor in the debates about the partition of Palestine and the recognition of the State of Israel. Its public expression was organized by the American Christian Palestine Committee (ACPC), formed in 1946 through a merger between the APC and the CCP. After Britain rejected the Anglo-American Committee's recommendations, the ACPC sought to mobilize Christians in favor of a Jewish commonwealth on the basis of Jews' unique status as a religious group as well as an ethnicity, the precedent of the Balfour Declaration, and Christian complicity in the Holocaust.[103]

It remains unclear whether these efforts had any direct effect on President Truman's decision to pledge support for a Jewish commonwealth in October 1946—and ultimately to recognize the State of Israel.[104] As a senator, Truman had been among the original members of the reborn APC. He also led a party that included a statement demanding "the opening of Palestine to unrestricted Jewish immigration and colonization, and such a policy as to result in the establishment there of a free and democratic Jewish commonwealth" in its platform, partly due to the influence of Truman's fellow APC member Senator Wagner.[105]

Yet Truman's sympathy for Zionism did not necessarily translate into action. As president, he opposed the bipartisan Taft-Wagner resolution declaring approval for a Jewish commonwealth, preferring to wait for the report of the Committee of Inquiry. After the committee issued its findings, Truman complained of incessant lobbying by Zionists, who were unsatisfied with these proposals.[106] Truman was also skeptical of the idea that Jews were God's chosen people. In a 1945 diary entry, he wrote: "The Jews claim God Almighty picked 'em out for special privilege. Well I'm sure he had better judgment. Fact is, I never thought God picked any favorites."[107]

Historians have debated endlessly about which factors were conclusive for Truman's policy toward Israel. Several point out that while he was not publicly devout, he was a serious reader of the Bible who was familiar with the prophecies of restoration.[108] Others contend that he was motivated primarily by political concerns: the election of 1948 was expected to be close, and Truman needed the help of Jewish voters.[109] This debate is fascinating, but in some ways beside the point. Statesmen always have complicated and sometimes contradictory reasons for their decisions. Truman's significance for Christian Zionism rests less on the private motives that led him to decide that the United States would recognize the State of Israel than on the symbolic significance of his doing so. Whether he intended to do so or not, Truman realized a hope cherished by many American Christians since the early republic. He deployed the power of the new Israel, founded under the guidance of divine Providence, in the service of reestablishing the old Israel.

Even if his decision in 1948 was driven by electoral calculation, Truman relished this mythopoeic role after leaving office. In an incident that has become famous among students of religion in American politics, Truman compared himself to the anointed restorer of Israel from the Babylonian captivity. "I am Cyrus!" he told an audience the Jewish Theological Seminary in New York.[110]

Yet if Truman was among the "heirs of Cyrus," as historian Paul Charles Merkley has described America's pro-Zionist presidents, he was a scion of distinctly liberal aspect.[111] What he honored in the biblical people of Israel was not its status as the vehicle of God's will, but its testimony to a religious perspective to which all people had access. At an address honoring the Passover holiday delivered shortly before he succeeded to the presidency, Truman explained that it "was the Hebrews who first fought the worship of pagan idols in the western world and who preached eternal faith in one God—the God in whom we all put our trust."[112] He was describing universal deity of liberal Protestantism rather than the God of the covenant. In an address to the Federal Council of Churches in March 1946, he noted that Americans "are a people who worship God in different ways. But we are all bound together in a single unity—the unity of individual freedom in a democracy."[113] Truman's kind of religion was realized in politics rather than in ceremony.

In this respect, Truman's decision to act as an American Cyrus signals a new phase of America's relationship to what had once been a semi-imaginary holy land. Modifying America's Protestant-inspired civil religion in a way that made Jews full participants, Truman opened the way for a special relationship between the United States and the Jewish State. Religious intellectuals had already coined a term for this vision: Judeo-Christian civilization.[114]

PART III
God's Country

On June 7, 1981, Israeli jets bombed the French-built nuclear reactor at Osirak, about eighteen miles south of Baghdad. The reactor was not yet operational, and Iraqi officials denied that it was part of a weapons program. According to the Israeli government, however, its very existence posed a mortal danger to the Jewish State.[1] This justification was widely rejected in the United States. Two days after the strike, the *New York Times* editorialized: "Israel's sneak attack . . . was an act of inexcusable and short-sighted aggression."[2] In a rare instance of agreement with the *Times* editorial board, President Ronald Reagan instructed UN ambassador Jeanne Kirkpatrick to support a resolution condemning Israel. Before the unanimous vote by the Security Council, Kirkpatrick described the raid as "shocking" and compared it to the Soviet invasion of Afghanistan.[3]

Despite criticism from the White House, Israel was not without American supporters. Soon after the bombing, Israeli prime minister Menachem Begin called on preacher and political organizer Jerry Falwell to organize conservative Christians on Israel's behalf. Believing that American prosperity and even survival depended on its attitude toward God's most favored nation, Falwell was happy to comply. "If this nation wants her fields to remain white with grain," he wrote in *Listen, America!*, a manifesto for the Moral Majority, "her scientific achievements to remain notable, and her freedom to remain intact, America must continue to stand with Israel."[4] In September, Begin and Falwell held a widely publicized meeting at Blair House, the executive branch's guest facility opposite the White House. In a statement following the summit, Falwell explained his support for Israel by citing

God's promise to "bless those who bless" Abraham. "I believe history supports the premise that God deals with nations as they deal with Israel," he told reporters.[5]

The "theo-political alliance" between conservative American Christians and a right-wing Israeli government was regarded as a novelty when it was announced.[6] And in some respects, it was. For much of the twentieth century, America's most prominent Christian supporters of Israel were political liberals associated with traditional denominations. From the establishment of the State of Israel up to Reagan's inauguration, figures including Reinhold Niebuhr, the Methodist historian Franklin Littell, and Robert Drinan, a Catholic priest who represented Massachusetts in Congress, were among the public faces of Christian Zionism.[7] Rather than end-times prophecy, these figures emphasized Christians' moral debt to Jews and Israel's credentials as a liberal democracy.[8]

Yet the love affair between conservative evangelicals and Israel was also more continuous with the liberal Christian Zionism of the postwar years than it appeared to be. Although it could be—and was—synthesized with dispensationalist themes, the moralized and often militarized vision of Judeo-Christian civilization to which the new brand of Christian Zionism appealed was not derived from obscure nineteenth-century theologians.[9] Instead, it emerged from Cold War–era attempts to find the meaning of American power in the travails of the people and the Land of Israel—a project that had been blessed by theological liberals before it was taken up by conservatives.

There is something paradoxical about the way in which the belief that the Promised Land lies thousands of miles away, between the Mediterranean Sea and the Jordan River, bolstered Americans' sense of their own national purpose. Yet many American Christians perceived in Israel and Israeli Jews a better, more heroic version of themselves. By projecting American ideals and identities onto the biblical landscape, they also promoted those principles at home. To that extent, they could regard themselves as honorary citizens of God's country.

5 | The God of the Armies of Israel: Zionism and Judeo-Christian Civilization

> Then David said to the Philistine, "You come to me with a
> sword and with a spear and with a javelin; but I come to you
> in the name of the Lord of hosts, the God of the armies of
> Israel, whom you have defied."
> —1 Sam. 17:45, Revised Standard Version

Exodus was one of the most highly anticipated film releases of 1960. Based on a best-selling novel and cast with stars including Paul Newman and Eva Marie Saint, the production had the makings of a hit. Among other notable features, it was the highest-profile film yet to be shot in the State of Israel—a fact that attracted considerable attention from the press.[1] While it earned nominations for several Academy Awards and $20 million at the box office, however, *Exodus* was not an artistic success. A review in the *New Yorker* observed that director Otto Preminger "permits nearly everyone in his large cast to state his ideological and political convictions before and after each new turn of events, and the result is an awesome talkfest that is all too rarely interrupted by the popping of rifles."[2] Beyond its reliance on expository dialogue, *Exodus* suffered from a tendency toward caricature. The heroes—principally Jewish and American—were very good. The villains—mostly British and Arab—were very bad.

If these qualities limited *Exodus*'s success as an entertainment, they also made it instructive as a document of American culture. Blending vague religiosity with history lessons, the speeches that critics mocked made the case that there was a latent affinity between America and the Jewish State. An exchange between Paul Newman and Eva Marie Saint about midway through the film is representative of this dynamic. On a journey to visit his parents' kibbutz, Newman's character, Ari Ben Canaan—literally, the son of Canaan—invites Saint's Kitty Fremont to join him in surveying the Galilean landscape. Pointing out landmarks, he asks if she knows her Bible. She does, Kitty explains, "in a Presbyterian sort of way."[3] A trained nurse from Indiana, Kitty is a mainline Protestant rather than a fundamentalist captivated by end-times prophecy. Despite her modesty, Kitty identifies Mount Tabor from the Book of Judges. It is "[w]here Deborah gathered her armies . . . where she stood when she watched Barak march out to fight the Canaanites."

Ari is impressed. He explains that his father was inspired by the same story to rename himself when he arrived in Palestine as part of the first *aliyah*: "Barak, the son of Canaan, and this valley became a Jewish land once again." In addition to grounding Zionism in the biblical narrative, Ari's speech suggests a parallel between his people and the settlers who sought their destiny in the American West. In the popular imagination, they, too, were stern, Bible-inspired pioneers, who wanted to live in peace but were prepared to defend themselves if forced to do so. These stories overlap in Ari's justification of Zionism. When he asserts, "This is my country," Kitty reassures him: "I do know. I understand."[4]

This suggestive way making connections between Jews and Christians, Americans and Israelis was not original to *Exodus*. In mass media as well as intellectual journals, American Christians developed favorable interpretations of Israel as a partner in a special relationship based on common history and values. Skeptics about American support for the State of Israel worried that it would become aligned with the Soviet Union or interfere with America's strategic goals in the Middle East. As the Cold War intensified, however, Israel came to be seen as a bulwark of Judeo-Christian civilization.

Israel's Early Years

On May 14, 1948, the State of Israel declared its independence. Eleven minutes later, President Truman approved a statement recognizing the "[Jewish] provisional government as the de facto authority of the new State of Israel."[5] The terseness of the statement belied its controversial significance. Although U.S. recognition was regarded as a fait accompli by the time it was actually announced, Truman's secretary of state, General George C. Marshall, had threatened to resign over the issue.

Divisions in opinion extended to the general public. Polls showed that nearly three times as many Americans sympathized with the Jews over the Arabs in the conflict in Palestine—about a third, compared with roughly 12 percent. Yet only a minority of the population held strong views on the issue. And even though a plurality favored the Jewish side, Americans overwhelmingly opposed U.S. military intervention in the region.[6]

Christian supporters of Zionism tried to shift opinion in favor of the Zionist cause.[7] On a theoretical level, their case was based on the rehabilitation of nationalism. Challenging the internationalism and pacifism that characterized liberal Protestantism in the 1920s and 1930s, American Christian Palestine Committee (ACPC) chairman Carl Voss acknowledged that while "it is clear that a truly internationalist attitude is the consummation we all pray for, the struggles within the United Nations itself show us how far we still are from a world without nationalism and separate national organisms."[8] In addition to his defense of nationalism in general, Voss made a religious case for a Jewish state. Without taking a position on the mystery of the relation between the people of Israel and the church, he maintained: "Every student of Jewish history knows that the Jewish religion is inextricably intertwined with the existence of the Jewish people. . . . Jewish nationhood and Jewish religion are intimately connected with the hope for restoration to Zion."[9] To reject Zionism, Voss suggested, was to refuse to take covenant seriously.

With war raging in Palestine, appeals by Voss and his allies were mostly talk. After the cessation of hostilities, the ACPC developed a new strategy to promote its message. In April 1949, weeks after the conclusion of the armistice that separated Israel from territory controlled by Jordan, the ACPC dispatched a "study tour" to Israel. Arriving on May 1, the group was apparently the first delegation of American Christians to visit Palestine since Israel's declaration of independence.[10] The composition of the group gives a hint about the ACPC's target audience. Mostly journalists, ministers, and academics from cities in the Northeast and the upper Midwest, the group's members had progressive politics and mainline denominational affiliations. It was the sort of company in which Kitty Fremont would have felt comfortable.

The group's findings, published in a volume distributed by the ACPC, were consistent with these affiliations. Common themes included condemnation of the Arab attacks, wonder at the social and political accomplishments of the new state, and assurances that Jews would be good stewards of sites sacred to Christians. Only one contributor, Minneapolis Lutheran pastor Reuben K. Youngdahl, offered prophetic justifications for Jewish restoration. For other contributors, Israel was as much a triumph of Western civilization as it was a work of God.[11]

Not all commentators on Jews or Middle Eastern affairs accepted the claim that support for the State of Israel followed from Christian premises. Insisting on the injustice of a Jewish state in lands inhabited predominantly by Arabs and the theological superficiality of Christian appropriations of Jewish concepts, critics argued that the ACPC was tempting American Christians into a dubious compromise with the same nationalism that had only recently led the world into war.

Liberal Protestant Criticism of Israel

Christian objections to Zionism were muted during the war itself, as discussions of Jewish issues were dominated by horror at Nazi persecution (the full dimensions of the Holocaust were not yet widely recognized). But they resurfaced as the conflict entered its final phases and interest turned to the character of postwar order. In 1945, the American Council for Judaism (ACJ) published a digest called *Christian Opinion on Jewish Nationalism and a Jewish State*, which publicized objections by dozens of prominent churchmen.[12] In an implicit rebuke to Niebuhr's authority as the leading Christian spokesman on the issue, the volume included critical statements from Henry Sloane Coffin—the president of Union Theological Seminary—and Niebuhr's brother, Yale theologian H. Richard Niebuhr.[13]

Figures associated with missions in the Middle East were prominent among the Christian critics of Zionism. Some of the earliest Americans who followed God's call to the Middle East focused their attention on Jews. In 1818, Levi Parsons led an expedition to Jerusalem, where he hoped to convert the Jews when they returned from exile. By the second half of the nineteenth century, missionaries shifted their efforts to Arabs. The results include the foundation of institutions such as the American University of Beirut (AUB).

Missionaries worried that Zionism threatened these achievements. In 1944, the Committee on Work Among Moslems of the Foreign Missions Conference of North America warned: "The Arabs note that some American Christians feel it their Christian duty to assist the Jews in their aspirations for a national home in Palestine, but they also note that these same Christians have not been so vocal in attempting to open the doors of America to the persecuted Jews of Europe. It appears to many that we are asking the Moslem Arab to assume a more Christian attitude than Christians are willing to take."[14] In his statements on Zionism, Niebuhr had urged Christians not to ask Jews to play the suffering servant under unendurable circumstances. Missionaries contended that it was hypocritical to seek relief for Jews by shifting the burden onto others.

Missionaries also pointed out the incongruity of the United States supporting a militant nationalist movement so soon after fighting against another one. In the months leading up to Israel's declaration of independence, Bayard Dodge, the former president of the AUB, published articles opposing American recognition of a Jewish state. According to Dodge: "Almost everyone in America is anxious to help the Jews, who have suffered so much during the past decade."[15] Even so, he contended, Israeli independence would be counterproductive both for the Jews and for America. Dodge particularly worried that a Jewish state would promote Soviet influence in the region. Even if it were not a formal ally of the USSR, its mere existence would drive a diplomatic wedge between Arab nations and their Western patrons.[16] Dodge further informed readers that "not all Jews are Zionists and not all Zionists are extremists."[17] He singled out the ACJ and its leader, Baltimore rabbi Morris Lazaron, as representatives of respectable Jewish opinion. For Dodge, the distinction between good Jews and bad Jews was clear. The former promoted a "universal religious message" hardly different from Christianity. The latter pursued political goals based on the Old Testament.

Arguments in this vein received institutional support from the Committee for Peace and Justice in the Holy Land. The committee was not a religious organization per se.[18] Its membership, which included Fosdick, Coffin, and the missionary Daniel Bliss, nevertheless had a clerical flavor.[19] The churchmen's goal was to refute claims that Zionism was somehow justified by Christianity. In Coffin's opinion, only "biblical literalists" accepted the idea that the people and the Land of Israel were destined to be reunited.[20] In a fiery 1949 article, Coffin denounced "emotionally nationalistic Jews who have fervently supported [Israel's] establishment" and would "continue to bring pressure on our government to sustain it with loans and to stand for its interests in the always confused and conflicting chaos of Near Eastern politics."[21] Against this pressure, Coffin insisted that "our foreign policy must be designed in the interests of this country and of the commonweal of mankind, not of any other state—Eire or Israel or what not—for which some group of partially Americanized Americans profess a sentimental attachment."[22]

Coffin's patrician disdain for meddling Jews and Irish Catholics provides a striking contrast to Voss's insistence that Americanism and Zionism were compatible. Reiterating arguments by Brandeis and Niebuhr, Voss insisted that the existence of independent homelands would actually enhance "hyphenated" Americans' loyalty to the United States. In fact, Voss praised Zionism as a counterpart to Irish republicanism. As these ethnic appeals suggest, Voss and the ACPC were aligned with the Democrats, while Coffin and other Christian critics of Zionism leaned toward the GOP, which remained the party of the WASP establishment.[23]

In the wake of the Holocaust, questioning the loyalty of American Jews turned out to be unpopular.[24] Christian critics of the new State of Israel gained more traction when they emphasized the plight of Arabs driven from their homes or forced to live under Israeli control.[25] According to the *Christian Century*, a policy that opposed repatriation of the refugees or "oppresses the Moslem minority within [Israel's] boundaries" was unacceptable. As an affront to justice, it could never lead to peace.[26] Karl Baehr, executive secretary of the ACPC and leader of the first study tour, countered that the Muslim minority was itself the problem. Reviving a proposal by former president Hoover also endorsed by Niebuhr, he suggested population transfer as "a creative solution to a situation of bitter conflict."[27] For Baehr and Niebuhr, the solution was separate states for Jews and Muslims. They demonstrated little concern for the fate of Arab Christians.[28]

ACPC spokesmen stressed what they regarded as the imbalance of population and military resources between Israel and its neighbors. They argued that Americans and Christians were normally inclined to help the weaker party—and that they should continue to do so in this case. Yet the Jews were not just another small nation struggling against mighty adversaries. Because the Jewish predicament was a consequence of Christian hostility, Christians had a responsibility to ensure that Jews were secured against existential threats. This was a religious as well as a moral argument. As theologian A. Roy Eckardt declared in the first of many studies of Jewish-Christian relations: "On the basis of a conviction that national and racial groups are part of the divine plan of creation and that a given people thus has a right to collective survival, we have a theological foundation for justifying the demand of the Jews for a homeland."[29]

But why did the Jewish State have to be in Palestine? In principle, a haven from oppression could be achieved anywhere. But Christian Zionists emphasized that such a refuge would be consistent with Jewish aspirations only if were placed within the traditional Promised Land. Even when they did not accept literal interpretations of the prophecies, Christian Zionists presented the establishment of the State of Israel as vindication of covenantal theology. Voss wrote: "Even the irreligious cannot forget the ancient promise: 'The Lord made a covenant with Abraham, saying, "Unto thee and thy seed have I given this land."'"[30]

Covenant, of course, is a perennial theme in American thought. The Puritans were inspired by the idea that God establishes relationships with nations, whose progress He guides toward the achievement of His purposes. During the Cold War, covenantal themes returned to prominence as a way of understanding America's task in the struggle against Communism. These interpretations of American purpose suggested that an alliance between the United States and the State of Israel was not only strategically useful but might also be providential.

Judeo-Christian Civilization and the Cold War

On December 22, 1952, Dwight D. Eisenhower delivered a speech at the Waldorf Astoria Hotel in New York to the Freedoms Foundation, an educational organization of which he had been appointed honorary chairman. Recounting wartime discussions, the president-elect described the difficulty he experienced in explaining American democracy to Soviet military commander Georgy Zhukov. According to Eisenhower, Communists like Zhukov could not understand America because "our form of Government has no sense unless it is founded in a deeply felt religious faith, and I don't care what it is. With us of course it is the Judo-Christian [sic] concept but it must be a religion that all men are created equal."[31]

Eisenhower's remark was not widely noticed when it was delivered. It achieved proverbial status a few years later, when Will Herberg, a labor activist, sociologist, and associate of Reinhold Niebuhr, made it the centerpiece of *Protestant, Catholic, Jew*, his groundbreaking analysis of religion in mid-century America. In Herberg's opinion, "[e]very American could understand" that Eisenhower's statement was "the expression of the conviction that at bottom the 'three great faiths' were really 'saying the same thing' in affirming the 'spiritual ideals' and 'moral values' of the American Way of Life."[32] The "Judeo-Christian concept" was a way of including all Americans—Protestants, Catholics, and Jews—in a common front against Soviet tyranny.[33]

Judeo-Christianity had mixed implications for the new Jewish State. On the one hand, it implied that Christians were bound to Jews, and to the State of Israel, in a fundamental manner that overrode their many disputes. German-born theologian and ACPC supporter Paul Tillich answered the question "Is there a Judeo-Christian tradition?" in the affirmative.[34] Among the points of agreement that Tillich identified was a common attitude toward history. Rather than a cycle or a random flux of events, Christians and Jews understood history as a process oriented toward a divine purpose.[35] Herberg noted that this understanding was inseparable from the promise of return to the Promised Land: "The destiny of Israel *begins* and *ends* in Zion."[36]

On the other hand, the emphasis that Eisenhower placed on confronting the Soviet Union suggested that history pointed in a different direction. Such was the view of his secretary of state, John Foster Dulles, who had come to public attention as a Presbyterian layman, whose service included work as an advocate for Harry Emerson Fosdick in his ecclesiastical trial for heresy. For Dulles, America's importance for Christianity lay in its stand against Communism.[37] Jews and Judaism played only a minor role in his conception of God's will.[38]

Dulles was not hostile to Israel per se. Although he maintained connections with anti-Zionist Christian circles, he resigned from the ACJ-affiliated Holy Land Emergency Liaison Program because it was too critical of Israel.[39] Even so, the Eisenhower administration sought a rebalancing of American influence in the Middle East.[40] In the words of the National Security Council planning staff, "Israel will not, merely because of its Jewish population, receive preferential treatment over any Arab state; and thereby demonstrate that our policy toward Israel is limited to assisting Israel in becoming a viable state living in amity with the Arab states and that our interest in the well-being of each of the Arab states corresponds substantially with our interest in Israel."[41]

Debates about the religious meaning of U.S. foreign policy came to a head during the 1956 Suez crisis. Enraged by the coordinated Israeli and Anglo-French invasion of Egypt, the Eisenhower administration threatened economic and political sanctions unless the attackers withdrew. France and Britain did so quickly, removing their forces within weeks. Israel's withdrawal was more protracted and ultimately incomplete, as it retained parts of the Sinai Peninsula—its first acquisition of territory beyond the 1949 armistice lines.

For Dulles and Eisenhower, the diplomatic issue was straightforward. It would be difficult to criticize Soviet aggression if American allies were permitted to make war at will. A moral principle was also at stake. By opposing an Anglo-Franco-Israeli power grab, the United States demonstrated that it was above the transparent self-interest that motivated colonial powers.

Christian supporters of Israel rejected this logic as a betrayal of the Judeo-Christian synthesis that Eisenhower himself had proclaimed. Asserting his authority as the most influential religious commentator on foreign affairs, Niebuhr criticized the administration not only for "shattering the Western alliance" but also for squandering the American "spiritual investment" in the State of Israel.[42]

Niebuhr accused the administration of two errors. First, he charged it with "absolute pacifism" descended from liberal Protestantism.[43] This was rather bizarre as a characterization of Eisenhower, the former Supreme Allied Commander. Yet Niebuhr had some basis for his indictment against Dulles, who had been a leading figure in pacifist circles for decades before being reborn as a Cold Warrior. In Niebuhr's view, the administration's refusal to support the British, French, and Israelis against Nasser exposed its commitments to the alliance between democracies as empty moralizing, comparable to toothless condemnations of Hitler in the 1930s.

The second error was a failure to appreciate that the significance of Israel transcended strategic calculation. Niebuhr agreed with Dulles that the Cold War was a religious conflict.[44] But this was precisely why it was important to place the security of Israel at the center of American policy. In addition to being a small and embattled nation, it was a "glorious spiritual and political achievement" that embodied Western civilization.[45] America would be renouncing its own historical task if it were to "allow 'any nation so conceived and so dedicated to perish from the earth.'"[46]

Niebuhr's enlistment of Israel in the Western religious and political synthesis was not limited to his writings on politics. Amplifying arguments about the Jewish origins of Christianity that he had first presented as a graduate student, Niebuhr asserted in theological texts that "when it is true to itself, [Christianity] is Hebraic rather than Hellenic."[47] The affinity between the two religions rested on their shared understanding of history as the story of a covenant. In a survey of American history that he coauthored with historian Alan Heimert, Niebuhr described the American national origin myth: "Like Israel of Old, we were a messianic nation from our birth. . . . [W]e were born to exemplify the virtues of democracy and to extend the frontiers of the principles of self-government throughout the world."[48]

Not that a theological-political mission was an unmixed blessing: in *The Irony of American History*, Niebuhr warned against "pretensions of innocency" based on the belief that "[w]e were God's 'American Israel.'"[49] In Niebuhr's view, the hope that America could evade the wrenching dilemmas that lesser nations faced led directly to the blunder in responding to Suez. Chosen peoples were called to be wise as well as good.[50]

Always hesitant to read the prophecy as a prediction for the future, Niebuhr pronounced himself "embarrassed when Messianic claims are used to substantiate the right of the Jews to the particular homeland in Palestine; or when it is assumed that this can be done without injury to the Arabs."[51] Nevertheless, he suggested that the Americans and Jews, the United States and the State of Israel were yoked together in a providential task. Despite all the risks of combining politics with religion, "there is the strange miracle of the Jewish people, outliving the hazards of the diaspora for two millennia and finally offering their unique and valuable contributions to the common Western civilization, particularly in the final stage of its liberal society."[52] In order to fulfill its role as defender of Western civilization, America was called to defend the "peculiar historical miracle" in the Middle East.

Muslims were not participants in the providential alliance that Niebuhr described. Indeed, he claimed that "the rise of Communism in our world is comparable to the rise of Islam and its challenge of Christian civilization in the high Middle Ages."[53] Unlike Judeo-Christianity, Islam and Communism were pseudo-religions that divinized specific political regimes. As such, they were natural opponents of the United States as well as of the State of Israel. Even though Niebuhr criticized interpretations of the Cold War as a replay of the Crusades, then, he too used the image of a besieged Christendom to dramatize the international situation. The Jewish State was integral to that portrayal; Arabs' religious and national claims were not.

Catholic Rapprochement

In addition to attitudes toward history, relations between American Protestants and Jews had a point of contact in the Old Testament. In search of consensus regarding the people and Land of Israel, both Protestants and Jews could appeal to texts about the covenant with Abraham and the prophets. These sources were less important to Catholics. Emphasizing the traditions and institutions of the Church rather than scripture, they were less likely to find meaning in the travails of the biblical Israel. Catholics were also resistant to chiliasm and millenarianism, with important consequences for their understanding of America. Historian Daniel Howe writes: "Catholic rejection of the doctrine of the millennium affected the attitude of the church in America in at least two ways. It meant that the church lacked the millennial sense of urgency, widespread among evangelical Protestants, to remake the world and fit it for Christ's return; it also meant that Catholics did not share in the belief that the United States had a special role, analogous to that of ancient Israel, as an example of divine providence to the rest of the world."[54]

The Vatican's generally critical position on Zionism posed another obstacle to a Catholic embrace of the Jewish State. Pope Benedict XV gave vague endorsement to the Balfour Declaration in 1917. He did not, however, interpret the document as implying Jewish sovereignty.[55] On the day that Israel declared independence, the Vatican newspaper *L'Osservatore Romano* reminded readers: "Modern Israel is not the heir to biblical Israel. The Holy Land and its sacred sites belong only to Christianity: the True Israel."[56] After 1948, papal statements avoided references to the State of Israel. Instead, they tended to discuss the "Holy Land" or "Palestine."[57]

A more receptive attitude toward Zionism began to emerge in the 1940s. Among its pioneers was Boston's Cardinal Cushing, a leading advocate of rapprochement between American Catholics and Jews. In 1945, Cushing sponsored a pro-Zionist conference on Palestine and permitted priests in his archdiocese to attend. After nearly half a century of organized activity, this was apparently the first American Zionist event to feature an official Catholic presence.[58] Catholics could also find intellectually ambitious overtures to Zionism in the work of the Thomist philosopher Jacques Maritain. In his wartime writings, Maritain linked the movement for a Jewish national home to the defense of Western civilization using arguments that recall Niebuhr's.[59]

Theological research followed political developments. In 1958, priest Edward H. Flannery published "Theological Aspects of the State of Israel" in the *Bridge*, a publication of the recently founded Institute for Judaeo-Christian Studies at Seton Hall University. When Flannery surveyed the literature, he found only five studies of the subject—none of which was originally published in English.[60] His article seems to be the first sustained consideration of the topic by an American Catholic theologian. Rejecting charges that the Catholic tradition was inherently anti-Zionist, Flannery contended that the "belief the Jews could never again regain their lost nationhood did not have its origin in Scripture or in a dogmatic patristic tradition."[61] He blamed fourth-century figures, especially Saint John Chrysostom, for expounding the idea that the extension of the covenant to Gentiles excluded the Jews. Sounding almost like a seventeenth-century Puritan, Flannery turned back to Saint Paul's Epistle to the Romans. He concluded that "the present state of Israel may be a stratagem of divine providence" intended to prepare the Jewish people for a distant future when they would finally accept Christ.[62]

Flannery's arguments, amplified by the award-winning 1965 volume *The Anguish of the Jews*, provided encouragement to Catholic supporters of Israel.[63] So did the doctrinal changes of the Second Vatican Council. The council's statement on relations with non-Christian religions, known as *Nostra Aetate*, did not include a revision of the church's stance toward the State of Israel. But it did reject the deicide charge and included a paraphrase of Saint Paul's insistence that God did not repent or revoke his calling to the Jews (Rom. 11:29).[64] In the view of John M. Oesterreicher, director of the Institute for Judaeo-Christian Studies and a participant in the council's deliberations, the statement's interpretation of Romans acknowledged an irrevocable promise that provided the basis for Catholic endorsement of Israel on theological grounds, even if it did not directly offer such an endorsement.[65]

Theological reassessments of Israel did not immediately make their way downstream to laypeople. Lagging behind the hierarchy, Catholic educational materials continued to feature teachings of supersessionism and Jewish responsibility for the crucifixion.[66] On the whole, however, American Zionists had reason to expect support for Israel from Catholics as well as Protestants in the 1960s. Particularly after Egypt, Israel's main regional adversary, moved closer to the USSR, leading representatives of the American religious triad could agree on Israel's right to exist and to defend itself.[67] That unity extended to popular culture—from which more Americans received their ideas about religion and politics than from learned publications.

Judeo-Christian Civilization in Popular Culture

In addition to the steady supply of articles and lectures, what Eisenhower called the "Judo-Christian concept" produced a burgeoning genre of popular culture. From the end of World War II to the mid-1960s, the Holy Land, Palestine, and Israel were the subjects of dozens of books and films aimed at a broad audience. These works played a major role in a process that historian Michelle Mart has described as the "Christianization" of Israel.[68] Artistic confections—ranging from Scholem Asch's novels inspired by the New Testament to dramatizations of Bible stories such as the films *Samson and Delilah* (1949), *David and Bathsheba* (1951), *The Robe* (1953), and *Solomon and Sheba* (1959) to sword-and-sandal epics with modern sources like *Ben-Hur*

(1959)—suggested that Jews and Christians shared more than divided them. As Asch put it in a 1945 work, *One Destiny: An Epistle to the Christians*: "The Jewish-Christian idea makes you equal partners in our Jewish one, in spite of the fact that we belong to separate faiths. For if faith in the Messiah makes you partners to the promise and—through that—inheritors of the legacy for those springing from Abraham, Isaac, and Jacob, then our belief in a single God and in the truthfulness of the prophecies makes us equal partners in the civilization, the fruit and the blessings, which the realization of the promise has brought to humanity. . . . [W]e are equal partners in our common heritage."[69]

The United States was often presented as the natural defender of that heritage. In *The Ten Commandments* (1956), director Cecil B. DeMille assured audiences that the battle between freedom under law (represented by the Israelites) and arbitrary despotism (represented by the Egyptians) "continues throughout the world today."[70] The message was clear. As "one nation under God," the United States was discharging ancient Israel's task in modern times. *The Ten Commandments* communicated this message in images as well as in words. Film scholar Michael Wood notes that in its last shot, Charlton Heston's Moses holds a pose that resembles the Statue of Liberty.[71]

A contribution to an old tradition of patriotic appropriation, *The Ten Commandments* turned America into the new people of Israel. *Ben-Hur* inverted this analogy. As scholar Hilton Obenzinger remarks, it was essentially a "Western dime novel" with togas and chariots replacing ten-gallon hats and stagecoaches.[72] The familiar motifs in *Ben-Hur* were not coincidental. In addition to drawing inspiration from cinema Westerns, its literary source was contemporary to the construction of this powerful American myth. The film was based on the best-selling 1880 novel *Ben-Hur: A Tale of the Christ* by Lew Wallace, former Union general, governor of New Mexico, and U.S. minister to the Ottoman Empire. Countering demeaning depictions of Jews as deceitful and weak, Wallace's novel presented them as proto-pioneers fighting for their rights.[73]

Mixing historical metaphors, the film version of *Ben-Hur* also made implicit connections between Jewish resistance to Roman rule and American independence. The actors portraying Romans use clipped English accents.

Charlton Heston's Judah Ben-Hur, on the other hand, speaks colloquial American. In the film, empire is depicted as decadent, oppressive, and vaguely British. The plainspoken virtues that audiences might regard as typically American are on the side of the Jews.

Not simply a parable of occupation and resistance, *Ben-Hur* is "a tale of the Christ." As such, it adds a theological message to the political one. Although he finally gets revenge on the Roman oppressors, Judah finds peace only when he recognizes Jesus as the Messiah. The names alone tell the story. Even when it appealed to shared origins, Judeo-Christian popular culture often depicted Christianity as the future and Judaism as the past.

Films that focused on the modern State of Israel provided a partial corrective to this narrative. *Sword in the Desert* (1949) was the earliest such offering. Set in late summer or fall 1947, soon after the real-life incident that inspired the novel and film *Exodus*, the plot revolves around Mike Dillon, a hard-boiled American freighter captain who helps Jewish refugees run the British blockade. Forced to go ashore to collect payment, he is successively captured by the Zionist underground and by British forces, before escaping from a British prison with the Zionists' help. Like Humphrey Bogart's Rick in *Casablanca*, Dillon is cynical about politics but becomes increasingly sympathetic to a just cause. At the end of the film, he promises to return to Palestine with more refugees, despite the trouble that his previous load cost him.

The action and setting of *Sword in the Desert* are not obviously religious. Rather than referring to the Bible, as in *Exodus*, Zionist characters in the film speak the language of secular nationalism. Even so, the relation between Christians and Jews is central to the climax. In a daring raid, Jewish forces break Dillon out of prison while the guards are distracted by Christmas celebrations. The camera lingers over inmates behind barbed wire, resembling victims of a concentration camp, while the soldiers sing "Silent Night." Christian hypocrisy is depicted as the obstacle to freedom and dignity in the very birthplace of Jesus. Yet the film holds out hope for a new relationship between Christians and Jews. Its final shot depicts Dillon and a Jewish comrade making their way toward Bethlehem. Brilliantly illuminated from above, it is literally a shining city on a hill.

Sword in the Desert plays up the similarity between Zionism and national movements to which American audiences might already be sympathetic. The

Zionist forces include an Irish demolitions expert, who joined the struggle in order to exact revenge for British rule of his country. The British, meanwhile, are depicted as effete snobs. They are a far cry from the noble Tommies of wartime propaganda.

Sword in the Desert evokes the concentration camps but does not address the Holocaust directly. *The Juggler* (1953), based on a novel by screenwriter Michael Blankfort, places genocide at the center of Israel's story.[74] Kirk Douglas plays Hans Muller, a German Jewish entertainer whose family was murdered by the Nazis. He finds refuge in Israel but kills a police officer in a fit of paranoia. Muller spends the rest of the film on the run before finally giving himself up to the authorities. *The Juggler* is notable for offering an entirely Jewish perspective—there are no American or even Gentile characters. The film builds a case for Zionism by forcing the audience to see the world through a Jewish refugee's eyes, including striking images of an Israeli landscape that *The Juggler* was the first American film to capture on location.

If *The Juggler* dramatized the challenges that refugees faced after their arrival in the Promised Land, *Lisa* (1962) presented the difficulties they faced in getting there. The plot centers on Lisa Held, an Auschwitz survivor who makes her way to Mandatory Palestine with the help of a Dutch detective. Despite entreaties to testify at the Nuremberg tribunal by an American Methodist who works with the Zionist underground, she insists on pursuing a new life among her people. In addition to depicting Israel as the natural destination for European Jews, *Lisa* highlights Gentiles' duty to make amends for the Holocaust. Inspector Jongman assists Lisa due to guilt about his failure to save his Jewish girlfriend during the war.

Cast a Giant Shadow (1966), also starring Kirk Douglas, is not a good movie, but is perhaps the most explicit cinematic appeal for a special relationship between the United States and Israel. Inspired by the true story of an American soldier, Colonel David "Mickey" Marcus, who was recruited to train the Haganah militia, the film presents American assistance as the necessary condition of Israel's independence. Indeed, the Haganah are depicted as almost helpless without Marcus's guidance. The first scene of *Cast a Giant Shadow* shows the nativity display of a New York department store, suggesting that the people and the Land of Israel gave the gift of Christianity to America, laying the foundation for its political and economic success. America then returns the favor by providing the know-how and resources to realize the dream of restoration.

It would be an exaggeration to describe these works as intentional appeals to Christian Zionism. Nevertheless, they promoted the assumption that Zionism was not just compatible with Christianity and Americanism but was an expression of the same values. In *Exodus*, Kitty Fremont assured Ari Ben Canaan that she understood his passion for the land. Much of the audience probably felt the same way.

David Becomes Goliath

By the early 1960s, the State of Israel had been integrated into a broader vision of American history and responsibility that characterized liberal perspectives on the Cold War. While the Eisenhower administration kept Israel at arm's length, President John Kennedy assured Golda Meir, then Israel's foreign minister: "The United States has a special relationship with Israel in the Middle East, really comparable only to that which it has with Britain over a wide range of world affairs."[75] Conversations among politicians are not necessarily reliable expressions of their true beliefs, yet this statement represented an extraordinary rhetorical promotion. Even if he was merely cultivating Meir, Kennedy was taking over Harry Truman's role as the American Cyrus, suggesting that the State of Israel was not just another ally but a partner in America's highest aspirations.

Following a low point in relations under his predecessor, Kennedy began a diplomatic rapprochement between the United States and the State of Israel.[76] His successor, Lyndon Johnson, pursued a relationship of outright patronage. By the mid-1960s, the United States had replaced West Germany and France as Israel's most important supplier of arms. The realpolitik basis for this development should not be neglected: the sale of American tanks and airplanes was a quid pro quo for restrictions on Israel's nuclear program, as well as an attempt to balance Soviet aid to Egypt, Syria, and Iraq. But it was consistent with the civil-religious affinity encouraged from pulpits as well as motion-picture screens.

The apparent strength of this connection helps explain the expectations of American Zionists—both Jewish and Christian—in the crisis that became the Six-Day War. As Egypt built up forces in the Sinai, demanded the removal of UN peacekeeping units, and closed the Straits of Tiran to Israeli shipping, Christian intellectuals demanded that the United States honor its ostensible commitments to Israel.[77] In a public statement issued on May 27, 1967, eight prominent figures called on "our fellow Americans of all persuasions and groupings and on the administration to support the independence, integrity, and freedom of Israel." In addition to Niebuhr, the statement was signed by John C. Bennett, then president of Union Theological Seminary; the editors of the Catholic magazines *America*, *Commonweal*, and *Catholic World*; and Martin Luther King, Jr.[78]

Other writers appealed explicitly to Judeo-Christian heritage. In a letter to the *New York Times*, Jewish historian Barbara Tuchman, a descendant of Wilson's ambassador to the Ottoman Empire during World War I, insisted: "Israel represents the land and the nation which were the source of the Judaeo-Christian tradition to which we and the other Western nations belong and which, presumably, we uphold."[79] The charge was partly based on Tuchman's research, which helped popularize the idea of a Judeo-Christian nexus. Her 1956 book, *Bible and Sword*, was perhaps the first work of public scholarship to emphasize the Puritan origins of Christian interest in Jewish restoration.[80]

Despite the relative prominence of Jews and Israel in American reflections on moral responsibility and the sources of Western civilization, such appeals were not as successful as their authors hoped. They left no trace on the Johnson administration's handling of the issue. After the war, Johnson gave a stirring public tribute to the "common love of human freedom" and "common faith in a democratic way of life" ostensibly inspired by the Hebrew prophets.[81] During the crisis itself, the president rejected calls to intervene on Israel's behalf.

It was not surprising that the administration would pay little attention to the blandishments of clergymen and scholars. More shocking, at least to supporters of Israel, was the cold response from religious institutions, including the National Council of Churches and the World Council of Churches. The bastions of establishment Protestantism offered only bland endorsements of peace and the rights of all parties.[82] Reactions from some Christian public figures were positively scathing. In a widely discussed letter to the *New York Times*, Henry P. Van Dusen—a former president of Union Theological

Seminary and a Dulles confidante—charged Israel with committing "the most violent, ruthless (and successful) aggression since Hitler's blitzkrieg across western Europe in the summer of 1940, aiming not at victory but at annihilation."[83] Van Dusen's letter was controversial not only because of its author's prominence (like Niebuhr, he had appeared on the cover of *Time* magazine) but also because of the way it flipped the script of liberal Christian attitudes toward Zionism. By charging Israel with aggression, Van Dusen transformed the analogy from the 1930s on which Christian supporters of Israel often based their arguments. Now it was the Israelis rather than the Arabs who were behaving in a manner comparable to the Third Reich.

It is difficult to get a handle on the division of opinion within mainline churches and the Christian intellectual community. In a survey of responses, A. Roy Eckardt and his wife and coauthor, Alice, claimed that "the majority of spokesmen who identify themselves in some way with Christianity tend to speak for the Arab side, while the majority of those who do not so identify themselves (and are not identifiable as Jews) speak largely for the Israeli cause."[84] Van Dusen had a different view: he presented critics of Israel as an embattled minority confronted by moral blackmail from a pro-Israel establishment.

The variety of audiences for statements on Israel may help to explain some of the variation in opinion. Ecumenical institutions and national elites were cautious in their responses. Local figures, especially in cities with large Jewish populations, seemed more supportive of Israeli policy. In Boston, Cardinal Cushing and other area religious leaders issued what was billed as a "Declaration of Moral Principle," arguing that Christians could not be neutral in a conflict that threatened to repeat the Holocaust.[85] In Los Angeles, 150 clerics published a "statement of conscience" insisting that Arab recognition of Israeli sovereignty be the central feature of any peace settlement.[86] Citing polling data, Reform rabbi and interfaith activist Marc Tanenbaum argued that "the generalization that 'the Christians' failed the Jews of Israel by their silence is inaccurate, misleading, and not substantiated by evidence."[87] Rather than a failure of American Christians as a group or even of specific churches, Tanenbaum charged that the liberal "establishment" displayed insufficient enthusiasm for the Israeli cause.

Tanenbaum discerned cracks in the base of American Christian approval for Israel, which had seemed solid just a few years earlier. Their most obvious cause was the growth of Israel's power. According to Reform rabbi Balfour Brickner, whose given name testifies to his parents' enthusiasm for Zionism, "attitudes of church people are hardening. No longer is Israel the 'heroic little David, magnificently pitted against an Arab Goliath.'"[88] It was easy for liberal churchmen and intellectuals to sympathize with an embattled Israel. But what they regarded as a conscientious duty to defend the weak was more difficult to square with Israel's status as a regional giant. The New Testament scholar Krister Stendahl, who developed a pioneering interpretation of Saint Paul that emphasized the continuing role of the people of Israel in the apostle's theology, explained: "A militarily victorious and politically strong Israel cannot count on half as much good will as a threatened Jewish people in danger of its second holocaust."[89] The Hollywood caricature had gone out of date.

The status of Jerusalem was a particularly hot issue. Although they affirmed Israel's sovereignty within the 1949 boundaries, many mainline Christians argued that Jerusalem should be internationalized, corresponding to the original partition plan. It was one thing for Jews to possess a state in part of the historical land of promise. It was quite another for them to assert control over the sacred places of three faiths.[90] While tri-faith America and Judeo-Christian civilization were based on the assumption that there were only superficial differences between great religions, the controversy about Jerusalem suggested otherwise. Bennett suggested that even if "Jewish self-understanding does require as a goal the occupation of Jerusalem," Christians were required to distinguish between religious attachment and political control.[91] Yale divinity professor Willard G. Oxtoby left no question about his sympathies. Since Jordan had posed "no serious threat to Israel's economy and trade," Israel's motive must have been a messianic desire to "possess the land completely, to be once more in Zion."[92] In Oxtoby's judgment, such a desire should be unacceptable to those who understood that Christ's kingdom was not of this world.

In a statement published in the *New York Times* on July 12, 1967, Niebuhr, Eckardt, Stendahl, and thirteen other theologians took an opposing view. They insisted: "Jerusalem should remain unified." Unlike the May statement, this document offered an explicitly theological defense of Israeli policy: "Judaism has at its center an indissoluble bond between the people of

Israel and the land of Israel. For Christians, to acknowledge the necessity of Judaism is to acknowledge that Judaism presupposes inextricable ties with the land of Israel and the City of David, without which Judaism cannot be truly itself. Theologically, it is this dimension to the religion of Judaism which leads us to support the reunification of the city of Jerusalem."[93]

Israel's military success reactivated tensions that had been latent in liberal versions of Christian Zionism for decades. But the controversies might not have been so bitter if they had not been carried out in the shadow of the Vietnam War. When Christian intellectuals debated Israel, they were not just thinking of the Jewish State. They were also thinking of America, the new Israel pursuing a different destiny in Vietnam.

The problematic analogy between the Middle East and Southeast Asia emerged early in the controversies provoked by the 1967 war. By that time, virtually all the figures discussed in this chapter opposed the Vietnam War. Several, including Niebuhr, were prominent in the leading religious antiwar group, Clergy and Laymen Concerned About Vietnam (CALCAV).[94] Yet there appeared to be a contradiction between their endorsement of American guarantees to Israel—backed by military intervention, if necessary—and criticism of American policy in Vietnam. Yale professor of Christian ethics David Little charged that "doves in one setting [have] become hawks in another."[95] The change was regarded as suspect by the religious antiwar community. The editors of the *Christian Century* professed that "we do not understand nor do we indulge in the rationalistic gymnastics engaged in by Christian leaders who, having worked hard to get U.S. military power out of Vietnam, insist that the power of the United States be unleashed in the Middle East on the side of Israel."[96] Beyond the theoretical contradiction, the *Century* feared damage to the antiwar cause: "The greatest harm done by this ideological flip-flop was the blow it struck the peace movement in the United States and particularly the injury to Clergy and Laymen Concerned about Vietnam, an organization to which many of the switch-and-fight people belong."[97]

Some Christian supporters of Israel welcomed the breakdown of consensus as an opportunity to develop a more outspoken and consistent Christian Zionism. Among mainline Protestants, A. Roy Eckardt revisited the role of Israel in Christianity, emphasizing its theological centrality as well as

Christians' moral debt to Jews.[98] Among Catholics, Robert Drinan, dean of the Boston College Law School and later a Democratic member of Congress, joined Oesterreicher and Flannery as an advocate for a theologically-grounded rapprochement with Jews and the State of Israel.[99] The energetic Franklin Littell founded Christians Concerned for Israel, later renamed the National Christian Leadership Conference for Israel, to promote these views among adherents of all denominations.[100] It was an echo of the inter-faith vision captured by the title of Herberg's famous work.

As their arguments grew more impassioned, however, liberal supporters of Israel became increasingly marginal within their own religious and political communities. In 1972, the magazine's critical coverage of Israel resulted in the removal of Niebuhr's name from the masthead of *Christianity and Crisis*. Angered by the magazine's publication of an article by the Israeli anti-Zionist activist Israel Shahak, Niebuhr's widow, Ursula, requested that Niebuhr no longer be listed as founding editor. Littell went further, charging that the editorial position of *Christianity and Crisis* had become indistinguishable from the view of Germans who compromised with Hitler.[101]

These debates were covered extensively in the mainstream press, which still regarded liberal churches and churchmen as worth covering.[102] As the religious Left exchanged letters to the editor, though, "the right had discovered Israel."[103] After 1967, mainline intellectuals and clergy drifted away from Israel, which they increasingly regarded as an outpost of imperialism, colonialism, and other sins. Meanwhile, Zionism emerged as a component of a different style of Christian politics.

6 | I Will Bless Those Who Bless You: Zionism and the Christian Right

> I will make you into a great nation and I will bless you; I will make your name great and you will be a blessing. I will bless those who bless you, and whoever curses you I will curse; and all the peoples on earth will be blessed through you.
>
> —Gen. 12:2–3, New International Version

The theological roots of the politically conservative, prophetically inflected version of Christian Zionism that emerged in the 1970s lie in the tension between modernists and fundamentalists in the early twentieth century. Speaking broadly, modernists argued that religion is subject to progressive improvement. Sacred texts, therefore, should be read as the work of human writers whose language and ideas reflected comparatively primitive times. Fundamentalists responded that the truths of Christianity were fixed and could be found in inerrant scripture.[1]

Fundamentalism did not necessarily entail dispensationalist eschatology, but dispensationalist ideas played a central role in the movement. Scholars trace the use of the term "fundamentals" to designate the basic principles of Christianity to a series of conferences on the Bible and prophecy organized by the dispensationalist James Brookes. The conferences featured contributions from dispensationalists and served as a platform for their ideas.[2] *The Fundamentals: A Testimony to Truth*, the programmatic pamphlets that gave the movement its name, strengthened the association between fundamentalism and dispensationalism. The essay "Prophecy Fulfilled: A Potent Argument for the Bible" was written by Arno Gaebelein, a German-born dispensationalist who learned Hebrew and Yiddish in order to preach the Gospel to Jews.[3]

Another vehicle for dispensationalism was the Scofield Reference Bible. Since it appeared in 1909, the Scofield Bible has sold millions of copies and never been out of print.[4] The importance of the Scofield Reference Bible was not in the translation that it contained, which was a modification of the King James Version. Instead, it lay in the notes and cross-references that Scofield, a protégé of Brookes and a participant in the prophecy conferences, interspersed with the biblical text in a manner reminiscent of the Geneva edition of the sixteenth century.

Like those in the Geneva Bible, the Scofield notes were permeated with restorationist themes. The commentary on "covenant" in Genesis, for example, stated: "Two dispossessions and restorations have been accomplished. Israel is now in the third dispersion, from which she will be restored at the return of the Lord as King."[5] For Scofield, the people of Israel were the living link between the covenantal past and the prophetic future.[6]

Like Blackstone, however, Scofield departed from the restorationist tradition in his account of the Jewish return to the Land of Israel. Classic restorationists assumed that Jews would adopt Christianity before or in conjunction with that great event. Scofield pushed off conversion to the last moment before the Second Coming, describing Jews as "the people of God who will have returned to Palestine *in unbelief.*"[7] This modification made fundamentalism compatible with Zionism in a way that the old restoration theories were not. Fundamentalists thus greeted the Balfour Declaration in November 1917 and the capture of Jerusalem by the British army the following month as proof that Daniel's final week was commencing.[8] In May 1918, the audience at the Philadelphia Prophecy Conference was informed: "We have entered on a prophetic era. We are looking upon the things which Moses and the prophets and Christ himself has [*sic*] foretold."[9]

Although it helped secure a Jewish presence in Palestine, World War I did not lead to Armageddon as quickly as some fundamentalists had expected. The darkening international prospect of the 1930s provided another occasion for prophetic interpretation of current events. The brevity of the pacific interlude that followed the war was consistent with fundamentalists' expectations of disorder and decline. From their perspective, the Versailles Treaty, the League of Nations, and other instruments of the postwar settlement were based on the blasphemous assumption that man had it within his power to establish lasting peace.

Belief that strife and war were inevitable did not make fundamentalists supportive of fascism. On the contrary, the prophecy writer Harry Ironside wondered whether Mussolini might be the Antichrist.[10] Hitler held even less appeal. Some fundamentalists dabbled in anti-Semitic conspiracy theories. In principle, however, they regarded enemies of "the Jew" as enemies of God. Even enemies could further the Lord's work, though. The creationist Harry Rimmer asserted: "All that Hitler has accomplished by his European-wide persecution may be summed up in a sentence: he has accelerated the return of Israel to Palestine, thus apparently hastening his own doom! By driving the 'preserved people' back into the preserved land, Hitler, who does not believe the Bible and who sneers at the Word of God, is helping to fulfill its most outstanding prophecy! Thus does the wrath of men sometimes serve the purposes of God."[11]

Fundamentalists had not been enthusiastic about American participation in World War I. Their modernist critics used this hesitation against them, insinuating that premillennialism encouraged political quietism and even disloyalty.[12] Partly to dispel this accusation, many became advocates of the Allied cause in World War II.[13] Yet the defense of democracy was not the only reason that fundamentalists encouraged the United States to fight in Europe. If "the Axis powers win this war," Rimmer reasoned, "Italy will take Palestine for her part of the share of the spoils. In that case the Jews will be driven forth from their own land, and once more the returned remnant of that persecuted people will be homeless."[14] If the Allies were victorious, on the other hand, the "result of that triumph will be the complete and unrestricted fulfillment of the Balfour declaration. England will wholeheartedly proceed to honor her commitments to Zion, and the Jews will return in vast number to their own land. . . . [A] Jewish state will appear to take its place in the councils of the nations."[15]

Rimmer's emphasis on England as the patron of Zionism indicates the marginality of the American Cyrus trope to early fundamentalists. Liberal Christians influenced by postmillennialism were more inclined than fundamentalists and dispensationalists to regard America as the main source of support for Jewish return. That is one reason Blackstone found allies outside fundamentalist circles. The list of signatories and endorsers of his second memorial included the arch-modernist Shailer Matthews, who accused dispensationalists of shirking their civic responsibilities after the United States entered World War I.

So it is not surprising that fundamentalists had little presence in the organized Christian Zionism of the war years. The ACPC and its predecessors were stocked with theological liberals and representatives of mainline denominations. Daniel A. Poling, editor of the *Christian Herald* magazine, represented the conservative position. But he was a nondispensationalist, described by *Time* as a "gentle fundamentalist" rather than the full-strength version.[16]

It was as spectators more than participants, then, that fundamentalists greeted the declaration of Israel's independence. Although they presumably numbered among the plurality of Americans sympathetic to the Jewish side in the Middle East conflict, fundamentalists and their arguments barely registered in the public debate. In 1948, theologian A. Roy Eckardt contended that fundamentalists were an insignificant factor in the developing relationship between American Christians and the Jewish State. That assessment would have seemed ludicrous just a few decades later.[17]

Christian Zionism Outside the Public Eye

Fundamentalists and dispensationalists shared a wary attitude toward politics. While they did not always observe Darby's admonitions against voting or Brookes's warnings against patriotic preachers—making exceptions for movements to ban the sale of alcohol and prevent the teaching of evolution—fundamentalists were skeptical that political mobilization was worth the effort.[18] Jesus was coming for believers. Their primary task was to prepare themselves for the next world rather than working to improve this one.

Fundamentalists therefore greeted improving prospects for Zionism with warm but distanced approval. M. R. DeHaan, who hosted the *Radio Bible Class* on the ABC network, wrote admiringly of Zionist lobbying and denounced the original partition plan as "a crime which God will not permit to go unjudged."[19] Yet he did not encourage his audience to take part, even by means as minimal as writing to elected officials. In a pamphlet on the issue,

DeHaan wrote that the "practical application" of prophecy was to provide "assurance of the unity and the infallibility and the harmony of this precious Book, the Word of God."[20] For DeHaan, Zionism was a confirmation of faith, not a program for action.

That faith was soon rewarded. When the State of Israel was proclaimed, a Christian radio station in Los Angeles pronounced it "the most significant event since Jesus Christ was born."[21] In one of his several memoirs, Christians United for Israel leader John Hagee recalls being "mesmerized" when reports of the new state were broadcast to his home in Texas. For the young Hagee, "the birth of the State of Israel confirmed the accuracy of Bible prophecy."[22]

Because Hagee is often treated as paradigmatic of Christian Zionism, it is worth dwelling briefly on his recollections. Hagee describes himself as "cradle-roll Zionist."[23] The biographical accounts in his books, however, are characterized by a significant elision. After describing his preacher father's teaching about prophecy and announcement of the great news, Hagee moves to a discussion of his first visit to Israel, in 1979, and his decision to organize an event to honor Israel in response to the Osirak raid.[24] The story leaves a blank spot of three decades.

What happened in the interval? One change was growing awareness of the Holocaust.[25] In another autobiographical account, Hagee mentions three books that influenced his thinking about Jews and Israel. They were Father Edward Flannery's *The Anguish of the Jews*; philosopher Dagobert Runes's *The War Against the Jew*; and John Toland's biography of Hitler.[26] Hagee is not alone among American Christians in having been affected by the Shoah. The CUFI official David Brog describes today's Christian Zionists as "obsessed" with the Nazi genocide.[27]

Another change was the emergence of a more engaged version of conservative Protestantism. Represented by the National Association of Evangelicals, founded in 1942, so-called neo-evangelicalism sought to uphold the principles of biblical inerrancy and personal commitment to Christ while manifesting "a social consciousness and responsibility which was strangely absent from fundamentalism."[28] Neo-evangelical leaders included Harold Ockenga, Carl F. H. Henry, and Arno Gaebelein's son Frank. But its most familiar face was Billy Graham, who would come almost to personify the term.

Though Graham generally tried to avoid partisan politics, he made public support for the State of Israel a centerpiece of his long ministry.[29]

Eschatology was not the only reason for neo-evangelicals' interest in Jews and Israel, but it was among the elements of fundamentalism that carried over into their movement. In his 1951 volume *World Crises and the Prophetic Scriptures,* Wilbur Smith, professor of the English Bible at the neo-evangelical stronghold Fuller Theological Seminary, argued that the establishment of the State of Israel was the "greatest event in Palestine certainly since the destruction of Jerusalem, infinitely more important than the Crusades."[30] The reason was that Israel's national "restoration is clearly, unmistakably predicted." Rejecting interpretations of prophecy that identified Christians as the people of Israel, Smith insisted: "The promises simply cannot be made to refer to the church, . . . for, as Dr. Gaebelein said years ago in referring to Amos 9:15: 'The "Church" was never plucked out of a land. It is Israel.'"[31] Smith emphasized that dispensationalists were not the only ones to teach the restoration of Israel; in addition to Gaebelein and Blackstone, he cited Increase Mather and New York University professor George Bush. The goal was to place his arguments in a lineage extending through the Second Great Awakening back to the Puritans. Smith insisted, correctly, that Christian Zionism was far from a recent development.

Whether or not they were innovations, Smith's interpretations were open to dispute. In the Christmas issue of 1956, its first year of publication, the leading journal *Christianity Today* published an exchange between Smith and Bible scholar Oswald T. Allis. Smith reiterated his view that the establishment of the State of Israel represented "God's victory for that portion of the earth which He has called His own land."[32] Allis countered that the "attempt to restore the Jews to Palestine has proved to be unjust in itself" and, more importantly, had no theological justification.[33] In Allis's judgment, Smith was guilty of "Judaizing" Christianity by erroneously insisting that the kingdom of God involved the satisfaction of national and territorial claims.[34]

Beyond disputes about prophecy, the State of Israel's position on religious freedom was an obstacle to the neo-evangelicals' embrace of the new nation. Christians enjoyed freedom of worship and access to holy sites under Israel's control (excluding the Old City of Jerusalem, which remained under Jordanian administration until 1967). Missionary activity, however, was subject to social disapproval and some bureaucratic obstacles.[35] Because neo-evangelicals defined themselves through their commitment to public witness, they experienced these hindrances as affronts. Through the 1950s, the cause connected with Israel that most attracted their attention was the elimination of restrictions on proselytization. Carl Henry even accused Israel of practicing the same intolerance toward Christianity that the Romans displayed.[36]

Despite these challenges, neo-evangelicals found in Israel a model of religious and political virtue. In Graham's judgment, "America is in desperate need of a moral and spiritual transfusion that will cause her to recapture some of the strength and idealism that made us the greatest nation in the world."[37] Graham located a source of that vitality during a widely publicized pilgrimage to Israel in 1960. Despite pressure to refrain from mentioning Jesus in his public addresses and an incident in which he was denied the use of a stadium in Tel Aviv, Graham returned to the United States singing Israel's praises.[38] In a *Time* magazine article published a few weeks later, Graham described "how in a visit to the Holy Land, I followed in the steps of some of the great nonconformists of the Bible, men such as Elijah, Amos, Micah," observing that these prophets "had the courage to stand up for moral right—alone if necessary."[39] It was this kind of courage, declared Graham, that Americans should emulate. In order to preserve its domestic prosperity and international influence, the country required "men who will live up to their idealism and who refuse to be moral copycats."[40]

Graham's conflation of modern Israel, the biblical heritage, and moral individualism rested on hints and his personal example more than detailed arguments. Allaying fears that the Jewish State was hostile to Christian faith, he encouraged Christians to see America and Israel as part of a unified story of struggle and triumph, beginning in biblical times and continuing through the present. At some point in the future, Graham acknowledged, that story might end in fiery judgment. At the moment, though, Americans and Israelis were players on the same team.

An appealing expression of this affinity between America and Israel could be found in popular music. Singers Pat Boone and Johnny Cash, both of whom developed friendships with Graham, produced works emphasizing Israel's political and religious legitimacy in a distinctly American idiom. In fact, Boone wrote the lyrics and performed the theme song for the film *Exodus*, crooning, "This land is mine, God gave this land to me." Historian Shalom Goldman observes that the *Exodus* theme and Cash's rendering of gospel numbers invoked Bible stories and the landscape of the Holy Land in a way that made Israel more meaningful to ordinary Americans than commentaries on scripture, sermons, or magazine articles were able to. Like movies of the period, music closed the historical and geographic distance between biblical Israel, the modern Jewish State, and America.[41]

In some cases, popular culture and politics overlapped more closely. Fred C. Schwarz, a Jewish convert to Christianity who led the Christian Anti-Communist Crusade, directed the band at some of his rallies to play "Milk and Honey," the theme song of a Broadway show about the founding of Israel.[42] Schwarz's choice of musical repertoire reflected growing comfort with Israel's quasi-socialist economy, which had disturbed early fundamentalists. After the Suez crisis and Nasser's turn toward Moscow, Israel was regarded as a reliable ally against the USSR despite its deviations from free enterprise.

Schwarz was not the only professional anti-Communist to draft Israel into the Cold War. Former FBI agent Cleon Skousen, best known as the author of the exposé *The Naked Communist*, was also an enthusiastic prophecy commentator. Skousen was a devout Mormon, and his reading of the prophecies included elements associated with the double Zion theory. On the whole, however, he sketched a conventional account of Jewish return based on Ezekiel.[43] The Soviet Union, as Skousen saw it, was the main threat to progress in this direction—and to "Judaic-Christian" civilization in general.[44] For Skousen, Jews and Christians, Israelis and Americans were confronting the same adversary.[45]

Historian Paul Boyer has shown how the threat of nuclear conflict renewed interest in prophecy.[46] The 1950s and early '60s saw the publication of works on prophecy by fundamentalists and fundamentalist-leaning evangelicals that promised the imminent end of the world. Many authors were associated with the Dallas Theological Seminary (DTS), a bastion of dispensationalism.[47] Older works such as Joseph Seiss's lectures on the Book of Revelation were also published in more accessible editions.[48] The State of Israel often played a central role in the argument. DTS president John F. Walvoord reminded readers that the establishment of the State of Israel "constitutes a preparation for the end of the age . . . and the fulfillment of Israel's prophetic destiny."[49]

Like DeHaan, Walvoord did not suggest that his readers take any practical steps connected with these events. Other prophecy writers contended that American Christians had an active role to play before the last days began. G. Douglas Young urged readers to promote the flourishing of Israel during whatever time intervened between the present and the commencement of Daniel's seventieth week.[50] He attempted to set an example by establishing an Israel-American Institute in Jerusalem, in cooperation with the Israeli ministries of education and religious affairs.[51] Young also encouraged Western governments not to force Israel to make concessions in peace negotiations. In a favorable allusion to Reinhold Niebuhr, Young wrote that the conflict could not be resolved unless Christians adopted a "realistic" understanding of its cause, which he identified as Arab intransigence.[52]

Burgeoning excitement about the State of Israel among conservative Protestants reflected the cultural and political setting. Even so, the emergence of American Christian Zionism on the right did not occur automatically. It required the shock of Israel's victory in the Six-Day War to galvanize a combination of dispensationalist eschatology, American patriotism, and pop-culture fixation into a movement.

A Glorious Redemption Draws Near

Israel's victory in June 1967 astonished the world. In six days and without foreign intervention, Israel destroyed forces widely regarded as superior and gained control of territory far beyond the armistice lines. The acquisition of the Golan Heights and the Sinai Peninsula was regarded as the most important strategic consequence of the war. But the most dramatic event from a religious perspective was Israel's capture of the Old City of Jerusalem. In a report on the events of June 7, the *New York Times* described a scene out of a Hollywood epic as Israeli troops marched through the Mandelbaum Gate blowing shofars.[53] The actual situation was more fraught. Shlomo Goren, head rabbi of the Israel Defense Forces, had to be talked out of a plan to inaugurate the messianic age by blowing up the mosques on the Temple Mount.[54]

This turn of events electrified conservative Christians. Like Rabbi Goren, they were inclined to believe that Israel's success was not just a feat of arms but reflected God's guidance of history. Skousen declared the war nothing less than a "rendezvous with destiny."[55] In a survey of the recent developments, *Christianity Today* reminded readers that the "Christian can best understand the imbroglio in the Middle East through his knowledge of prophetic Scriptures."[56] Although it warned against forecasting specific events or imposing rigid timelines, the unsigned editorial concluded: "The prophetic clock of God is ticking while history moves inexorably toward the final climax."[57]

This interpretation of the war was not accepted by all neo-evangelicals. The next month, *Christianity Today* published a commentary by the Presbyterian minister and archaeologist James Kelso that characterized Israel's victory as a lamentable triumph of might over right. To Israel, Kelso wrote, "Arabs are simply dogs. In the Orient, a dog is a thing to get rid of."[58]

Billy Graham offered a different opinion. Declaring that "Jews are God's chosen people," he expressed approval for the outcome of the war and support for the annexation of parts of Jerusalem. Hesitant about making religion a political wedge, Graham did not recommend that the United States adopt a specific policy regarding the territories occupied by Israel. But he did insist that American Christians "cannot place ourselves in opposition to Israel without detriment to ourselves."[59]

Within the year, Wilbur Smith and Arnold Olson, president of the Evangelical Free Church of America, published books that drew out the implications of this idea. Although they avoided apocalyptic date setting, both writers emphasized the necessity of Jewish control of Jerusalem to the fulfillment of God's plan. Citing the Book of Daniel, Smith proposed that "for the first time in all these two thousand years, we are amazingly near" the kingdom of God.[60] The traditional view was that this would come about in conjunction with the Jews' conversion. Without rejecting that doctrine, Olson urged Christians to reconsider their emphasis on missions and allow God to turn Jews' hearts on His own schedule. In the meantime, Olson argued, Christians should support the State of Israel as it actually existed. Citing G. Douglas Young's efforts to build working relationships with Israelis, Olson contended that the scriptural basis for Christian attitudes should be Genesis 12: "I will bless those who bless you."[61]

Conversion was not the only event that had to be moved on the apocalyptic timeline. Unlike previous versions, the 1967 edition of the Scofield Reference Bible—edited by a team including the convert from Judaism and prophecy writer Charles L. Feinberg, Frank Gaebelein, Wilbur Smith, and John F. Walvoord—stated that the Rapture would occur *after* the people of Israel returned to the Land of Israel.[62] The change tied the fate of Christians to their relationship with Israel. If God blessed those who blessed the Jews and cursed those who cursed them, He might deny participation in the Rapture to Christians who were insufficiently supportive of the Jewish State.

Debates about these changes were on display at a 1971 prophecy conference held in Jerusalem. Attracting participation by Ockenga, Henry, Smith, Young, Olson, Walvoord, and other neo-evangelical and fundamentalist leaders, the conference was intended to establish a united front on issues related to Israel. In his introduction to the proceedings, journalist Robert Walker identified five areas of agreement among the participants: that the prophecies expounded "God's moral purpose and man's destiny"; that Jesus was the prophesied messiah; that God was judge of nations; that belief in Christ's resurrection was necessary to personal salvation; and that Christ would soon return.[63]

Historian Daniel G. Hummel notes that neo-evangelicals like Henry, who were skeptical about mixing politics and religion were unable to reach consensus with pro-Israel activists like Young and Olson and strict dispensationalists like Walvoord.[64] Yet the symbolism of the conference was perhaps more important than any formal resolutions. Whatever their interpretations of prophecy, participants appeared to agree that it was being realized in the State of Israel, simply by attending the conference. As Henry put it: "On your long flight to the Holy Land the moment finally came when you saw the flashing signal: 'Fasten Seat Belts'; the closing hour of the journey was near. . . . So it is with the expectant church; with all the light of prophecy signaling the final arrival hour at hand, with all the prophetic signs exhorting preparedness, she readies for momentary landing. Here in the land of promise many interpret the regathering of Israel from the ends of the earth as one fulfillment of the prophetic Word; we anticipate a further fulfillment of that same Word in the risen One's return."[65]

Graham declined to join the conference in Jerusalem, fearing that it might prove controversial. His public-relations team, however, promoted similar claims in the musical film *His Land*, which presented the State of Israel as a "miracle of restoration" that served as "God's timepiece."[66] At a time when foreign-affairs broadcasting was dominated by sober reporting of the major networks, this groovy spectacle presented Israel in a new and stylish way. *His Land* confirmed Israel's status as God's country in a distinctively contemporary visual and musical language.[67]

Important as it seems in retrospect, growing fervor among conservative Protestants did not make an immediate impression on organized American Zionism. A 1968 report, "Christian Reactions to the Middle East Crisis," prepared for the American Jewish Committee, hardly bothered to discuss evangelical and fundamentalist responses.[68] A few years later, it would become impossible to ignore the political and theological currents drawing them toward Israel. More than any other event, the publication of a single book marked the change.

The Fuse of Armageddon

The Late Great Planet Earth is among the greatest successes in modern publishing history. By the turn of the twenty-first century, it had sold 28 million copies—quite a feat for a work that suggested that the world might not survive past 1988.[69] The author was Dallas Theological Seminary graduate Hal Lindsey. Just forty when *The Late Great Planet Earth* appeared, Lindsey had previously worked for the Campus Crusade for Christ, which sought to evangelize a younger and more upscale demographic. *The Late Great Planet Earth* shared this goal. In its outlines, the book replicated the dispensationalist scenario as it was taught at DTS. It divided history into periods, argued that the present dispensation would culminate in the Rapture, and described the seven-year tribulation that would separate the Rapture from Christ's physical return amid the battle of Armageddon. Jews and Israel played the central role. According to Lindsey, the State of Israel was the "paramount prophetic sign" and the "fuse of Armageddon."[70]

Readers steeped in neo-evangelicalism or fundamentalism found few interpretive novelties in *The Late Great Planet Earth*, but they were not its intended audience. Two appealing features distinguished Lindsey's presentation from works on similar themes by Dallas stalwarts like J. Dwight Pentecost or John F. Walvoord and helped make it a popular sensation.

The first was its style. Inheritors of the strategy of "out-Bibling" critics, old-fashioned commentators offered detailed and sometimes excruciating textual analysis. The following passage from Walvoord's *Israel in Prophecy* is representative of the genre:

> The remaining minor prophets continue this theme. Zephaniah closes chapter 3 with the picture of Israel regathered and rejoicing in the Lord in their ancient land. Zechariah speaks at length on the future blessings of Israel, describing the streets full of happy children in Zechariah 8:5 and Israel is being regathered from the east and from the west in chapter 8:7, 8. Jerusalem is pictured as the capitol of the earth in 8:22. . . . The concluding chapter of Zechariah, beginning as it does with the second coming of Christ, pictures that change in the land in the millennial kingdom and the wealth and prosperity and spiritual blessings of Israel. All of these prophecies imply that the promises of the land are going to be fulfilled and Israel will once again be established in the area promised to the seed of Abraham.[71]

Accustomed to addressing uninitiated audiences, Lindsey avoided Walvoord's dry style. Rather than moving systematically through Bible passages, *The Late Great Planet Earth* included mostly brief quotations and summaries. In addition to making things easier on readers, Lindsey's breezy use of sources lent authority to his claims. Because he showed readers only the passages that were consistent with his reading, he was able to avoid knotty questions of interpretation.[72]

This rhetorical decision had important consequences. *The Late Great Planet Earth* allowed readers to think that Christian Zionism was read directly out of scripture, rather than being the product of a long intellectual history. Lindsey's intentionally casual mode of address made his argument even more accessible. American evangelists going back to the Second Great Awakening made efforts to speak to their audiences in a conversational, unaffected manner. The American studies scholar Melani McAlister points out that Lindsey followed their example in a 1960s idiom, prefacing brief, easily digestible sections with headings like "What's Your Game, Gog?"[73]

The second feature was Lindsey's increased focus on politics. Identification of the establishment of the State of Israel and the capture of the Old City of Jerusalem as prophetic signs were routine in evangelical and fundamentalist literature. But Lindsey provided an unusually detailed analysis of current events. According to Lindsey, the Six-Day War was not the only indication of God's sovereignty over history. The counterculture and risk of a population bomb were also indications that Daniel's seventieth week was about to commence.[74] So was the spread of Communism—a topic on which Lindsey took cues from Skousen.[75] Lindsey qualified his observations with reminders that the ability to foretell the future was limited to prophets. Nevertheless, he argued that Jesus promised to return a generation after the fulfillment of the prophecies and that a "generation" in the Bible is equivalent to about forty years. "If this is a correct deduction," Lindsey concluded, "then within forty years or so of 1948, all these things could take place."[76]

The Late Great Planet Earth was the best-selling pop-apocalypse, but it was not the only contribution to the genre. Books in the same mold included the novel *666*, by Salem Kirban, and the Lindsey-style prophecy study *Satan in the Sanctuary*, by Thomas S. McCall and the convert from Judaism Zola Levitt. Like *The Late Great Planet Earth*, these works made few modifications to the dispensationalist narrative. What they lacked in originality, they made up for in liveliness. In addition to rendering obscure prophecies as a gripping adventure story, *666* used newspaper clippings and recent stock photos to show that the events it described might already be in progress.[77]

One prophecy that appeared to be on the cusp of fulfillment was the construction of a third temple in Jerusalem. Rabbi Goren's demolition plan was vetoed on the spot, but members of Israel's Orthodox communities urged the rebuilding of the temple on its ancient site. This provocative suggestion attracted keen attention from American Christians, particularly those with dispensationalist leanings.[78] Their interest was driven by an obscure passage in the Book of Daniel. In his prophecy of the seventy weeks, Daniel speaks of a great desecration occurring halfway through the last week. Combining Daniel's statement with the mystical Babylon narrative of Revelation, prophecy writers argued that this so-called abomination of desolation would involve worship of the Antichrist in the rebuilt temple.[79]

Speculation about the identity of the Antichrist is a feature of chiliastic and millenarian traditions going back to Irenaeus. In more recent times, the candidates have included popes, Napoleon Bonaparte, Franklin Roosevelt, and Mussolini. The problem with these identifications was that they called the authority of prophecy into question when their targets failed to perform the foretold deeds. Like calculating the date of the Second Coming, actually naming the Antichrist carried a high risk of disappointment. The new literature avoided this danger by resisting the temptation to name names while offering tantalizing speculations about the Antichrist's characteristics. Its authors agreed that would be a man of prodigious savvy and charisma who might come to prominence by bringing peace to the apparently intractable Middle East.

The national and religious origins of the Antichrist were the subject of considerable dispute. One school of thought held that the association of the mystical Babylon with Rome meant that the Antichrist would be Italian, or at least Catholic. Another maintained that the Antichrist had to be a Jew in order to fulfill his role as the inversion of Christ.[80] Among early fundamentalists, Arno Gaebelein contended that the Antichrist would most likely be a Jew.[81]

Authors of the pop-apocalypse literature of the 1970s rejected the Jewish Antichrist theory. Considering the events of the twentieth century, they argued that it made no sense for a Jew to subject his own people to the sort of tribulation that scripture described. Instead, the Antichrist was depicted as a Gentile and a fanatical Jew hater—a sort of greater Hitler. According to Arthur Bloomfield: "Previously nations have been concerned only with driving the Jews out of their particular countries; [the] Antichrist's concern will be to annihilate all the Jews in the world."[82] As with Hitler, however, the Antichrist's persecution of the Jews would achieve an unintended result. Facing worldwide tribulation, Jews would be further concentrated in Israel.

Televangelist Oral Roberts informed readers in his pilgrimage report and eschatology study *The Drama of the End Time* that, at the end of his life, William E. Blackstone arranged for boxes of Bibles to be stored in the caves of Petra, where he expected Jews who survived the tribulation to seek refuge. The Bibles were to be marked in those passages that "show the Jewish people how they have been deceived, betrayed by the Antichrist, and that Jesus Christ is truly their Messiah, their only hope."[83] Pop-apocalypse writers made the same prediction. Drawing on the statement in Revelation that 144,000 Jews would be "sealed" in God's name during the last days (Rev. 7:3–4), Kirban foresaw mass conversions to Christianity.[84]

Attention to theological and hermeneutic nuances of these debates distinguished discussions of Israel in comparatively highbrow periodicals like *Christianity Today* or *Eternity* from works in the pop-apocalyptic genre.[85] Yet the latter were more widely circulated and made a greater impact on ordinary people. This influence was partly due to their exciting content and accessible style but also reflected their attention to the role of the United States. Even while they excluded America from sacred geography, eschatological narratives built around Jews and Israel helped Americans find their place in sacred history.

America the Redeemer?

At first glance, the assessment of America that emerges from midcentury discussions of prophecy is distinctly pessimistic. The United States was depicted as a cesspool of moral corruption and political decadence. At the Jerusalem conference, Wilbur Smith contended: "Modern man has never witnessed such a flood of lawlessness as prevails in our world today," singling out the United States for criticism.[86] Harold Ockenga concurred; in addition to a crime wave, he noted disturbing outbreaks of egocentrism, disobedience to parents, and sexual hedonism. Ockenga concluded: "Another scripture, seemingly being fulfilled in our day, is that of Paul in 2 Timothy 3:1–7. . . . 'In the last days, perilous times shall come.'"[87] These bleak assessments echoed classic dispensationalist critiques of progressivism and nationalism. The fact that only Christ could establish the reign of peace meant that Christians should not expect much from the broader society or politics. This message could be deflating to Americans accustomed to regarding the United States as an instrument of Providence. According to Paul Boyer: "As Darby's premillennial dispensationalism became an increasingly important strand of U.S. prophecy writing, belief in America's special millennial destiny diminished accordingly."[88]

It is true that dispensationalists warned against mistaking the United States for God's country. James Brookes wrote that "it is no uncommon thing to hear from the pulpit idle talk affirming the inalienable rights of man to life, liberty, and the pursuit of happiness, to trial by jury, to vote, and to other fancied privileges. Such language may sound very well from the lips of politicians, but surely the child of God ought to know that man has no inalienable rights, except the right to be damned."[89] By insisting that God made a covenant with only one nation—Israel—Brookes and other dispensationalists offered a powerful check to Americans' pretensions to be a new chosen people.

Yet Blackstone's appeals for an American Cyrus show that warnings against divinizing the United States were not incompatible with belief in a special destiny. Israel would be the setting of the apocalyptic drama and Jews the main actors. Yet America might have been drafted by God to play a supporting role. In the Bible, God used Gentile states and empires to execute His plans for Israel. Why should He not do the same in these latter days?

The idea that America rose to power for a special purpose is a recurring theme in postwar prophecy literature. William L. Hull, a Canadian fundamentalist who ministered to the imprisoned Adolf Eichmann, speculated that God granted the United States prosperity so its citizens could fund the "incoming of the exiles" to Palestine.[90] Walvoord agreed, speculating that America was rich because the "United States for the most part has been kind to the Jew. Here the seed of Abraham has had religious freedom and opportunity to make wealth."[91] By allowing Jews and Gentiles to accumulate resources and direct their fortunes toward Israel, America could play the part of Cyrus despite its alarming moral and spiritual deficiency. According to Walvoord: "History has many records of great nations which have risen to unusual power and influence only to decline because of internal corruption or international complications. It may well be that the United States of America is today at the zenith of its power much as Babylon was in the sixth century BC prior to its sudden downfall."[92]

American Christians, then, should not hope to take Israel's place in God's affection. But they could bask in the reflected glory of Israel by acknowledging its chosenness. God Himself promised to bless those who blessed the Jews. So long as it supported Israel, America would enjoy more divine favor than it actually deserved. The catch was that America's relationship to God was conditional, unlike Israel's irrevocable covenant. If it became derelict in its duty, God would withdraw His support.

The fate of Britain was a powerful warning of this possibility. Although it had been an important source of support for early Zionism, American prophecy writers linked the decline of British power after World War II to the anti-Zionist policies that characterized the last years of the Palestine Mandate. In 1943, Rimmer predicted that Britain would win the war in order to fulfill the Balfour Declaration.[93] At the Jerusalem conference nearly three decades later, Ockenga observed that the "question may well be raised as to whether the decline of Britain is not connected with her perfidy in reference to Israel."[94]

It might be thought that believers in a so-called pretribulational Rapture would have little reason to worry about this outcome. Because they expected to be removed from the earth before God poured out His wrath on the nations, the fate of the nations might seem irrelevant. Walvoord interpreted God's eventual judgment on the United States as a consequence of the disappearance of the righteous, whose steadfast friendship for Jews and Israel previously forestalled the divine hand. "It is evident," he wrote, "that if Christ came for His church and all true Christians were caught out of this world, America then would be reduced to the same situation as other countries. . . . The drastically changed situation would no longer call for material or political blessing upon the United States."[95]

The trouble was that no one could be sure when the Rapture would occur. Rather than promoting the true goal of the church, withdrawal from politics might defy His plan and endanger the continuation of His blessings. Even though they opposed conceptions of America as a new Israel, some prophecy interpreters offered provided a justification for an active American role in world affairs—at least until the last moment, when God would return His hand to the tiller of history.

The Yom Kippur War provided encouragement to this conclusion. Israel's victory in 1967 appeared to be based almost entirely on its own resources. In

1973, its narrow escape was thought to depend on diplomatic and military assistance from the United States. Believing that Israel was in mortal danger, Billy Graham abandoned his customary reticence and lobbied President Nixon to sell it F-15 fighter jets.[96] For his part, Walvoord read the decision by the Nixon administration to supply Israel's military needs in prophetic terms. In *Armageddon, Oil, and the Middle East Crisis*, he wrote: "The United States was the sole support of Israel. . . . This was just the beginning of new political and economic arrangements which were much like those predicted by the prophets. The world was moving toward a dramatic realignment of nations similar to that predicted as leading to Armageddon."[97]

Realignment in the Middle East was consistent with the theologized reading of the Cold War that many conservative Christians favored. If the United States was obeying God's will by supporting Israel, the Soviet Union was working for Satan by supporting the Arabs. Indeed, this evil parallel to the increasingly special relationship between the United States and Israel seemed to be written directly in scripture. It goes back to Ezekiel: after foretelling the return of the exiles, Ezekiel prophesies an invasion of the Promised Land. At its head is a certain Gog, who leads many nations against the restored Israel.

The link to Russia rests on Ezekiel's description of Gog as *rosh*. In Hebrew, *rosh* means "chief" or "head." For that reason, many translations describe Gog as ruler of lands called Magog, Meshech, and Tubal (Ezek. 38:2). But other versions treat *rosh* as a proper noun referring to a place. In that case, the line could be construed to identify Gog as the chief *of* Rosh, as well as commander of a horde that also includes Persia, Cush (traditionally identified as Ethiopia), and Put (often assumed to be Libya).

The German Bible scholar Wilhelm Gesenius was apparently the first to suggest that "Rosh" meant Russia, but the hypothesis was popularized among English speakers by the Scottish premillennialist John Cumming.[98] The identification of Gog as prince of Rosh was then included in the Scofield Reference Bible. The 1967 version states: "The reference is to the powers in the north of Europe, headed by Russia. . . . Gog is probably the prince, Magog, his land. Russia and the northern powers have long been the persecutors of the dispersed Israel, and it is congruous both with divine justice and with the covenants of God that destruction should fall in connection with the attempt to exterminate the remnant of Israel in Jerusalem. The entire prophecy belongs to the yet future days of the Lord."[99]

In addition to naming Israel's adversaries, an interpretation of Ezekiel focused on Russia helped clarify the sequence of events that would precede the appearance of the Antichrist. Posing as a man of peace, he might lead the international response to a Russian incursion into the Middle East. Writers on prophecy were divided about the motive for Russia's possible attack. Echoing concerns about resource depletion, Kirban speculated that a food crisis might lead Russia to seize fertile lands that Israel had reclaimed from the desert. Lindsey contended that valuable minerals in the Dead Sea could be the intended prize.

Whatever its proximate cause might be, a showdown between Russia—which prophecy writers treated interchangeably with the USSR—and Israel was inevitable. Because it was foretold by prophecy, the United States could not hope to prevent this confrontation. Both interest and duty, however, required America to hold the line as long as possible. For McCall and Levitt, the superpowers' contest for influence in the Middle East was "the enemies of God versus the friends of God."[100] The Cold War and Israel's security were two elements of the same struggle.

Prophecy writers worried that the religious nature of that struggle would be ignored in favor of secular geopolitics. Reacting to the oil embargo that OPEC imposed in response to Western support for Israel in the 1973 war, televangelist Jack Van Impe warned Americans not to give in to economic blackmail. If they betrayed Israel in exchange for cheap energy, they would find themselves on the wrong side of God. "Now that Arab oil is necessary for Americans to continue their love affair with affluence," Van Impe wrote, "one wonders how long this nation will officially stand on the side of the Jews. . . . Jewish favor has always been fragile, and oil may grease the slide in America. If so, the 'Land of the Free' is about to enter its darkest hour."[101]

A pessimistic assessment of American prospects, however, did not imply that the United States stood outside God's plan. To the contrary, it reinforced the idea that America was responsible for upholding the Judeo-Christian alliance until the last days. David Allen Lewis, Franklin Littell's fundamentalist successor as president of the National Christian Leadership Council for

Israel (NCLCI), put it this way: "A study of prophecy, rightly undertaken, does not promote escapism, defeatism, or irresponsibility. It is a call to be a participant in the ongoing plan and purpose of God. We are laborers together with the Lord. . . . God is not looking for spectators, He is looking for workers."[102]

Falwell and the New Christian Right

It is a central argument of this book that Christian Zionism is an older feature of American culture than most citizens and even some scholars recognize. Its sources stretch back to the English Reformation—and, in some ways, to the early church. In America, there were Christian advocates of the establishment of a Jewish state in the biblical Promised Land before Theodor Herzl founded the formal Zionist movement. As earlier chapters showed, some of them even argued that the United States was chosen by God to bring this about.

Yet the term "Christian Zionism" was introduced to the American lexicon relatively recently.[103] Scholar Stephen Spector has found that it was applied as a pejorative to G. Douglas Young—who thanked his critics for the compliment.[104] But it does not seem to have appeared in the mainstream media before the 1980s. The meaning of the phrase had to be explained to readers after its first appearance in the *New York Times*. A report of a rally celebrating the founding of the International Christian Embassy to protest Western governments' refusal to recognize Jerusalem as Israel's capital, the article introduces "Christians who call themselves Zionists."[105]

What accounts for the lateness of this development? The answer has less to do with any conceptual innovation than with a changing relationship between religion and politics. Fundamentalists and conservative evangelicals did not disappear from public life after the setbacks of the Scopes trial and the repeal of prohibition. Nevertheless, they played a less prominent role in the second third of the twentieth century than they had in its first. A younger generation was provoked by cultural upheavals, desegregation controversies, and the nationalization of legal abortion to renewed engagement with politics in the 1970s and 1980s. The Moral Majority, founded in 1979, was the largest and most dramatic product of this trend.

The Moral Majority was not primarily a Christian Zionist organization. Jerry Falwell's "Biblical Plan of Action" paid greater attention to abortion and homosexuality than it did to Jews or Israel.[106] Falwell did, however, synthesize support for Israel with his broader agenda. In Falwell's presentation, Israel was not an isolated issue that might attract the attention of clergy interested in Jewish-Christian relations or readers of the prophecy literature. It became a characteristic feature of the "new Christian Right" that helped define the Reagan era.[107]

In statements intended for a relatively wide audience, Falwell was tactful concerning the future of the Jewish nation. Avoiding discussion of the tribulation or the Second Coming, he emphasized Israel's friendship with America and its status as a bastion against Communism.[108] Falwell was less guarded in publications for insiders, which unfolded the dispensational timeline involving the Rapture, the rise of the Antichrist, the "slaughter" of "[m]illions of devout Jews," and the final battle of Armageddon.[109]

For some dispensationalists, this eschatology implied a distanced relation to international affairs. For Falwell, by contrast, action was the test of faith. Abstract belief was not enough to satisfy God. According to Moral Majority deputy Ed Dobson: "[Y]ou are judged by what you do."[110] By that standard, God might be thought to demand action to hasten the end of the world.[111] Falwell and his allies rejected that assumption, insisting that it is impossible to force God's hand. The prophecies would be fulfilled according to the divine schedule. In the meantime, Christians were responsible for demonstrating their faith by means of work in the world. Confronting charges that Christian conservatives believed the world so sinful that it ought to be destroyed, Dobson answered: "Our enthusiastic political involvement is proof that we are not among those evangelicals whose apocalyptic views are a pretext for this worldly despair."[112]

Rather than provoking conflict or abandoning Israel to its fate, then, Christian Right leaders encouraged the American faithful to support Israel in all its endeavors. By blessing the Jewish State with electoral or institutional support, they demonstrated their own piety. These actions would attract God's favor for themselves and for the United States. Tim LaHaye assured readers: "As long as there is a strong Israeli air force with the capability of nuclear retaliation, Russia will not attack the United States. Before they can suppress the world with their totalitarian ideology, they must first knock out the United States. And to do that, they must first remove Israel. . . . Thus Israel's safety and military strength are our own nation's best interest for survival."[113] According to journalist Mike Evans, "Israel is our only totally reliable ally against Soviet expansion. . . . [I]f Israel falls, the United States can no longer remain a democracy."[114]

Theologians associated with Falwell cautioned that blessing Israel did not imply carte blanche to act unjustly. "If Israel involves herself in sin," wrote John S. Feinberg, a professor at Liberty Baptist Seminary (later part of Liberty University) and son of Charles L. Feinberg, "we should not condone it, try to rationalize it, or justify it on the grounds that Israel is God's nation so she can do whatever she wants."[115] Sin, however, lay in the eye of the beholder. In practice, conservative Christians found justifications for Israel's controversial policies, including its invasion of Lebanon in 1982. In the Liberty-affiliated *Fundamentalist Journal*, columnist and Moral Majority official Cal Thomas noted that the "taking of innocent life, including innocent Palestinian life, should, of course, be condemned. But after a visit to the places of PLO and Syrian carnage, one is left wondering where all this concern was when innocent Jews and Christians were being murdered in a massive scale. . . . It is curious that such atrocities could have been carried out for so long without arousing the passions and protests of Christians around the world."[116]

Although they denounced the PLO and Israel's neighbors in resounding tones, Christian Zionists remained convinced that Russia was the destined enemy.[117] In a sequel to *The Late Great Planet Earth* published in 1981, Hal Lindsey wrote that the "Soviet Union and its satellites have now reached the position of military superiority and strategic world power to fulfill their predicted dreadful role in history."[118] It was America's responsibility to resist Soviet encroachments in the Middle East "until the Lord comes to evacuate his people."[119] Christian Zionism continued to be framed by the Cold War.

Political scientist Donald Vinz observed that this analysis of America's relationship with Israel thus had a "heads I win, tails you lose" character.[120] If America remained strong, that was because it supported Israel, confirming

Genesis 12. If America declined, that was because it had failed to support Israel adequately, corresponding to prophecies that foresaw international disorder in the run-up to the Second Coming. Either way, the Bible was right.

One way to secure a blessed future for America was to ensure that the United States continued to provide Israel with military aid. In the 1980s, Christian Zionists urged President Reagan and Congress not only to give Israel access to the latest technology but also to deny that technology to its regional rivals. In one of their first attempts to pressure the White House, Christian Zionists urged the Reagan administration not to sell radar-detection planes to Saudi Arabia. The effort was unsuccessful—an outcome that they blamed on the influence of oil money. Although they would later be characterized as part of the most powerful lobby in Washington, Christian Zionists saw themselves as embattled outsiders.[121]

A second form of concrete support was tourism. American Christians had been making pilgrimages to Israel since its founding. Falwell pioneered a new kind of religious tourism, recruiting large groups to visit Israel on tightly scripted trips. Grace Halsell, a former speechwriter for Lyndon Johnson, wrote one of the earliest books about Christian Zionism. She described her tour group as "encapsulated, as in a space ship."[122] Almost ignoring modern Jewish life and the Arab population, the itinerary was mostly limited to sites of prophetic interest.

Such activities were highly congenial to Israeli governments, particularly after Menachem Begin took office in 1977. A pugnacious nationalist with no hesitation about taking friends as he found them, Begin and his government welcomed support from American Christians.[123] It is not true, as was rumored, that Israel provided Falwell with an airplane to assist him in his work. But he was presented with the 1981 Jabotinsky Award in recognition of his services.[124] Reports of contacts with highly placed Israelis became characteristic of the Christian Zionist literature in the 1980s. Although they never seemed to include any surprising information, these conversations created the impression of tight links between Christian conservatives in America and the religious and political establishment in Israel.

After Begin left office, no Israeli politician was more assiduous in cultivating these appearances than Benjamin Netanyahu, whose father, historian Benzion Netanyahu, acted as an informant to American visitors. In 1985, the younger Netanyahu, then serving as Israel's ambassador to the UN, addressed the National Prayer Breakfast in Honor of Israel at the meeting of the National Association of Religious Broadcasters, thanking Christian conservatives for their support.[125] Although not affiliated with the White House, the event's name evoked the annual National Prayer Breakfasts established under President Eisenhower to present the United States as a nation "under God."[126] Like Begin and Falwell's meeting at Blair House, Netanyahu's address intentionally evoked a providential relationship between the two countries.

Christian conservatives expected this message to appeal to American Jews. Despite overtures by interfaith activists like Marc Tanenbaum, that expectation went mostly unrealized. One reason was the social distance between urban, highly educated American Jews and sometimes defiantly provincial conservatives. As the American Jewish Committee official A. James Rudin tactfully put it: "[A]ccidents of demography and geography have often prevented Jews and evangelicals from interacting with one another in a meaningful way."[127] Rather than relying on caricatures and stereotypes, Rudin encouraged members of both groups to get to know each other better. Then they would recognize their agreement regarding Israel, even though they might be at odds on other matters.

Consensus proved elusive because of the profound theological and political principles at stake. The most immediate obstacle was the emphasis on conversion that had long defined fundamentalists and neo-evangelicals' interest in Jews. Echoing Saint Paul's promise in Romans 11, they argued that return to the land was merely a stage toward their salvation. According to Falwell: "The Jews are returning to their land of unbelief. They are spiritually blind and desperately in need of their Messiah and Savior."[128]

This did not mean that Jews had to be converted collectively or immediately. On the contrary, LaHaye insisted: "Not until Russia is supernaturally destroyed by God on the mountains of Israel will the nation turn en masse to Him."[129] Falwell denied any interest in missions targeted at Jews.[130] For most Jews, however, that was small consolation. Whether conversion was supposed to occur immediately or at some point in the future, the eschatological narrative seemed to make Jews puppets in what Oral Roberts called the "drama of the end time." Falwell and other Christian conservatives disclaimed any intention of influencing Israel's policies. But their emphasis on prophetic fulfillment encouraged skepticism about a negotiated peace or a territorial compromise.[131]

The most lurid suspicions were false: the Zionists of the new Christian Right did not seek to hasten Armageddon. At least where Israel was concerned, though, they tended to subsume foreign policy under sacred history. For evangelical and fundamentalist supporters of Israel, politics was conditioned by divine purposes. Man's role was to recognize and accommodate himself to that design, which would ultimately play out in the landscape promised to Abraham.

But this vision of America's role was nothing new. Inspired by prophecy as well as covenant, it was perhaps closer to the theological understanding of a city upon a hill familiar to the Puritans than to President Reagan's utopian appropriations of the phrase.[132] Rather than possessing wealth and power because it had been chosen by God, conservative Christian Zionists argued that America enjoyed these goods so that it could help complete to a divine plan centered on Israel. In Genesis 12, God promises to bless those who bless Abraham. For the Christian Right of the 1980s, there were plenty of blessings to go around.

Conclusion

On October 3, 2002, *60 Minutes* aired a report titled "Zion's Christian Soldiers." Brisk and direct, the segment introduced viewers to "Fundamentalist Christian Evangelicals" who believe that "the Jewish State should control all of the Biblical Jewish homeland."[1] Among spokesmen for this group, the ubiquitous Jerry Falwell received the most screen time. But other luminaries of the Reagan-era Christian Right, including the Religious Roundtable founder, Ed McAteer, were duly quoted. Although neutral in tone, the report was unmistakably skeptical. Its audience was informed that Christian conservatives support Israel because they see "the return of the Jews to their ancient homeland . . . as a precondition for the Second Coming of Christ." Drawing on the *Left Behind* novels, the report sketched a scenario that culminates "in Israel where, according to the Book of Revelations [*sic*], the final battle in the history of the future will be fought on an ancient battlefield in northern Israel called Armageddon. . . . The blood will rise as high as a horse's bridle at Armageddon, before Christ triumphs to begin his 1,000 year rule."[2] Jewish and Israeli sources described their discomfort with this vision, which seems to sacrifice Jews to the greater glory of God. McAteer, on the other hand, acknowledged no qualms, saying, "I believe that we are seeing prophecy unfold so rapidly and dramatically and wonderfully and, without exaggerating, [that] makes me breathless."[3]

This solemn depiction of a clash between fanaticism and reason on *60 Minutes* was part of a wave of attention to Christian Zionism in the first decade of the twenty-first century. Struggling to make sense of events including the election of a president with ties to the Christian Right, the 9/11 attacks, and the intensifying clashes between Israelis and Palestinians, observers discovered in Christian Zionism a symptom of a world apparently gone mad. Some of the coverage was narrowly factual, focusing on the growing role of Christian Zionists in an emboldened pro-Israel coalition. But much of it evoked fears that an "American theocracy" would pursue doomsday policies rather than world peace.[4]

The politics of the apocalypse made for good headlines, but imagination sometimes outstripped the evidence. There was no proof that Christian Zionists wielded as much clout in Washington as either they or their critics claimed. Like other political factions, Christian Zionists held rallies, circulated petitions, and wrote letters to elected officials. No investigation, however, demonstrated that these strategies diverted U.S. foreign policy far from its recent course. According to many analysts, the Bush White House pursued the same goals in its relations with Israel—security cooperation, promotion of economic ties, and a negotiated two-state settlement—as had the Clinton administration.[5] As historian Walter Russell Mead pointed out in *Foreign Affairs*, the reality was that a majority of Americans regarded Israel as a friend and had for years. U.S. foreign policy reflected that fact, no matter who sat in the Oval Office.[6]

Christian Zionism was also blamed for some of the Bush administration's less popular stances. During the Iraq War, rumors circulated that the president was obsessed with Bible prophecy and had even told Jacques Chirac that "Gog and Magog are at work in the Middle East."[7] In his review of a biography of George W. Bush that includes an account of the alleged episode, historian William Inboden, who served in a variety of national security roles in the period, dismissed this charge as "utterly and completely false."[8] If the Second Gulf War was a disastrous folly, it was not the result of end-times theology.

The lack of evidence supporting fears of a fundamentalist takeover does not mean that Christian Zionists were irrelevant. Although they were not planning U.S. foreign policy in secret meetings, their talent for organization and habit of turning out to vote made them valued friends and feared enemies of candidates for office, especially in constituencies with large numbers of evangelical voters. Efforts to maintain their influence, however, encouraged shifts away from the rhetoric of the Moral Majority. Partly as a response to criticism from Jews, themes of covenant have become more prominent than prophecy in Christian Zionist appeals. The change is not merely instrumental. In most cases, it represents a sincere attempt to find a more productive and respectful basis for relations between the two religions. Rather than Daniel's seventieth week or Isaiah's foretelling of the restoration of Jerusalem, the core idea of Christian Zionism is that God's relationship with the Jewish people was not severed with the advent of Christ. What many Christian Zionists hope to do is return that idea to the centrality that they believe it deserves.

It is also important to recall that the idea of an American calling to help complete God's plan for the Jews was not invented by the Christian Right of the 1980s. On the contrary, it is a recurring theme of American thought. Since the Puritans, many inhabitants of what is now the United States have tried by make sense of their own identity by affirming God's election of the nation of Israel. It is neither surprising nor sinister that this component of our national myth endures.

For some critics, the intertwinement of Christian Zionism with American exceptionalism renders it more ideological than genuinely religious. It is possible, however, that renewed appreciation for the concept of covenant could serve as an antidote to what *New York Times* columnist Ross Douthat calls "bad religion." Douthat cautions that "if we think of ourselves as in any way analogous to Israel, it must be *only* by way of analogy. There is only one true Israel and even the greatest nation can hope only to be an '*almost*-chosen people.'"[9] The reference is to Abraham Lincoln's warning that Americans should not regard themselves as morally perfect or immune to divine judgment.

In its origins, this was precisely the implication of Puritans' insistence that God was not finished with the Jews. Because the covenant with Abraham and his descendants remained valid, they were encouraged to resist the temptation to regard themselves as successors to the chosen people and the objects of God's unique favor. That might function today as a way of warning Americans against exaggerated nationalism. Perhaps that is part of what

Saint Paul was getting at when he described the mystery of Israel's salvation as a rebuke to arrogance among Gentiles.

But does Christian Zionism have a future? A decade ago, many observers were confident that conservative Protestants provided a stable base of support for Israel within the American public. In 2006, Mead contended that "evangelical power is here to stay"—and with it, the influence of Christian Zionism.[10]

More than ten years later, the picture is less clear. Evangelicals remain America's largest religious group. But their demographic advantage has been eroded by the rising number of Americans who are religiously unaffiliated. According to a 2014 survey by the Pew Research Center, about 23 percent of Americans can be described as "nones." That almost matches the quarter of the population who identify as evangelicals and exceeds the number who identify with any other Christian community.[11]

The political clout of evangelicals and other conservative Christians has declined in consequence. Once confident that they represented a moral majority, many now hope for protection as a threatened minority.[12] Despite the election of Donald Trump with overwhelming support from these voters, their status in Republican and conservative politics has irrevocably changed. What once seemed to be almost an overwhelming electoral coalition in itself is now just one interest group among many.

There is also reason to think that Christian Zionism is losing its appeal among those who were recently its most energetic supporters. Citing resistance from prominent American church figures and the growing visibility of the Palestinian Christian community, Christian Middle East activist Robert Nicholson observed that "more and more American evangelicals are being educated to accept the pro-Palestinian narrative—on the basis of their Christian faith."[13] The CUFI official David Brog has even warned of "the end of evangelical support for Israel."[14] He points ominously toward mainline Protestants' drift away from Israel after 1967.

Only prophets can foretell the future, but obituaries for Christian Zionism seem premature. The specific form of Christian Zionism that emerged in the 1970s seems to be waning. But one argument of this book is that Second

Coming narratives and a hawkish twist on Cold War foreign policy are not the only justification for Christian support of the State of Israel. The end times are not the end of the story.

The future of Christian Zionism may turn out to be less American than its recent past, however. While a secularizing trend continues at home, the focus of Christian Zionism seems be moving away from the United States, as religious movements that began there spread throughout the world.[15] In 2014, the *New York Times* reported the construction of an enormous replica of Solomon's temple by a Pentecostal congregation in São Paolo, Brazil. The temple's entrance is guarded by a menorah that resembles one displayed outside the Knesset in Jerusalem, as well as flags of Israel, the United States, Brazil, and other nations. "There is just one biblical faith; it is impossible to disassociate Christianity from its Jewish roots," a spokeswoman for the Universal Church explained.[16] Wherever Christians agree, they keep God's country in their prayers.

Notes

Introduction

1. James Inhofe, "Peace in the Middle East," March 4, 2002, http://www.inhofe.senate.gov /newsroom/speech/peace-in-the-middle-east-speech.

2. Ibid.

3. Ibid.

4. Ibid.

5. Ibid.

6. Ralph Reed, "We People of Faith Stand Firmly with Israel," *Los Angeles Times*, April 21, 2002, http://articles.latimes.com/2002/apr/21/opinion/oe-reed21.

7. Ibid.

8. Quoted in Craig Horowitz, "Israel's Christian Soldiers," *New York*, September 29, 2003, http://nymag.com/nymetro/news/religion/features/n_9255.

9. See John Hagee, "Why Christians Should Support Israel," http://www.jhm.org/Home /About/WhySupportIsrael.

10. John J. Mearsheimer and Stephen M. Walt, *The Israel Lobby and U.S. Foreign Policy* (New York: Farrar, Straus and Giroux, 2007), 107–8, 132–39. Clifford Kiracofe, Jr., offers a similar assessment, in *Dark Crusade: Christian Zionism and U.S. Foreign Policy* (New York: I. B. Tauris, 2009).

11. Shalom Goldman, *Zeal for Zion: Jews, Christians, and the Idea of the Promised Land* (Chapel Hill: University of North Carolina Press, 2009), 90.

12. Yaakov Ariel, "It's All in the Bible: Evangelical Christians, Biblical Literalism, and Philosemitism in Our Times," in *Philosemitism in History*, ed. Jonathan Karp and Adam Sutcliffe (Cambridge: Cambridge University Press, 2012), 263.

13. Nahum Sokolow, *History of Zionism, 1600–1918* (London: Longman, 1919), 1:162, 174. On Gawler's relationship with Montefiore, see Abigail Green, *Moses Montefiore: Jewish Liberator, Imperial Hero* (Cambridge, MA: Belknap Press, 2010), 215–20.

14. Eitan Bar-Yosef, "Christian Zionism and Victorian Culture," *Israel Studies* 8, no. 2 (Summer 2003): 32.

15. Stephen Spector, *Evangelicals and Israel* (New York: Oxford University Press, 2009), 2.

16. David K. Shipler, "1,000 Christian 'Zionists' in Jerusalem," *New York Times*, September 25, 1980, cited in Spector, *Evangelicals and Israel*, 2.

17. Victoria Clark, *Allies for Armageddon: The Rise of Christian Zionism* (New Haven, CT: Yale University Press, 2007), 3.

18. Gershom Gorenberg, *The End of Days: Fundamentalism and the Struggle for the Temple Mount* (New York: Oxford University Press, 2000), 160.

19. Timothy P. Weber, *On the Road to Armageddon* (Grand Rapids, MI: Baker Academic, 2004), 18.

20. Caitlin Carenen, *The Fervent Embrace* (New York: New York University Press, 2012).

21. Jonathan Edwards, "Notes on the Apocalypse," in *Works of Jonathan Edwards Online*, vol. 5, *Apocalyptic Writings*, 133–34.

22. Robert O. Smith, *More Desired than Our Owne Salvation: The Roots of Christian Zionism* (New York: Oxford University Press, 2013), 66.

23. Gerald R. McDermott, "A History of Christian Zionism," in *The New Christian Zionism*, ed. idem (Downers Grove, IL: IVP, 2016), 46.

24. John Winthrop, "A Modell of Christian Charitie," in *God's New Israel: Religious Interpretations of American Destiny*, ed. Conrad Cherry (Chapel Hill: University of North Carolina Press, 1998), 40–41.

25. Ezra Stiles, "The United States Elevated to Glory and Honor" (New Haven, CT, 1783), 6.

26. Reinhold Niebuhr, "Our Stake in the State of Israel," *New Republic*, February 3, 1957, 12.

27. Starting points for this debate include Stephen Sizer, *Christian Zionism: Road-Map to Armageddon?* (Leicester, UK: IVP, 2004); and Gary M. Burge, *Whose Land? Whose Promise? What Christians Are Not Being Told About Israel* (Cleveland: Pilgrim Press, 2013).

28. The earliest treatment of this idea for a general audience is Peter Grose, *Israel in the Mind of America* (New York: Knopf, 1983). For a more recent attempt, see Michael Oren, *Power, Faith, and Fantasy: America in the Middle East, 1776 to the Present* (New York: W. W. Norton, 2007).

29. Robert F. Drinan, *Honor the Promise: America's Commitment to Israel* (New York: Doubleday, 1977), 3.

30. Stephen Prothero, *Religious Literacy: What Every American Needs to Know* (New York: HarperCollins, 2008), 18–19.

31. Mark Lilla, *The Stillborn God* (New York: Vintage, 2008), 23.

32. Paul Kahn, *Political Theology: Four New Chapters on the Concept of Sovereignty* (New York: Columbia University Press, 2012), 3.

Part I

1. David Hackett Fischer, *Albion's Seed: Four British Folkways in America* (New York: Oxford University Press, 1989), 118–19.

2. Ibid., 140.

3. Chandler Robbins, *History of the Second Church, or Old North Church, in Boston* (Boston, 1852), 26.

4. Robert Middlekauff, *The Mathers: Three Generations of Puritan Intellectuals, 1596–1728* (Berkeley: University of California Press, 1999), 88. On the so-called Thursday Lectures, see Arthur B. Ellis, *History of the First Church in Boston, 1630–1880* (Boston, 1881), 34–35; Robbins, *History of the Second Church*, 29; Michael G. Hall, *The Last American Puritan: The Life of Increase Mather* (Middletown, CT: Wesleyan University Press, 1988), 72.

5. Cotton Mather, *Parentator: Memoirs of Remarkables in the Life and Death of the Ever-Memorable Dr. Increase Mather* (Boston, 1723), repr. in *Two Mather Biographies: Life and Death and Parentator*, ed. William J. Scheick (Cranbury, NJ: Associated University Presses, 1989), 200.

6. The rumored Messiah was Sabbatai Sevi. See Gershom Scholem, *Sabbatai Sevi: The Mystical Messiah* (Princeton, NJ: Princeton University Press, 1976). On Sevi's background and influence,

including links to English millenarianism, see Matt Goldish, *The Sabbatean Prophets* (Cambridge, MA: Harvard University Press, 2004), esp. chap. 1.

7. Increase Mather, *The Mystery of Israel's Salvation, Explained and Applyed* (London, 1669), 159.

8. C. Mather, *Parentator*, 117. Unless otherwise noted, all emphasis and capitalization are in the original.

9. For versions of this interpretation, see Perry Miller, *Errand into the Wilderness* (Cambridge, MA: Harvard University Press, 2000), 6–7; Emory Elliott, "From Father to Son: The Evolution of Typology in Puritan New England," in *Literary Uses of Typology from the Late Middle Ages to the Present*, ed. Earl Miner (Princeton, NJ: Princeton University Press, 1977), 206–7. For a critique, see Richard M. Gamble, *In Search of the City on a Hill* (New York: Continuum, 2012), chap. 7.

10. Reinier Smolinski, "Israel Redivivus: The Eschatological Limits of Puritan Typology in New England," *New England Quarterly* 63, no. 3 (1990): 358–59.

11. Nicholas Guyatt convincingly defends a providentialist interpretation of Puritan culture in *Providence and the Invention of the United States* (New York: Cambridge University Press, 2007).

12. Peter Bulkeley, *The Gospel Covenant* (London, 1651), 19.

13. James Ceaser, "The Origins and Character of American Exceptionalism," *American Political Thought* 1, no. 1 (Spring 2012): 12–13.

14. Elias Boudinot, *A Star in the West* (Trenton, NJ, 1816), 297.

Chapter 1

1. Gamble, *In Search of the City on a Hill*, 28–29.

2. Robert Bellah, *The Broken Covenant: American Civil Religion in Time of Trial* (Chicago: University of Chicago Press, 1992), 15.

3. John Cotton, "Gods Promise to His Plantation" (London, 1630), 6.

4. Conor Cruise O'Brien, *God Land: Reflections on Religion and Nationalism* (Cambridge, MA: Harvard University Press, 1988), 31–32.

5. Philo, "Against Flaccus," *Philo*, vol. 9, trans. F. H. Colson (Cambridge, MA: Harvard University Press, 1995), 329.

6. Unless otherwise noted, Bible quotations are from the New Revised Standard Version.

7. See Elaine Pagels, *Revelations: Visions, Prophecy, and Politics in the Book of Revelation* (New York: Penguin, 2013).

8. Justin Martyr, *The First Apology, The Second Apology, Dialogue with Trypho, Exhortation to the Greeks, Discourse to the Greeks, the Monarchy or the Rule of God*, trans. Thomas B. Falls (Washington, DC: Catholic University of America Press, 1948), 277. My interpretation of Justin follows Robert L. Wilken, *The Land Called Holy: Palestine in Christian History and Thought* (New Haven, CT: Yale University Press, 1992), 56–57.

9. Justin Martyr, *The First Apology, The Second Apology, Dialogue with Trypho, Exhortation to the Greeks, Discourse to the Greeks, the Monarchy or the Rule of God*, 322.

10. Ibid., 339–40.

11. Andrew Crome, *The Restoration of the Jews: Early Modern Hermeneutics, Eschatology, and National Identity in the Works of Thomas Brightman* (New York: Springer, 2014), 32.

12. Irenaeus, *Against Heresies*, ed. Alexander Roberts and James Donaldson (Lexington, KY: Ex Fontibus, 2010), 650.

13. Ibid.

14. Ibid., 645.

15. For a survey of these debates, see Jeremy Cohen, "The Mystery of Israel's Salvation: Romans 11:25–26 in Patristic and Medieval Literature," *Harvard Theological Review* 98, no. 3 (2005): 247–81.

16. Wilken, *The Land Called Holy*, 77.

17. David Nirenberg, *Anti-Judaism: The Western Tradition* (New York: W. W. Norton, 2003), 109–12.

18. Paula Frederiksen, *Augustine and the Jews* (New York: Doubleday, 2008), 280–86, 349.

19. Saint Augustine, *City of God*, trans. Henry Bettenson (New York: Penguin, 1984), 178.

20. Gerald R. McDermott, "A History of Christian Zionism," in *The New Christian Zionism*, ed. idem (Downers Grove, IL: IVP, 2016), 56.

21. Marjorie Reeves, *The Influence of Prophecy in the Later Middle Ages: A Study in Joachimism* (South Bend, IN: University of Notre Dame Press, 2011), 48, 222, 237, 299, 305.

22. Robert E. Lerner, *The Feast of Saint Abraham: Medieval Millenarians and the Jews* (Philadelphia: University of Pennsylvania Press, 2000), 118–19.

23. Martin Luther, *Commentary on Romans*, trans. J. Theodore Mueller (Grand Rapids, MI: Kregel, 1976), xiii.

24. Ibid., 161.

25. Ibid., 161–62.

26. Yaakov Ariel, *An Unusual Relationship: Evangelical Christians and Jews* (New York: New York University Press, 2013), 17–18.

27. David S. Katz and Richard Popkin, *Messianic Revolution* (New York: Hill & Wang, 1998), 46–47.

28. John Calvin, *Commentaries on the Epistles of Paul the Apostle*, trans. John Owen (Grand Rapids, MI: Eerdmans, 1947), 410. In addition to summarizing Paul, Calvin echoes Psalm 89, in which God reiterates that "I will not violate my covenant, or alter the word that went forth from my lips" (Ps. 89:34).

29. Ibid., 438.

30. Gideon Shimoni, *The Zionist Ideology* (Hanover, NH: University Press of New England, 1995), 60–65.

31. Bulkeley, *The Gospel Covenant*, 1.

32. *The Geneva Bible: A Facsimile of the 1560 Edition* (Madison: University of Wisconsin Press, 1967), title page.

33. Ibid. (Old Testament), 6.

34. Ibid. (Old Testament), 304.

35. Ibid. (Old Testament), 303.

36. Ibid. (Old Testament), 345.

37. Augustine, *City of God*, 907, 915.

38. John Calvin, *Institutes of the Christian Religion*, ed. John T. McNeill (Philadelphia: Westminster Press, 1960), 2:996.

39. Jerry L. Walls, "Introduction," in *The Oxford Handbook of Eschatology*, ed. idem (New York: Oxford University Press, 2008), 13. See also Timothy P. Weber, "Millennialism," in ibid., 374.

40. Quoted in Crome, *The Restoration of the Jews*, 51.

41. Thomas Draxe, *The Worldes Resurrection or the General Calling of the Iewes* (London, 1608), 64. See also pp. 89, 94.

42. On Brightman's version of the apocalyptic timeline, see Robert O. Smith, *More Desired than Our Owne Salvation* (New York: Oxford University Press, 2013), 72–74.

43. Thomas Brightman, *Revelation of the Revelation* (London, 1611), 549.

44. Ibid., 550.

45. Brog, *Standing with Israel* (Lake Mary, FL: FrontLine, 2006), 13–14.

46. Brightman, *Revelation of the Revelation*, 551.

47. For a comparison of Mede's and Brightman's eschatologies, see Robert G. Clouse, "The Rebirth of Millenarianism," in *Puritan Eschatology: Puritans, the Millennium, and the Future of Israel*, ed. Peter Toon (London: James Clarke, 1970), 56–61.

48. R. Smith, *More Desired than Our Owne Salvation*, 94.

49. Henry Finch, *The Calling of the Iewes* (London, 1621), 6.

50. Ibid., 7.

51. Ibid.

52. Ibid., 103.

53. William Laud, *A Sermon Preached Before his Majesty* (London: 1621), 23.

54. Ibid., 24.

55. Conrad Cherry, "The Colonial Errand into the Wilderness," in *God's New Israel*, ed. idem, 26–27.

56. Ibid., 322.

57. Edward Johnson, *A History of New-England* (London, 1651), 117. The unofficial title is based on the running title that appears throughout the body of the text rather than the one on the title page. Johnson's work has been known as the *Wonder-Working Providence* since the late seventeenth century. For a discussion of these issues, see Edward Johnson, *Johnson's Wonder-Working Providence, 1628–1651*, ed. J. Franklin Jameson (New York: Charles Scribner's Sons, 1910), 3–5.

58. John Cotton, *Moses His Judicialls and Abstract of the Laws of New England*, ed. Worthington Chauncy Ford (Cambridge, MA: John Wilson, 1902), 15. Cf. John Cotton, *A Discourse About Government in a New Plantation Whose Design Is Religion* (Cambridge, 1663), 16. On the role of Hebraism in Puritan legal thought, see Michael Hoberman, *New Israel/New England: Jews and Puritans in Early America* (Amherst: University of Massachusetts Press, 2011), 27–29.

59. Smolinski, "Israel Redivivus," 357–95.

60. Bulkeley, *The Gospel Covenant*, 3, 6–7 (emphasis in original).

61. Ibid., 16–17.

62. Ibid., 21.

63. John Cotton, *The Powring Out of the Seven Vials; or an Exposition of the 16. Chapter of Revelation with an Application of It to Our Times* (London, 1642), 158.

64. Johnson, *Wonder-Working Providence*, 233.

65. John Cotton, *A Brief Exposition of the Whole Book of Canticles* (London, 1642), 196.

66. B. S. Capp, *The Fifth Monarchy Men: A Study in Seventeenth-Century English Millenarianism* (Totowa, NJ: Rowman & Littlefield, 1972), cited in Katz and Popkin, *Messianic Revolution*, 68–69.

67. "Peters or Peter, Hugh," *Dictionary of National Biography*, ed. Sidney Lee (New York: Macmillan, 1896), 45:69–77. On Peters's chiliasm, see Glenn A. Moots, *Politics Reformed: The Anglo-American Legacy of Covenant Theology* (Columbia: University of Missouri Press, 2010), 94–95.

68. Peters is mentioned as a sympathizer of Menasseh's, in Nahum Sokolow, *History of Zionism, 1600–1918* (London: Longmans, Green, 1919), 183, 446. For a comprehensive analysis of the episode, see David S. Katz, *Philo-Semitism and the Readmission of the Jews to England, 1603–1655* (Oxford: Oxford University Press, 1982).

69. B. S. Capp, "Extreme Millenarianism," in *Puritans, the Millennium, and the Future of Israel: Puritan Eschatology 1600 to 1660*, ed. Toon, 71–72.

70. Menasseh ben Israel, *The Hope of Israel* (London, 1650), 43.

71. C. Mather, *Parentator*, repr. in *Two Mather Biographies*, ed. Scheick, 117.

72. This biographical sketch is based on Robert Middlekauff, *The Mathers: Three Generations of Puritan Intellectuals, 1596–1728* (Berkeley: University of California Press, 1999), 80–88.

73. C. Mather, *Parentator*, 117. See also Mason I. Lowance, Jr., *Increase Mather* (New York: Twayne, 1974), 154; Perry Miller, *The New England Mind: From Colony to Province* (Cambridge, MA: Belknap Press, 1953), 187.

74. I. Mather, *The Mystery of Israel's Salvation*, 2.

75. Ibid., 3.

76. Ibid., 6.

77. Ibid., 9.

78. Ibid. (author's preface), unpaginated. See also Increase Mather, *A Dissertation Concerning the Future Conversion of the Jewish Nation* (London, 1709), 11.

79. I. Mather, *The Mystery of Israel's Salvation*, (author's preface), unpaginated. For a discussion of Beza's influence on Puritan writers, see Linda Munk, *The Devil's Mousetrap: Redemption and Colonial American Literature* (New York: Oxford University Press, 1997), 122.

80. I. Mather, *The Mystery of Israel's Salvation*, (author's preface), unpaginated.

81. Theodore Dwight Bozeman, *To Live Ancient Lives: The Primitivist Dimension in Puritanism* (Chapel Hill: University of North Carolina Press, 1988), 323–24.

82. John Davenport, "An Epistle to the Reader," in I. Mather, *The Mystery of Israel's Salvation*, unpaginated.

83. I. Mather, *The Mystery of Israel's Salvation* (author's preface), unpaginated.

84. Ibid., 127–28.

85. Ibid., 128.

86. William Twisse, epistle 62, *The Works of the Pious and Profoundly Learned Joseph Mede, B.D.* (London, 1677), bk. 4, 799.

87. Joseph Mede, epistle 63, in ibid., 800.

88. I. Mather, *A Dissertation Concerning the Future Conversion of the Jewish Nation*, 32–33.

89. Increase Mather, *A Brief History of the Warr with the Indians in New-England* (Boston: John Foster, 1676), 9.

90. Nicholas Noyes, *New-Englands Duty and Interest to Be an Habitation of Justice and Mountain of Holiness Containing Doctrine, Caution, & Comfort* (Boston, 1698), 68–69.

91. Ibid., 60. Noyes's argument illustrates the complexity of the analogy to Israel in jeremiad tradition. Puritan divines used Israel to model the consequences of disobedience to God's covenant: exile, persecution, and general misery. Puritan ministers argued that New England risked the same fate because of its sins.

92. Samuel Sewall, *Phaenomena quaedam Apocalyptica* (Boston, 1697), unpaginated. See also J. W. Davidson, *The Logic of Millennial Thought: Eighteenth-Century New England* (New Haven, CT: Yale University Press, 1977), 67.

93. S. Sewall, *Phaenomena quaedam Apocalyptica* (Boston, 1697), 49.

94. Ibid., 32.

95. Ibid., 2, 41–42. See also Richard H. Popkin, "The Rise and Fall of the Jewish Indian Theory," in *Menasseh ben Israel and His World*, ed. Yosef Kaplan, Henry Méchoulan, and Richard H. Popkin (Leiden: Brill, 1989), 63–82.

96. Michael G. Hall, *The Last American Puritan: The Life of Increase Mather* (Middletown, CT: Wesleyan University Press, 1988), 77.

97. Samuel Mather, *Figures and Types of the Old Testament* (London, 1683), 180, 217, 481. See also Mason I. Lowance, *The Language of Canaan: Metaphor and Symbol in New England from the Puritans to the Transcendentalists* (Cambridge, MA: Harvard University Press, 1980), 6.

98. Reiner Smolinski, "Apocalypticism in Colonial North America," in *The Continuum History of Apocalypticism*, ed. Bernard J. McGinn, John J. Collins, and Seymour J. Stein (New York: Continuum, 2003), 450. Cf. Davidson, *The Logic of Millennial Thought*, 61–63.

99. Cotton Mather, *Theopolis Americana: An Essay on the Golden Street of the Holy City* (Boston, 1710).

100. Quoted in Lee B. Friedman, *Cotton Mather and the Jews* (New York: American Jewish Historical Society, 1918), 203.

Chapter 2

1. Richard S. Patterson and Richardson Dougall, *The Eagle and the Shield: A History of the Great Seal of the United States* (Washington, DC: Department of State, 1976), 22–24.

2. Recent contributions to the literature on this subject include Eran Shalev, *Rome Reborn on Western Shores: Historical Imagination and the Creation of the American Republic* (Charlottesville: University of Virginia Press, 2009); Robert A. Ferguson, *Reading the Early Republic* (Cambridge, MA: Harvard University Press, 2004), chap. 6; Carl J. Richard, *The Founders and the Classics: Greece, Rome, and the American Enlightenment* (Cambridge, MA: Harvard University Press, 1994).

3. For a survey of uses of the Bible in the early republic, see John Fea, "Does America Have a Biblical Heritage?," in *The Bible in the Public Square*, ed. Mark A. Chancey, Carol Meyers, and Eric M. Meyers (Atlanta: SBL Press, 2014).

4. Donald S. Lutz, "The Relative Influence of European Writers on Late Eighteenth-Century American Political Thought," *American Political Science Review* 78, no. 1 (March 1984): 192.

5. Steven Prothero, *The American Bible* (New York: HarperOne, 2012), 18–33.

6. David Austin, ed., *The Millennium* (Elizabethtown, NJ, 1794), 415.

7. Eran Shalev, *American Zion: The Old Testament as a Political Text from the Revolution to the Civil War* (New Haven, CT: Yale University Press, 2013).

8. Nicholas Street, *The American States Acting over the Part of the Children of Israel in the Wilderness* (New Haven, CT, 1777).

9. Timothy Dwight, *The Conquest of Canäan* (Hartford, 1785). See also idem, *A Discourse of Some Events of the Last Century* (New Haven, CT, 1801), 42.

10. Abiel Abbot, *Traits of Resemblance in the People of the United States to Ancient Israel* (Haverhill, MA, 1799), 12. Unless otherwise noted, all capitalization and emphasis are in the original.

11. Elias Boudinot, *The Second Advent* (Trenton, NJ, 1815), 531–32.

12. Elias Boudinot, *A Star in the West* (Trenton, NJ, 1816), 297.

13. Perry Miller, *Errand into the Wilderness* (Cambridge, MA: Harvard University Press, 2000), 233.

14. Jonathan Edwards, "Some Thoughts Concerning the Present Revival of Religion in New England," in *Works of Jonathan Edwards Online*, vol. 4, *The Great Awakening* (New Haven, CT: Jonathan Edwards Center, Yale University), 353.

15. Michael J. McClymond and Gerald R. McDermott, *The Theology of Jonathan Edwards* (New York: Oxford University Press, 2012), 575. See also Gerald R. McDermott, *One Holy and*

Happy Society: The Public Theology of Jonathan Edwards (State College, PA: Penn State University Press, 1992), 60–61.

16. McClymond and McDermott, *The Theology of Jonathan Edwards*, 575.

17. Jonathan Edwards, "Notes on the Apocalypse," in *Works of Jonathan Edwards Online*, vol. 5, *Apocalyptic Writings*, 133–34.

18. Ibid.

19. Jonathan Edwards, "Blank Bible," in *Works of Jonathan Edwards Online*, vol. 24, *The Blank Bible*, 1028.

20. Samuel Collet, *Treatise of the Future Restoration of the Jews to Their Own Land* (London, 1747). On Collet, see Franz Kobler, *Vision Was There: A History of the British Movement for the Restoration of the Jews to Palestine* (London: Lincolns-Prager, 1956), 39.

21. Jonathan Edwards, letter of June 28, 1751, to the Rev. John Erskine, in *Works of Jonathan Edwards Online*, vol. 16, *Letters and Personal Writings*, 376.

22. Gerald R. McDermott, *Jonathan Edwards Confronts the Gods* (New York: Oxford University Press, 2000), 164. Despite his antipathy to Judaism, Edwards retained a lifelong fascination with the Hebrew language. See Shalom Goldman, *God's Sacred Tongue: Hebrew and the American Imagination* (Chapel Hill: University of North Carolina Press, 2004), 80–82.

23. These developments have been explored in classic works including John F. Berens, *Providence and Patriotism in Early America, 1640–1815* (Charlottesville: University of Virginia Press, 1978); Ruth Bloch, *Visionary Republic: Millennial Themes in American Thought, 1756–1800* (New York: Cambridge University Press, 1985); Nathan O. Hatch, *The Sacred Cause of Liberty: Republican Thought and the Millennium in Revolutionary New England* (New Haven, CT: Yale University Press, 1977).

24. Hatch, *The Sacred Cause of Liberty*, 39.

25. Samuel Dunbar, *The Presence of God with His People, Their Only Safety and Happiness* (Boston, 1760), repr. in *Political Sermons of the American Founding Era, 1730–1805*, ed. Ellis Sandoz (Indianapolis: Liberty Fund, 1991), 1:217–18.

26. Gordon Wood, *The Radicalism of the American Revolution* (New York: Vintage, 1991), 13–16. Eric Nelson challenges Wood's interpretation, in *The Royalist Revolution: Monarchy and the American Founding* (Cambridge, MA: Harvard University Press, 2014), 108–9.

27. Charles Chauncy, *Civil Magistrates Must Be Just, Ruling in the Fear of God* (Boston, 1747), repr. in Sandoz, *Political Sermons of the American Founding Era*, 1:141–42.

28. Thomas Paine, *Political Writings*, ed. Bruce Kuklick (New York: Cambridge University Press, 2000), 9–11.

29. Samuel Cooper, *A Sermon Preached Before His Excellency John Hancock, Esq.* (Boston, 1780), repr. in Sandoz, *Political Sermons of the American Founding Era*, 1:634.

30. Shalev, *American Zion*, chap. 2.

31. George Duffield, *A Sermon Preached on a Day of Thanksgiving* (Philadelphia, 1784), repr. in Sandoz, *Political Sermons of the American Founding Era*, 1:779.

32. Ibid., 784.

33. Ezra Stiles, "The United States Elevated to Glory and Honor" (New Haven, CT, 1783), 6.

34. Abiel Holmes, *The Life of Ezra Stiles* (Boston, 1798), 139, 169.

35. Elhanan Winchester, *A Century Sermon on the Glorious Revolution* (London, 1788), repr. in Sandoz, *Political Sermons of the American Founding Era*, 1:999–1000. See also Elhanan Winchester, *A Course of Lectures on the Prophecies That Remain to Be Fulfilled* (London, 1789).

36. Winchester, *A Century Sermon on the Glorious Revolution*, 1:997.

37. Bloch, *Visionary Republic*, 121.

38. Allen C. Guelzo, "Austin, David," *American National Biography Online* (2000).

39. Austin, *The Millennium*. The original citation for Bellamy is Joseph Bellamy, *The Millennium* (Boston, 1758).

40. David Austin, "The Downfall of Mystical Babylon," in *The Millennium*, ed. idem, 347.

41. Ibid., 382–83.

42. Ibid., 392–93.

43. The quotation from Hinsdale is reproduced from David Austin, ed., *The American Preacher, or, a Collection of Sermons from Some of the Most Eminent Preachers Now Living in the United States of Different Denominations of the Christian Church* (New Haven, CT, 1793), 4:128.

44. William Buell Sprague, "Austin, David," *Annals of the American Pulpit* (New York, 1859), 1:195, 202.

45. Due to his outstanding piety, modern Christian conservatives have claimed Boudinot as a kind of forgotten founder. But he attracts little attention beyond those circles. See Rick Santorum, *American Patriots: Answering the Call to Freedom* (Carol Stream, IL: Tyndale, 2012), chap. 11.

46. Boudinot, *The Second Advent*, iii–iv.

47. George Adams Boyd, *Elias Boudinot: Patriot and Statesman, 1740–1821* (Princeton, NJ: Princeton University Press, 1952), 252–53.

48. Elias Boudinot, *The Age of Revelation* (Philadelphia, 1801), 191, 285. See also idem, "Oration Before the Cincinnati," July 4, 1793, repr. in Mayo W. Hazeltine, *Orations from Homer to McKinley* (New York: Collier, 1902), 7:2664–65.

49. Boudinot, *The Age of Revelation*, xxii.

50. Ibid., 191, 131–32.

51. John Locke, *The Works of John Locke* (London, 1824), 7:392.

52. Boudinot, *The Age of Revelation*, 329.

53. Boudinot, *The Second Advent*, 22.

54. Ibid., 21.

55. Ibid., 33.

56. Ibid., 16–17.

57. Ibid., 17.

58. Ibid.

59. Ibid., 530.

60. Boudinot, *A Star in the West*, 297.

61. Jonathan Edwards, Jr., *Observations on the Language of the Muhhekaneew Indians* (New Haven, CT, 1788), 5, 14–15.

62. Boudinot, *A Star in the West*, 74, 123–24, 281–82. Stiles also speculated that the Lost Tribes might have made their way to Siberia. See Holmes, *The Life of Ezra Stiles*, 158–59.

63. Boudinot, *A Star in the West*, 192–93.

64. Ibid., 280.

65. Boudinot, *The Second Advent*, 353.

66. Ibid., 85.

67. Ibid., 298.

68. "Of the Return of the Jews to Their Own Land in the Millennium," *Theological Magazine* 2 (1797): 176, cited in Robert K. Whalen, "'Christians Love the Jews!' The Development of American Philo-Semitism, 1790–1860," *Religion and American Culture* 6, no. 2 (Winter 1996): 249.

69. Harriet Beecher Stowe, *Oldtown Folks* (Boston: Houghton Mifflin, 1911), 306.

70. Sam Haselby emphasizes Yankees' use of religious nationalism to maintain cultural and political influence, in *The Origins of American Religious Nationalism* (New York: Oxford University Press, 2015), 231–32.

71. John McDonald, *Isaiah's Message to the American Nation* (Albany, NY, 1814), 15. Photographically reproduced in *Call to America to Build Zion*, ed. Moshe Davis (New York: Arno Press, 1977). For background on McDonald, see Alan Taylor, *William Cooper's Town: Power and Persuasion on the Frontier of the Early American Republic* (New York: Vintage, 1996), 217–27.

72. McDonald, *Isaiah's Message*, 9.

73. Ethan Smith, *A View of the Hebrews* (Poultney, VT, 1823), 66.

74. Ibid.

75. Ibid., 139.

76. Ibid., 131.

77. Ibid., 148.

78. Fawn M. Brodie, *No Man Knows My History: The Life of Joseph Smith* (New York: Knopf, 1946), 46–47.

79. Richard Bushman, *Joseph Smith: Rough Stone Rolling* (New York: Vintage, 2007), 96–97.

80. III Nephi 20:29–32.

81. III Nephi 21:22–24.

82. *The Doctrine and Covenants* in *English Scriptures* (Salt Lake City: Church of Jesus Christ of Latter-Day Saints, 2013), 84.3–4, https://www.lds.org/scriptures/dc-testament/dc?lang=eng. Cf. ibid., 57.1–3, 101.70.

83. *The Articles of Faith of the Church of Jesus Christ of Latter Day-Saints*, no. 10, https://www .lds.org/scriptures/pgp/a-of-f/1?lang=eng, cited in David S. Katz and Richard Popkin, *Messianic Revolution* (New York: Hill & Wang, 1998), 86.

84. Orson Pratt, *The New Jerusalem; or, the Fulfillment of Modern Prophecy* (Liverpool, UK: 1849), 20.

85. Ibid., 24.

86. Ibid.

87. Duffield, *A Sermon Preached on a Day of Thanksgiving*, 784 (emphasis added).

88. Herman Melville, *Redburn, White-Jacket, Moby-Dick* (New York: Library of America, 1983), 506.

Part II

1. Tim Chapman, *Imperial Russia* (New York: Routledge, 2001), 128–29.

2. The original publication of the memorial appears to be "Pleading for the Jews: The Proposition to Reclaim Palestine for Their Use," *Chicago Daily Tribune*, March 7, 1891, 13. A pamphlet version of the memorial is reprinted as Blackstone, "Palestine for the Jews," in *Christian Protagonists for Jewish Restoration*, ed. Moshe Davis (New York: Arno Press, 1977), 1–14.

3. Blackstone, "Palestine for the Jews," 1.

4. Ibid., 2.

5. William Blackstone, *Jesus Is Coming* (Chicago: Fleming H. Revell, 1908), esp. chap. 15.

6. Blackstone, "Palestine for the Jews," 2.

7. William Blackstone, "May the United States Intercede for the Jews?," in *Christian Protagonists for Jewish Restoration*, ed. Davis, 17.

8. Adam Garfinkle argues that the formulation was popularized in America by the travel lecturer John Lawson Stoddard, who used it in a lecture series delivered in 1897. Given the simi-

larity of his language to the memorial and associated texts, which were widely reported, Stoddard may have been paraphrasing Blackstone. See Adam M. Garfinkle, "On the Origin, Meaning, Use and Abuse of a Phrase," *Middle Eastern Studies* 27, no. 4 (1991): 543–45.

9. William Blackstone to Harrison and Blaine, March 5, 1891, in *Christian Protagonists for Jewish Restoration*, ed. Davis, 13.

10. Benjamin Harrison, "Third Annual Message," December 9, 1891, http://millercenter.org /president/speeches/detail/3767.

11. Ibid.

12. Quoted in Shalom Goldman, "The Holy Land Appropriated: The Careers of Selah Merrill, Nineteenth-Century Hebraist, Palestine Explorer, and U.S. Consul in Jerusalem," *American Jewish History* 85, no. 2 (1997): 151.

13. Ibid.

14. In addition to Goldman's discussion *idem*, see Peter Grose, *Israel in the Mind of America* (New York: Knopf, 1983), 40–41.

15. Quoted in "Pleading for the Jews," *Chicago Daily Tribune*, 13.

16. Marnin Feinstein, *American Zionism, 1884–1904* (New York: Herzl Press, 1965), 99.

17. Blackstone, "Palestine for the Jews," 2.

18. Jonathan Moorhead, "The Father of Zionism: William E. Blackstone?," *Journal of Evangelical Theological Studies* 53, no. 4 (2010): 796.

19. Blackstone to Harrison and Blaine, *Christian Protagonists for Jewish Restoration*, ed. Davis, 14.

20. Timothy P. Weber, *On the Road to Armageddon* (Grand Rapids, MI: Baker Academic, 2004), 106.

21. Brett McCracken, "The Birth of Blackstone Hall," *Biola Magazine* (Winter 2016): 9, http://magazine.biola.edu/static/media/downloads/pdf/Biola_Magazine_Winter_2016_web.pdf.

22. Quoted in Michael B. Oren, *Power, Faith, and Fantasy: America in the Middle East, 1776 to the Present* (New York: W. W. Norton, 2007), 501.

Chapter 3

1. Increase Mather, *A Dissertation Concerning the Future Conversion of the Jewish Nation* (London, 1709), 12.

2. Donald M. Lewis, *The Origins of Christian Zionism: Lord Shaftesbury and Evangelical Support for a Jewish Homeland* (New York: Cambridge University Press, 2010), 42–44.

3. James Bicheno, *The Signs of the Times* (London, 1808), 45–46.

4. John P. Durbin, *Observations in the East, Chiefly in Palestine, Syria, and Asia Minor* (New York, 1845), 1:346.

5. See Mark A. Noll, *America's God: From Jonathan Edwards to Abraham Lincoln* (New York: Oxford University Press, 2002), pt. 3.

6. Daniel Walker Howe, *What Hath God Wrought: The Transformation of America, 1815–1848* (New York: Oxford University Press, 2007), 171.

7. Hannah Adams, *A Dictionary of All Religions* (London, 1824), 191–94.

8. Grose, *Israel in the Mind of America*, 7. The revaluation of the relation between divine redemption and human action was not limited to Christians. Jewish thinkers began to develop an "activist and naturalist messianism" around the same time. See Robert Eisen, *The Peace and Violence of Judaism: From the Bible to Modern Zionism* (New York: Oxford University Press, 2011), 186–87.

9. Lewis, *The Origins of Christian Zionism*, 75–80.

10. Elias Boudinot, "Inaugural Address," in *Constitution of the American Society for Meliorating the Condition of the Jews* (New York, 1820), 16–17.

11. George Stanley Faber, *A General and Connected View of the Prophecies* (London, 1808), 7–8; see also vii, 32–33, 73.

12. Mark A. Noll, *Princeton and the Republic, 1768–1822* (Vancouver: Regent College Publishing, 2004), 253–54; Scott Malcolmson, *One Drop of Blood: The American Misadventure of Race* (New York: Farrar, Straus and Giroux, 2000), 188–89.

13. Eddie S. Glaude, Jr. explores the role of the Exodus story in debates surrounding the ACS, in *Exodus! Religion, Race, and Nation in Early Nineteenth-Century Black America* (Chicago: University of Chicago Press, 2000), 45–53, 113, 124–25.

14. For a vivid account of Frey's milieu, see Paul E. Johnson and Sean Wilentz, *The Kingdom of Matthias: A Story of Sex and Salvation in Nineteenth-Century America* (New York: Oxford University Press, 1994), 33–34.

15. Joseph Samuel C. F. Frey, *Judah and Israel, or, the Restoration and Conversion of the Jews and the Ten Tribes* (New York, 1840), 288 (emphasis added). Unless otherwise noted, all capitalization and emphasis are in the original.

16. Noah defended his conduct in *Travels in England, France, Spain, and the Barbary States* (New York, 1819), appendix.

17. Adam Rovner documents Noah's exposure to these ideas in *In the Shadow of Zion: Promised Lands Before Israel* (New York: New York University Press, 2014), 18–23.

18. Mordecai Noah, *Discourse Delivered at the Consecration of the Synagogue Shearith Israel* (New York, 1818), 19.

19. Ibid., 27.

20. Ibid., 42.

21. Jonathan Sarna, *Jacksonian Jew: The Two Worlds of Mordecai Noah* (New York: Holmes & Meier, 1981), 56–57. Frey disapproved of the change, which he regarded as false advertising. See his *Judah and Israel*, 86–88.

22. Noah, *Discourse Delivered*, 5.

23. Jefferson to Noah, May 28, 1818, in Noah, *Travels*, appendix, 25.

24. Adams to Noah, March 15, 1819, repr. in Moshe Davis, *America and the Holy Land* (Westport, CT: Praeger, 1995), 26; John Adams, *The Diary of John Adams*, Adams Family Papers: An Electronic Archive, Massachusetts Historical Society, https://www.masshist.org/digitaladams/archive/doc?id=D18&hi=1&query=jews&tag=text&archive=diary&rec=1&start=0&numRecs=4.

25. Adams, *The Diary of John Adams*.

26. Sarna, *Jacksonian Jew*, 62–68.

27. Mordecai Manuel Noah, "Ararat Proclamation," in *The Selected Writings of Mordecai Manuel Noah*, ed. Michael Schuldiner and Daniel J. Kleinfeld (Westport, CT: Praeger, 1999), 109.

28. Ibid.

29. Ibid., 112.

30. Ibid.

31. Rovner, *In the Shadow of Zion*, 35.

32. Mordecai Manuel Noah, "Discourse on the Restoration of the Jews," in *The Selected Writings of Mordecai Manuel Noah*, ed. Schuldiner and Kleinfeld, 129.

33. See Shalom Goldman, *God's Sacred Tongue: Hebrew and the American Imagination* (Chapel Hill: University of North Carolina Press, 2004), 204–5.

34. Bush, *The Valley of Vision* (New York, 1844), ii.

35. Ibid.

36. Ibid., iii.

37. Ibid., 37.

38. Ibid., 39–40.

39. Ibid., 39.

40. Noah, "Discourse on the Restoration of the Jews," 128; idem, *Discourse on the Evidence of the American Indians Being the Descendants of the Lost Tribes of Israel* (New York, 1837), 39.

41. Noah, "Discourse on the Restoration of the Jews," 125.

42. Ibid., 135.

43. Ibid., 140–41.

44. Howe, *What Hath God Wrought*, 171.

45. Noah, "Discourse on the Restoration of the Jews," 147.

46. Durbin, *Observations in the East*, 1:330, 318.

47. Ibid.

48. Samuel G. Levine called this a "millenarian" as opposed to a "metaphorical" Zion. See his "Palestine in the Literature of the United States to 1867," in *Early History of Zionism in America*, ed. Isidore S. Meyer (New York: American Jewish Historical Society, 1958), 29, 32–34.

49. Hilton Obenzinger, *American Palestine: Melville, Twain, and the Holy Land Mania* (Princeton, NJ: Princeton University Press, 1999), chap. 4.

50. Lester I. Vogel, *To See a Promised Land: Americans and the Holy Land in the Nineteenth Century* (University Park, PA: Penn State University Press, 1993), 32–39.

51. Levi Parsons, *The Dereliction and Restoration of the Jews: A Sermon Preached in Park-Street Church Boston, Sabbath, Oct. 31, 1819, Just Before the Departure of the Palestine Mission*, photographic repr. in *Holy Land Missions and Missionaries* (New York: Arno Press, 1977).

52. Durbin, *Observations in the East*, 1:341.

53. Ibid.

54. Stephen Higginson Tyng, *Recollections of England* (London, 1847), 101–14.

55. Quoted in James A. Huie, *The History of the Jews: From the Taking of Jerusalem by Titus to the Present Time* (Andover, MA, 1843), 334.

56. Oren, *Power, Faith, and Fantasy*, 133–48.

57. Joseph Fielding Smith, *Essentials in Church History* (Salt Lake City: Deseret News Press, 1922), 284.

58. Steven D. Ricks, "From Joseph to Joseph," in *Covenant and Chosenness in Judaism and Mormonism*, ed. Raphael Jospe, Truman G. Madsen, and Seth Ward (Cranbury, NJ: Associated University Presses, 2001), 99.

59. Frank Fox, "Quaker, Shaker, Rabbi: Warder Cresson, the Story of a Philadelphia Mystic," *Pennsylvania Magazine of History and Biography* (April 1971): 147–94.

60. See Cresson's own account of the trial in *The Key of David* (Philadelphia, 1852).

61. Abraham J. Karp, "The Zionism of Warder Cresson," in *Early History of Zionism in America*, ed. Meyer, 12.

62. Herman Melville, *Clarel: A Poem and Pilgrimage in the Holy Land*, ed. Harrison Hayford et al. (Evanston, IL: Northwestern University Press, 1991), 62.

63. Edward Robinson, *Biblical Researches in Palestine, Mount Sinai, and Arabia Petraea* (Boston, 1856), excerpted in Robert T. Handy, *The Holy Land in American Protestant Life, 1800–1948: A Documentary History* (New York: Arno Press, 1981), 25. See also James T. Barclay, *The City of the Great King* (Philadelphia, 1857), 600–601.

64. Joseph A. Seiss, *The Last Times and the Great Consummation* (Philadelphia, 1863), 200.

65. Melville, *Clarel*, 381.

66. William Cowper Prime, *Tent Life in the Holy Land* (New York, 1857), 105. Prime was later satirized by Mark Twain as the pious guidebook writer Grimes. See Mark Twain, *The Innocents Abroad*, ed. Guy Cardwell (New York: Penguin, 2002), 384, 400, 414.

67. Durbin, *Observations in the East*, 1:346. Note the implied priority of return to conversion in Durbin's remark.

68. Lewis, *The Origins of Christian Zionism*, 144–45.

69. Beshara B. Doumani, "Rediscovering Ottoman Palestine: Writing Palestinians into History," *Journal of Palestine Studies* 21, no. 2 (1992): 8.

70. James H. Moorhead, *World Without End: Mainstream American Protestant Visions of the Last Things, 1880–1925* (Bloomington: Indiana University Press, 1999), 7.

71. Hollis Read, *The Hand of God in History* (Hartford, 1849). See also Robert G. Clouse, "The New Christian Right, America, and the Kingdom of God," in *Modern American Protestantism and Its World*, ed. Martin Marty (Munich: K. G. Saur, 1993), 285–86.

72. Although the focus here is on America, British Christian Zionism also derived strength from postmillennial ideas. Bicheno's eschatology was postmillennial, as were Lord Shaftesbury's beliefs. See Gerald R. McDermott, "A History of Christian Zionism," in *The New Christian Zionism: Fresh Perspectives on Israel & the Land*, ed. idem (Downers Grove, IL: IVP, 2016), 66–67.

73. Hollis Read, *The Coming Crisis of the World* (Columbus, OH, 1861), 48.

74. Martin Spence, *Heaven on Earth* (Eugene, OR: Pickwick, 2015), 56–57.

75. George Duffield, *Dissertation on the Prophecies Relative to the Second Coming of Jesus Christ* (New York, 1842), 259, 264. Duffield acknowledges that Edwards's eschatology was technically postmillennial but numbers him among the antecedents to premillennialism.

76. John Cumming, *The End, or the Proximate Signs of the Close of This Dispensation* (Boston, 1855), 213. See also Dwight Wilson, *Armageddon Now! The Premillenarian Response to Russia and Israel Since 1917* (Grand Rapids, MI: Baker Book House, 1977), 24–26.

77. Seiss, *The Last Times and the Great Consummation*, 4.

78. Isaac Wellcome, *History of the Second Advent Message* (Boston, 1874), 162–71.

79. Clarinda Minor, *Meshullam, or Tidings from Jerusalem* (Philadelphia, 1850). For a more extensive treatment of Minor, see Barbara Kreiger and Shalom Goldman, *Divine Expectations: An American Woman in Nineteenth-Century Palestine* (Athens: Ohio University Press, 1999).

80. The summary that follows is based on George Marsden, *Fundamentalism and American Culture* (New York: Oxford University Press, 2006), 48–55.

81. Richard Kyle, *The Last Days Are Here Again* (Grand Rapids, MI: Baker, 1998), 203; Timothy P. Weber, *Living in the Shadow of Armageddon: American Premillennialism, 1875–1982* (Chicago: University of Chicago Press, 1987), 19–20.

82. Paul Richard Wilkinson, *For Zion's Sake: Christian Zionism and the Role of John Nelson Darby* (Eugene, OR: Wipf & Stock, 2008), 119–23.

83. Paul Boyer discusses Increase Mather's version of the Rapture in *When Time Shall Be No More* (Cambridge, MA: Belknap Press, 1994), 75.

84. Timothy P. Weber, *On the Road to Armageddon: How Evangelicals Became Israel's Best Friend* (Grand Rapids, MI: Baker Academic, 2004), 26.

85. Quoted in R. Smith, *More Desired than Our Owne Salvation*, 159–60.

86. James H. Brookes, *Israel and the Church* (New York: Revell, n.d.), 11.

87. Ibid., 398. Brookes repeats the claim at ibid., 444–45.

88. Blackstone, *Jesus Is Coming*, 3.

89. Yaakov Ariel, *On Behalf of Israel* (New York: Carlson, 1991), 56.

90. Matthew Avery Sutton, *American Apocalypse: A History of Modern Evangelicalism* (Cambridge, MA: Harvard University Press, 2014), 34–35.

91. Blackstone, *Jesus Is Coming*, 235.

92. Quoted in "Pleading for the Jews," *Chicago Daily Tribune*, 13.

93. The proceedings of the meeting appeared as *Jew and Gentile: Being a Report of a Conference of Israelites and Christians* (Chicago: Fleming H. Revell, 1890), 23. Original capitalization.

94. Feinstein, *American Zionism*, 69.

95. Yaakov Ariel, *Evangelizing the Chosen People: Missions to the Jews in America, 1880–2000* (Chapel Hill: University of North Carolina Press, 2000), 13, 28, 34.

96. Avi Ravitsky, *Messianism, Zionism, and Jewish Religious Radicalism* (Chicago: University of Chicago Press, 1996), 26–32.

97. See Ariel, *On Behalf of Israel*, 60.

98. William Blackstone to Harrison and Blaine, March 5, 1891, in *Christian Protagonists for Jewish Restoration*, ed. Davis, 14.

99. David Vital, *The Origins of Zionism* (Oxford: Clarendon Press, 1975), 97–100.

100. Melvin I. Urofsky, *American Zionism from Herzl to the Holocaust* (Lincoln, NE: Bison, 1995), 17.

101. Blackstone, *The Millennium*, 50.

102. Jonathan Moorhead, "The Father of Zionism: William E. Blackstone?," 797–98.

Chapter 4

1. David Fromkin, *A Peace to End All Peace: The Fall of the Ottoman Empire and the Creation of the Modern Middle East* (New York: Holt, 2009), 196. Christopher Sykes, son of the British diplomat who gave his name to the agreement, became something of a Christian Zionist after World War II. See his study of the British military officer and Christian Zionist activist, *Orde Wingate: A Biography* (Cleveland: World Publishing, 1959), and *Crossroads to Israel* (London: Collins, 1965).

2. Yaakov Ariel, "William E. Blackstone and the Petition of 1916," *Studies in Contemporary Jewry* 7 (1991): 75, 84n55.

3. Jonathan Moorhead, "The Father of Zionism: William E. Blackstone?," *Journal of Evangelical Theological Studies* 53, no. 4 (2010): 798.

4. Ariel, "William E. Blackstone and the Petition of 1916," 76. Ariel argues that North's participation did not reflect an official endorsement by the Federal Council of Churches of Christ. For an alternative interpretation, see Timothy P. Weber, *Living in the Shadow of Armageddon: American Premillennialism, 1875–1982* (Chicago: University of Chicago Press, 1987), 140.

5. Stephen S. Wise, *Challenging Years: The Autobiography of Stephen Wise* (New York: Putnam's Sons, 1949), 186–87. For discussions of this incident, see also Paul Charles Merkley, *The Politics of Christian Zionism, 1891–1948* (Portland, OR: Frank Cass, 1998), 88–92; Michael T. Benson, *Harry S. Truman and the Founding of Israel* (Westport, CT: Praeger, 1997).

6. Edgar F. Daugherty, "The Fall of Jerusalem," *Christian Century*, December 20, 1917, 7–8.

7. "Shall We Have the Republic of Judea?," *Christian Century*, January 10, 1918, 9. Cf. Edgar DeWitt Jones, "Palestine, the Jews, and the World War," *Christian Century*, July 12, 1917, 12–13; "The Premillennial Manifesto," *Christian Century*, December 13, 1917, 7–8; Herbert L. Willett, Jr., "The Holy Land in the War," *Christian Century*, December 20, 1917, 14–15.

8. Gary Dorrien, *The Making of American Liberal Theology: Imagining Progressive Religion* (Louisville, KY: Westminster/John Knox, 2001), 1:xxiii.

9. On the *Century*'s role as a forum for mainline Protestantism, see Elesha J. Coffmann, *The Christian Century and the Rise of the Protestant Mainline* (New York: Oxford University Press,

2013), 5–8. The attitude expressed in these early statements does not support Fishman's characterization of the *Century* as consistently hostile toward Zionism. See Herzl Fishman, *American Protestantism and a Jewish State* (Detroit: Wayne State University Press, 1973), 28. On the broader trends in liberal Protestant thought, see Mark Tooley, "Mainline Protestant Zionism and Anti-Zionism," in *The New Christian Zionism*, ed. Gerald R. McDermott (Downers Grove, IL: IVP, 2016).

10. Shirley Jackson Case, *The Revelation of John: A Historical Interpretation* (Chicago: University of Chicago Press, 1919), 403–7.

11. Caitlin Carenen, *The Fervent Embrace* (New York: New York University Press, 2012).

12. James H. Moorhead, *World Without End: Mainstream American Protestant Visions of the Last Things, 1880–1925* (Bloomington: Indiana University Press, 1999), 39–47.

13. Walter Rauschenbusch, *A Theology for the Social Gospel* (New York: Macmillan, 1917), 4.

14. On the liberal clergy's enthusiastic embrace of Wilson's agenda, see Richard M. Gamble, *The War for Righteousness: Progressive Christianity, the Great War, and the Rise of the Messianic Nation* (Wilmington, DE: ISI Books, 2003), chaps. 6–7; Ray H. Abrams, *Preachers Present Arms* (Eugene, OR: Wipf & Stock, 2009).

15. Howard Brick, *Transcending Capitalism: Visions of a New Society in Modern American Social Thought* (Ithaca, NY: Cornell University Press, 2006), 75.

16. A. A. Berle, *The World Significance of a Jewish State* (New York: Mitchell Kennerly, 1918), 5.

17. Ibid., 7.

18. Ibid., 29.

19. Ibid.

20. Dwight Wilson, *Armageddon Now! The Premillenarian Response to Russia and Israel Since 1917* (Grand Rapids, MI: Baker House, 1977), 55.

21. Berle, *The World Significance of a Jewish State*, 15.

22. Ibid., 16.

23. Ibid., 44.

24. "National Home for the Jewish People," H.R. 360, 67th Congress (1922).

25. Stephanie Stidman Rogers, *Inventing the Holy Land: American Protestant Pilgrimage to Palestine* (Lanham, MD: Rowman & Littlefield, 2011), chap. 4.

26. Biographical information is derived from Robert Moats Miller, *Harry Emerson Fosdick: Preacher, Pastor, Prophet* (New York: Oxford University Press, 1985).

27. Quoted in ibid., 182.

28. Fosdick develops this argument at greater length in *Christianity and Progress* (Chicago: Revell, 1922).

29. Harry Emerson Fosdick, *A Pilgrimage to Palestine* (New York: Macmillan, 1927), 286.

30. Ibid., 290–93.

31. Ibid., 281.

32. Ibid., 293.

33. Ibid., 281.

34. "Fosdick Sees Ruin Ahead for Zionism," *New York Times*, May 25, 1926, 8, cited in Gershon Greenberg, *The Holy Land in American Religious Thought, 1620–1948* (Lanham, MD: University Press of America, 1994), 284.

35. Daniel P. Kotzin, *Judah L. Magnes: The American Jewish Nonconformist* (Syracuse, NY: Syracuse University Press, 2010), 85.

36. See Carl Hermann Voss, *Rabbi and Minister: The Friendship of Stephen S. Wise and John Haynes Holmes* (Amherst, NY: Prometheus Books, 1980).

37. John Haynes Holmes, *Palestine To-Day and To-morrow: A Gentile's Survey of Zionism* (New York: Macmillan, 1929), xiv, 259. Miller quotes Holmes' review of *A Pilgrimage to Palestine* in *Harry Emerson Fosdick*, 182.

38. Ibid., 141.

39. Ibid., 142.

40. Ibid., 131.

41. Ibid., 146.

42. Ibid., 255.

43. Ibid., xi.

44. Ibid., 168.

45. Arthur Schlesinger, Jr., "Niebuhr's Shadow," *New York Times*, June 22, 1992, http://www.nytimes.com/1992/06/22/opinion/reinhold-niebuhr-s-long-shadow.html.

46. Published as Abraham Joshua Heschel, "Reinhold Niebuhr: A Last Farewell," *Conservative Judaism* 25 (1971): 62–63.

47. Egal Feldman, "American Protestant Theologians on the Frontiers of Jewish-Christian Relations, 1922–82," in *Anti-Semitism in American History*, ed. David A. Gerber (Urbana: University of Illinois Press, 1986), 364.

48. Shailer Matthews, *Will Christ Come Again?* (Chicago: American Institute of Sacred Literature, 1917), 5–6. See Reuben Torrey's response, *Will Christ Come Again: An Exposure of the Foolishness, Fallacies, and Falsehoods of Shailer Matthews* (Los Angeles: Bible Institute of Los Angeles, 1918), 19.

49. Rauschenbusch, *A Theology for the Social Gospel*, 248.

50. Christopher Hodge Evans, *The Kingdom Is Always but Coming: A Life of Walter Rauschenbusch* (Grand Rapids, MI: William B. Eerdmans, 2004), 94–95, 228.

51. Charles C. Brown, *Niebuhr and His Age: Reinhold Niebuhr's Prophetic Role and Legacy* (Harrisburg, PA: Trinity Press, 2002), 19.

52. Reinhold Niebuhr, *Leaves from the Notebook of a Tamed Cynic* (Louisville, KY: Westminster/John Knox, 1980), 147.

53. Reinhold Niebuhr, "Judah Magnes and the Zionists," *Detroit Times*, December 28, 1929, 16.

54. Ibid.

55. Ibid.

56. Reinhold Niebuhr, *Moral Man and Immoral Society* (New York: Charles Scribner, 1960), xi. The book was originally released in 1932 by the same publisher.

57. See Richard Fox, *Reinhold Niebuhr: A Biography* (New York: Pantheon, 1985), 136.

58. Niebuhr, *Moral Man*, 3.

59. Ibid., 233.

60. Ibid., 61.

61. Ibid., 66.

62. Ibid., 62.

63. Ibid.

64. Deborah Lipstadt, *Beyond Belief: The American Press and the Coming of the Holocaust, 1933–1945* (New York: Free Press, 1986), 44.

65. Carenen, *The Fervent Embrace*, 15.

66. See R. Fox, *Reinhold Niebuhr*, 209.

67. Reinhold Niebuhr, "Germany Must Be Told," *Christian Century*, June 28, 1933, 1014–15.

68. Richard Breitman and Allan J. Lichtman, *FDR and the Jews* (Cambridge, MA: Belknap Press, 2013), chap. 4; J. Bruce Nichols, *The Uneasy Alliance: Religion, Refugee Work, and U.S. Foreign Policy* (New York: Oxford University Press, 1988), 42–43; Egal Feldman, *Dual Destinies: The Jewish Encounter with Protestant American* (Champaign: University of Illinois Press, 1990), 197–98.

69. Reinhold Niebuhr, "My Sense of Shame," *Hadassah Newsletter* 19, no. 3 (December 1938): 60.

70. *Zionism in Prophecy* (New York: Pro-Palestine Federation of America, 1936). The pamphlet is a close paraphrase of Russell's sermon "Zionism in Prophecy," repr. in *Pastor Russell's Sermons* (Brooklyn, NY: International Bible Students Association, 1917). The Jehovah's Witnesses later distanced themselves from arguments that Zionism was a fulfillment of prophecy. See Yona Malachy, *American Fundamentalism and Israel: The Relation of Fundamentalist Churches to Zionism and the State of Israel* (Jerusalem: Institute of Contemporary Jewry, 1978), 59–68.

71. Merkley, *The Politics of Christian Zionism*, 102, 109, 111–12; Fishman, *American Protestantism and a Jewish State*, 66–69.

72. Tooley, "Mainline Protestant Zionism and Anti-Zionism," 201.

73. John Judis, *Genesis: Truman, American Jews, and the Origins of the Arab-Israeli Conflict* (New York: Farrar, Straus and Giroux, 2014), 194.

74. Doreen Bierbrier, "The American Zionist Emergency Council: An Analysis of a Pressure Group," in *American Jewish History: Missions and Politics*, ed. Jeffrey S. Gurock (New York: Routledge, 1998), 8:393.

75. Carenen, *The Fervent Embrace*, 21–22.

76. Niebuhr, "Jews After the War," pt. 2, *Nation* (February 28, 1942): 254.

77. Ibid.

78. Reinhold Niebuhr, "Toward a Program for the Jews," *Contemporary Jewish Record* (June 1942): 242.

79. For a more extensive version of this argument, see Samuel Goldman, "A Glorious Spiritual and Political Achievement: Reinhold Niebuhr on Zionism, Israel, and Realism," in *American Political Thought* 6, no. 2 (2017), 432–454.

80. Lipstadt, *Beyond Belief*, 195–96.

81. Walter Laqueur, *The History of Zionism* (London: I. B. Tauris, 2003), 558; Andrew Preston, *Sword of the Spirit, Shield of the Faith* (New York: Anchor Books, 2012), 336–37.

82. Henry A. Atkinson, "'The Jewish Problem' Is a Christian Problem," *Christianity and Crisis*, June 28, 1943, 3.

83. Carl Hermann Voss and David A. Rausch, "American Christians and Israel," *American Jewish Archives* 40, no. 2 (1988), 42–43; Carenen, *The Fervent Embrace*, 25.

84. Michael B. Oren, *Power, Faith, Fantasy* (New York: W. W. Norton, 2007), 444.

85. For Christian Zionist responses to the Biltmore program, see *Truth About Palestine* (New York: Christian Council on Palestine, 1946), 23.

86. Merkley, *The Politics of Christian Zionism*, 142.

87. "Conflict over Palestine," *Federal Council of Churches Information Service* 33, no. 32 (October 7, 1944): 1–8.

88. "Resolutions Adopted by National Conference on Palestine," in *The Voice of Christian America* (Washington, DC: American Palestine Committee, 1944), 44–45.

89. Norman Littell, "The Christian Heritage," in *The Voice of Christian America*, 6.

90. Niebuhr, "Jews After the War," pt. 2, 255.

91. Niebuhr, "Toward a Program for the Jews," 241.

92. Niebuhr, "Jews After the War," pt. 2, 255.

93. Niebuhr, "The Partition of Palestine," *Christianity and Society* 13, no. 1 (1948): 4.

94. Niebuhr, "My Sense of Shame," 59–60.

95. Daniel Poling, "Our Good Faith at Stake," in *The Voice of Christian America*, 32–34.

96. Reinhold Niebuhr, "Statement to the Anglo-American Committee of Inquiry," *Jewish Frontier* 13 (February 1946): 40.

97. Ibid., 42.

98. Rafael Medoff, "A Further Note on the 'Unconventional Zionism' of Reinhold Niebuhr," *Studies in Zionism* 12, no. 1 (1991): 85.

99. Judis, *Genesis*, 214.

100. *Truth About Palestine*, 5.

101. "Will Recommend the Admission of 100,000 Jews to Palestine," *Christian Century*, May 8, 1946, 580.

102. The anti-Zionist Committee for Peace and Justice in the Holy Land was not established until February 1948, after the UN vote for partition.

103. Carl Hermann Voss, *A Christian Looks at the Jewish Problem* (New York: American Christian Palestine Committee, 1946). Cf. William L. Burton, "Protestant America and the Rebirth of Israel," in *American Jewish History: Missions and Politics*, ed. Jeffrey S. Gurock (New York: Routledge, 1998), 8:209.

104. See "Statement by the President Following the Adjournment of the Palestine Conference in London," American Presidency Project, University of California, Santa Barbara, http://www.presidency.ucsb.edu/ws/?pid=12520.

105. "Democratic Party Platform of 1944," American Presidency Project, University of California, Santa Barbara, http://www.presidency.ucsb.edu/ws/?pid=29598. The Republican Party included similar language in its 1944 platform, superintended by Wagner's ally on matters related to Zionism, Senator Robert Taft. On their efforts, see Robert A. Taft, "Address at Testimonial Dinner for Dr. Abba Hillel Silver," in *The Papers of Robert A. Taft*, ed. Clarence E. Wunderlin (Kent, OH: Kent State University Press), 3:32–37.

106. David McCullough, *Truman* (New York: Touchstone, 1992), 599.

107. Quoted in Judis, *Genesis*, 192–93.

108. Ronald Radosh and Allis Radosh, *A Safe Haven: Harry S. Truman and the Founding of Israel* (New York: Harper Perennial, 2010), 47–48; Paul Charles Merkley, *American Presidents, Religion, and Israel* (Westport, CT: Praeger, 2004), 4–5. See also Clark Clifford, *Counsel to the President* (New York: Random House, 1991), chap. 1.

109. Judis, *Genesis*, 271–72.

110. Quoted in Oren, *Power, Faith, and Fantasy*, 501.

111. Merkley, *American Presidents, Religion, and Israel*, chap. 1.

112. Quoted in Preston, *Sword of the Spirit*, 437.

113. Harry Truman, "Address in Columbus at a Conference of the Federal Council of Churches," March 6, 1946, Truman Library, http://www.trumanlibrary.org/publicpapers/index.php?pid=14 94.

114. See Mark Silk, "Notes on the Judeo-Christian Tradition in America," *American Quarterly* 36, no. 1 (1984): 66.

Part III

1. Lexie Verdon, "2-Minute Raid: Planning, Technology, and Subterfuge Aided in Pinpoint Bombing Mission," *Washington Post*, June 10, 1981.

2. "Israel's Illusion," *New York Times*, June 9, 1981.

3. Michael J. Berlin, "U.N. Council Condemns Israeli Raid," *Washington Post*, June 20, 1981.

4. Jerry Falwell, *Listen, America! The Conservative Blueprint for America's Moral Rebirth* (New York: Bantam, 1980), 98.

5. Martin Schram, "Jerry Falwell Vows Amity with Israel," *Washington Post*, September 12, 1981.

6. Ibid.

7. See Franklin Littell, "Israel and the Jewish-Christian Dialogue," in *The Religious Dimension of Israel: The Challenge of the Six-Day War*, ed. David Polish et al. (New York: Synagogue Council of America, 1968), and *The Crucifixion of the Jews* (New York: Harper & Row, 1975), chap. 5; Robert Drinan, *Honor the Promise* (New York: Doubleday, 1977), 220. See also Raymond A. Schroth, *Bob Drinan: The Controversial Life of the First Catholic Priest Elected to Congress* (New York: Fordham University Press, 2010), 273–78.

8. Political conservatives were relatively late converts to Zionism. The 1964 Republican platform written by supporters of Barry Goldwater was the first since 1940 *not* to include an expression of support for the Zionism or the State of Israel. The growth of the conservative movement after Goldwater did not lead to enthusiasm for Israel. In 1976, Ronald Reagan, who was challenging Gerald Ford for the GOP nomination, proposed that the platform include a statement encouraging Israelis and Palestinians to compromise. See "Reagan Urges GOP Platform to Declare Need for Compromises to Settle Mideast Conflict," Jewish Telegraphic Agency, August 12, 1976.

9. Jerry Falwell, *An Autobiography* (Lynchburg, VA: Liberty House, 1996), 387, 401.

Chapter 5

1. Bosley Crowther, "Film Cameras over the Holy Land," *New York Times*, May 15, 1960.

2. Roger Angell, "3:45 Flat," *New Yorker*, December 17, 1960, 136.

3. *Exodus* (United Artists, 1960).

4. Fremont shares a name with Western explorer and U.S. Army general John C. Fremont. It is not clear whether the similarity was intentional—Leon Uris's original novel makes no reference to the connection. Nevertheless, it might have resonated with film audiences: Fremont and his sidekick Kit Carson were staple figures in the Hollywood Western mythology.

5. "Statement of the President re: Recognition of Israel, May 14, 1948," correspondence file, 1916–50, Harry S. Truman Library, http://www.trumanlibrary.org/exhibit_documents/index.php?tldate=1948-05-14&groupid=3429&pagenumber=1&collectionid=ROIexhibit.

6. Eytan Gilboa, *American Public Opinion Toward Israel and the Arab-Israeli Conflict* (Lexington, MA: Lexington Books, 1987), 23 (tables 1–4), 26 (tables 1–5).

7. See Eric R. Crouse, *American Christian Support for Israel: Standing with the Chosen People, 1948–1975* (Lanham, MD: Lexington Books, 2015), 33.

8. Carl Voss, *Questions and Answers on Palestine* (New York: ACPC, 1947), 24.

9. Ibid.

10. Thomas Clark Pollock, "After Twenty-Five Years," in *A Christian Report on Israel* (New York: ACPC, 1949), 1. See also Caitlin Carenen, *The Fervent Embrace* (New York: New York University Press, 2012), 75–76.

11. Reuben K. Youngdahl, "A Reed That Cannot Be Broken," in *A Christian Report on Israel*, 28.

12. *Christian Opinion on Jewish Nationalism and a Jewish State* (Philadelphia: American Council for Judaism, 1945). See also Thomas A. Kolsky, *Jews Against Zionism: The American Council for Judaism, 1942–1948* (Philadelphia: Temple University Press, 1990), 107; but cf. Jack Ross, *Rabbi*

Outcast: Elmer Berger and American Jewish Anti-Zionism (Washington, DC: Potomac Books, 2011), chap. 5.

13. *Christian Opinion on Jewish Nationalism and a Jewish State*, 10–11, 22–23.

14. Gloria M. Wysner, "Dilemma in Palestine," *Bulletin of the Committee on Work Among Moslems* (November 1944): 7.

15. Bayard Dodge, "Peace or War in Palestine," *Christianity and Crisis*, March 15, 1948, 27.

16. Bayard Dodge, "Must There Be War in the Middle East?," *Reader's Digest* (April 1947): 41.

17. Ibid., 43. Cf. "Rabbi Magnes Supports a Federated Palestine," *Christian Century*, September 8, 1948, 900–901.

18. Hugh Wilford, *America's Great Game: The CIA's Secret Arabists and the Shaping of the Modern Middle East* (New York: Basic Books, 2013), 87–90. Robert Moats Miller asserts that the committee and its successor, the American Friends of the Middle East, received funding from the CIA and the oil industry. See Miller, *Harry Emerson Fosdick: Pastor, Preacher, Prophet* (New York: Oxford University Press, 1985), 192.

19. Martin Marty, *Modern American Religion: Under God, Indivisible 1941–1960* (Chicago: University of Chicago Press, 1996), 188–89.

20. Henry Sloane Coffin, "Politics and Missions," *Christianity and Crisis*, August 4, 1947, 5–6. See also Daniel Bliss, "Justice and Peace in the Holy Land," *Christian Century*, September 8, 1948, 909.

21. Henry Sloane Coffin, "Perils to America in the New Jewish State," *Christianity and Crisis*, February 21, 1949, 9.

22. Ibid., 10.

23. Voss, *Questions and Answers on Palestine*, 3.

24. Mark Hulsether, *Building a Protestant Left: Christianity and Crisis Magazine, 1941–1993* (Knoxville: University of Tennessee Press, 1999), 85.

25. See G. Daniel Cohen, "Elusive Neutrality: Christian Humanitarianism and the Question of Palestine, 1948–1967," *Humanity* 5, no. 2 (2014): 183–210.

26. "What's to Become of Arab Refugees?," *Christian Century*, February 2, 1949, 131; S. A. Morrison, "Israel and the Middle East," *Christianity and Crisis*, July 11, 1949, 96.

27. Karl Baehr, "The Arabs and Israel," *Christianity and Crisis*, October 3, 1949, 124.

28. See Theodore Huebner and Carl Hermann Voss, *This Is Israel: Palestine: Yesterday, Today, and Tomorrow* (New York: Philosophical Library, 1956), 154; Herman F. Reissig, "Another Look at the Arab-Israeli Problem," *Christianity and Crisis*, April 16, 1956, 46; James G. McDonald, "Toward Middle East Peace," *New York Times*, March 4, 1956, E10.

29. A. Roy Eckardt, *Christianity and the Children of Israel* (New York: King's Crown, 1948), 170.

30. Carl Hermann Voss, *The Palestine Problem Today: Israel and Its Neighbors* (Boston: Beacon Press, 1953), xiv.

31. "President-Elect Says Soviet Demoted Zhukov Because of Their Friendship," *New York Times*, December 23, 1952, 1, 16. For a discussion of the textual variants, reception, and frequent misquotation of Eisenhower's remark, see Patrick Henry, "'And I Don't Care What It Is': The Tradition-History of a Civil Religion Proof Text," *Journal of the American Academy of Religion* 49 (1981): 35–49. See also Kevin M. Kruse, *One Nation Under God: How Corporate America Invented Christian America* (New York: Basic Books, 2015), 69–72.

32. Will Herberg, *Protestant, Catholic, Jew: An Essay in American Religious Sociology* (Chicago: University of Chicago Press, 1983), 84.

33. See Raymond Haberski, Jr., *God and War: American Civil Religion Since 1945* (New Brunswick, NJ: Rutgers University Press, 2012), 36.

34. Paul Tillich, "Is There a Judeo-Christian Tradition?," *Judaism* 1, no. 2 (1952): 106.

35. Avihu Zakai finds precedents for Tillich's conception of history in Jonathan Edwards, in *Jonathan Edwards's Philosophy of History: The Reenchantment of the World in the Age of Enlightenment* (Princeton, NJ: Princeton University Press, 2003), 13–14. He does not consider the association of *kairos*—the moment of divine intervention in history—with the geopolitical restoration of Israel. See also ibid., 180–81.

36. Will Herberg, *Judaism and Modern Man: An Interpretation of Jewish Religion* (New York: Farrar, Straus and Young, 1951), 276.

37. Andrew Preston, *Sword of the Spirit, Shield of the Faith* (New York: Anchor Books, 2012), 455; John D. Wilsey, *American Exceptionalism and Civil Religion* (Downers Grove, IL: IVP, 2015), 131–38; William Inboden, *Religion and American Foreign Policy, 1945–1960* (New York: Cambridge University Press, 2008), 234–37.

38. See Michelle Mart, *Eye on Israel: How Americans Came to View the Jewish State as an Ally* (Albany: State University of New York Press, 2006), 107–8.

39. Robert S. Ellwood, *1950: Crossroads of American Religious Life* (Louisville, KY: Westminster/John Knox, 2000), 214. See also Wilford, *America's Great Game*, 177–81.

40. See Douglas Little, *American Orientalism: The United States and the Middle East Since 1945* (Chapel Hill: University of North Carolina Press, 2004), 88–90.

41. "Statement of Policy by the National Security Council," NSC 155/1, S/P–NSC files, lot 61 D 167, Near East (NSC 155), https://history.state.gov/historicaldocuments/frus1952-54v09p1/d145.

42. Reinhold Niebuhr, "Seven Great Errors of U.S. Foreign Policy," *New Leader*, December 24–31, 1956, 3–4.

43. Ibid.

44. Inboden, *Religion and American Foreign Policy*, 255.

45. Reinhold Niebuhr, "Our Stake in the State of Israel," *New Republic*, February 3, 1957, 11.

46. Ibid., 12.

47. Reinhold Niebuhr, *The Self and the Dramas of History* (New York: Charles Scribner's Sons, 1955), 78; see also idem, *Pious and Secular America* (New York: Charles Scribner's Sons, 1958), 108–10.

48. Reinhold Niebuhr and Alan Heimert, *A Nation So Conceived: Reflections on the History of America from Its Early Visions to Its Present Power* (London: Faber & Faber, 1963), 123.

49. Reinhold Niebuhr, *The Irony of American History* (Chicago: University of Chicago Press, 2008), 24.

50. Niebuhr and Heimert, *A Nation So Conceived*, 147–48.

51. Niebuhr, *Pious and Secular America*, 109.

52. Ibid., 111–12.

53. Niebuhr, *The Irony of American History*, 128. See also Jason W. Stevens, *God-Fearing and Free* (Cambridge, MA: Harvard University Press, 2010), 62.

54. Daniel Walker Howe, *What Hath God Wrought?: The Transformation of America, 1815–1848* (New York: Oxford University Press, 2007), 319–20.

55. Esther Yolles Feldblum, *The American Catholic Press and the Jewish State* (New York: Ktav, 1977), 17, 31.

56. Quoted in Pinchas Lapide, *Three Popes and the Jews* (New York: Hawthorn, 1967), 25, 282.

57. Feldblum, *The American Catholic Press and the Jewish State*, 72.

58. Doreen Bierbrier, "The American Zionist Emergency Council: An Analysis of a Pressure Group," in *American Zionism: Missions and Politics*, ed. Jeffrey Gurock (New York: Routledge, 1998), 8:403.

59. Jacques Maritain, "On Anti-Semitism," *Commonweal*, September 25, 1942, 534–37.

60. Edward H. Flannery, "Theological Aspects of the State of Israel," *Bridge* 3 (1958): 303n6.

61. Ibid., 312.

62. Ibid., 324.

63. Edward H. Flannery, *The Anguish of the Jews: Twenty-Three Centuries of Anti-Semitism* (New York: Macmillan, 1965).

64. "Declaration on the Relation of the Church to Non-Christian Religions," *Nostra Aetate*, http://www.vatican.va/archive/hist_councils/ii_vatican_council/documents/vat-ii_decl _19651028_nostra-aetate_en.html.

65. John M. Oesterreicher, *The Rediscovery of Judaism: A Re-Examination of the Conciliar Statement on the Jews* (South Orange, NJ: Institute for Judaeo-Christian Studies, 1971).

66. "Guidelines for Catholic-Jewish Relations" (U.S. National Conference of Catholic Bishops, 1967), http://www.usccb.org/beliefs-and-teachings/ecumenical-and-interreligious/jewish /upload/Guidelines-for-Catholic-Jewish-Dialogue-1967.pdf. See also John T. Pawlikowksi, *Cathechetics and Prejudice: How Catholic Teaching Materials View Jews, Protestants, and Racial Minorities* (New York: Paulist Press, 1973), 133.

67. Feldblum, *The American Catholic Press and the Jewish State*, 96.

68. Michelle Mart, "The 'Christianization' of Israel and Jews in 1950s America," *Religion and American Culture* 14, no. 1 (2004): 122–27.

69. Scholem Asch, *One Destiny: An Epistle to the Christians* (New York: G. P. Putnam's Sons, 1945), 87–88.

70. *The Ten Commandments* (Paramount Pictures, 1956).

71. Michael Wood, *America in the Movies* (New York: Columbia University Press, 1989), 187.

72. Hilton Obenzinger, "Holy Lands, Restoration, and Zionism in *Ben-Hur*," in *Bigger than Ben-Hur: The Book, Its Adaptations, and Their Audiences*, ed. Barbara Ryan and Millette Shamir (Syracuse, NY: Syracuse University Press, 2016), 81.

73. Louise Mayo, *Ambivalent Image: Nineteenth-Century America's Perception of the Jew* (Rutherford, NJ: Fairleigh Dickinson University Press, 1988), 27.

74. Michael Blankfort, *The Juggler* (New York: Dell, 1953).

75. Quoted in Yaacov Bar-Simon, "The United States and Israel Since 1948: A 'Special Relationship'?," *Diplomatic History* 22, no. 2 (Spring 1998): 231. For the original context, see Mordecai Gazit, "Israeli Military Procurement from the United States," in *Dynamics of Dependence: U.S. Israeli Relations*, ed. Gabriel Sheffer (Boulder, CO: Westview Press, 1987), 98.

76. See Warren Bass, *Support Any Friend: Kennedy's Middle East and the Making of the U.S.-Israel Alliance* (New York: Oxford University Press, 2004).

77. "Commitment to Israel," *America*, June 3, 1967, 802.

78. Irving Spiegel, "8 Church Leaders Ask Aid to Israel," *New York Times*, May 28, 1967; "The Moral Responsibility in the Middle East," display ad, *New York Times*, June 4, 1967. King later claimed that he had not read the statement and had reservations about Israel's policies. Nevertheless, he expressed general support for Israel and consistently rejected claims that Zionism was a form of racism. On these issues, see Martin Kramer, *The War on Error: Israel, Islam, and the Middle East* (New Brunswick, NJ: Transaction, 2016), 254–77. King offered a somewhat more extensive statement of his views in an interview with Abraham Heschel, published as "Conversation with Martin Luther King," *Conservative Judaism* 22, no. 3 (1968): 12.

79. Barbara Tuchman, "U.S. Role in the Mideast," *New York Times*, May 30, 1967.

80. Barbara Tuchman, *Bible and Sword: England and Palestine from the Bronze Age to Balfour* (New York: New York University Press, 1956). See, esp., chap. 7.

81. Lyndon Johnson, remarks at the 125th anniversary meeting of B'nai B'rith, September 10, 1968, American Presidency Project, http://www.presidency.ucsb.edu/ws/?pid=29109.

82. Judith H. Banki, *Christian Reactions to the Middle East Crisis* (New York: American Jewish Committee, 1968), 2.

83. Henry P. Van Dusen, "'Silence' of Church Leaders on Mideast," *New York Times*, July 7, 1967. Van Dusen's letter responds to Irving Spiegel, "Rabbis Score Christians for Silence on Mideast," *New York Times*, June 23, 1967, and "Rabbinical Leaders Criticize Christians," *New York Times*, June 27, 1967. On Van Dusen's role in this debate, see Jonathan Rynhold, *The Arab-Israeli Conflict in American Political Culture* (New York: Cambridge University Press, 2015), 122–24.

84. A. Roy Eckardt and Alice Eckardt, "Again, Silence in the Churches," pt. 2, "Christian and Arab Ideology," *Christian Century*, August 8, 1967, 992.

85. Marc H. Tanenbaum, "Israel's Hour of Need and Jewish-Christian Dialogue," *Conservative Judaism* 22, no. 2 (1968): 4.

86. "'Conscience Statement' on Middle East Issued," *Los Angeles Times*, July 26, 1967, B6.

87. Tanenbaum, "Israel's Hour of Need and Jewish-Christian Dialogue," 2, 7.

88. Balfour Brickner, "No Ease for Us in Zion," *Christianity and Crisis*, September 18, 1967, 200. Brickner's father was a rabbi and Zionist activist in Cleveland. See Wolfgang Saxon, "Balfour Brickner, Activist Reform Rabbi, Dies at 78," *New York Times*, September 1, 2005, https://query.nytimes.com/gst/fullpage.html?res=9801E1DB1731F932A3575AC0A9639C8B63.

89. Krister Stendahl, "Judaism and Christianity II: After a Colloquium and a War," *Harvard Divinity Bulletin* (Fall 1967): 7.

90. See "Israel Annexes Old Jerusalem," *Christian Century*, July 12, 1967, 884–85.

91. John C. Bennett, "A Response to Rabbi Brickner," *Christianity and Crisis*, September 18, 1967, 204.

92. Willard G. Oxtoby, "What Is the Christian Stake in a Jewish Dream?," *Presbyterian Life*, July 1, 1967, 26. Cf. David Noel Freedman, "Another View of the Middle East Crisis," *Presbyterian Life*, September 15, 1967, 28–29.

93. "Jerusalem Should Remain Unified," *New York Times*, July 12, 1967, 12.

94. Dan McKanan, *Prophetic Encounters: Religion and the American Radical Tradition* (Boston: Beacon Press, 2011), 218; Jill K. Gill, *Embattled Ecumenism: The National Council of Churches, the Vietnam War, and the Protestant Left* (DeKalb: Northern Illinois University Press, 2011), 180; Mark Silk, *Spiritual Politics: Religion and America Since World War II* (New York: Simon & Schuster, 1988), 148–50.

95. David Little, "Basis for U.S. Commitments in Asia," *New York Times*, June 25, 1967.

96. "Israel and the Christian Dilemma," *Christian Century*, July 12, 1967, 883.

97. Ibid.

98. A. Roy Eckardt and Alice Eckardt, *Encounter with Israel: A Challenge to Conscience* (New York: Association Press, 1970).

99. Robert Drinan, "The State of Israel: Theological Implications for Christians," *Conservative Judaism* (1968): 28–35, and *Honor the Promise*.

100. Paul Charles Merkley, *Christian Attitudes Toward the State of Israel* (Montreal: McGill-Queens University Press, 2007), 180. See Littell, "Israel and the Jewish-Christian Dialogue," and *The Crucifixion of the Jews*, chap. 5.

101. Hulsether, *Building a Protestant Left*, 137–39. Niebuhr's family has continued to defend his support for Zionism against criticism from the Christian Left. For a recent example, see Gustav Niebuhr and Elisabeth Sifton, *Huffington Post*, May 7, 2014, http://www.huffingtonpost.com/gustav-niebuhr/why-reinhold-niebuhr-supp_b_5280958.html.

102. William R. MacKaye, "Middle East War Issue Fractures Bond Linking Liberal Protestants," *Washington Post*, May 6, 1972.

103. Judith A. Klinghoffer, *Vietnam, Jews, and the Middle East* (New York: St. Martin's Press, 1999), 171.

Chapter 6

1. See Mark A. Noll, *The Scandal of the Evangelical Mind* (Grand Rapids, MI: Eerdmans, 1994), 122–37.

2. George M. Marsden, *Fundamentalism in American Culture* (New York: Oxford University Press, 2006), 46–51. The proceedings of the prophecy conferences are reprinted in Donald W. Dayton, ed., *The Prophecy Conference Movement: Fundamentalism in American Religion*, 6 vols. (New York: Garland, 1988).

3. Arno Gaebelein, "Prophecy Fulfilled: A Potent Argument for the Bible," in *The Fundamentals: A Testimony to the Truth*, ed. R. A. Torrey (Chicago: Testimony, 1915), vol. 11. On Gaebelein, see David A. Rausch, "Arno C. Gaebelein," *American Jewish History* 68 (September 1978): 43–55.

4. Timothy P. Weber, *On the Road to Armageddon* (Grand Rapids, MI: Baker Academic, 2004), 39–40.

5. *The Scofield Reference Bible* (New York: Oxford University Press, 1909), 25.

6. Ibid., 256, 442, 719, 723, 930, 974.

7. Ibid., 1337. Emphasis added.

8. Marsden, *Fundamentalism in American Culture*, 143–51.

9. Quoted in Victoria Clark, *Allies for Armageddon: The Rise of Christian Zionism* (New Haven, CT: Yale University Press, 2007), 127. See also Dwight Wilson, *Armageddon Now!: The Premillenarian Response to Russia and Israel Since 1917* (Grand Rapids, MI: Baker House, 1977), 44–47.

10. Harry Ironside, *Looking Backward over a Third of a Century of Prophetic Fulfillment* (New York: Loizeaux Bros., 1930), 28–30.

11. Harry Rimmer, *The Shadow of Coming Events* (Grand Rapids, MI: Wm. Eerdmans, 1946), 63–64. Harold Ockenga expressed similar sentiments. For a discussion of Ockenga's views, see Matthew Avery Sutton, *American Apocalypse: A History of Modern Evangelicalism* (Cambridge, MA: Harvard University Press, 2014), 220.

12. Joel A. Carpenter, *Revive Us Again: The Reawakening of American Fundamentalism* (New York: Oxford University Press, 1997), 39.

13. Sutton, *American Apocalypse*, 57.

14. Rimmer, *The Shadow of Coming Events*, 38. On Rimmer, see Ronald L. Numbers, *The Creationists* (Berkeley: University of California Press 1993), 60–71.

15. Harry Rimmer, *The Coming War and the Rise of Russia* (Grand Rapids, MI: Wm. Eerdmans, 1943), 79–80.

16. "A Gentle Fundamentalist," *Time*, December 11, 1964, 98.

17. A. Roy Eckardt, *Christianity and the Children of Israel* (New York: King's Crown, 1948), 77–79.

18. Sutton, *American Apocalypse*, 182.

19. M. R. DeHaan, *Palestine in History and Prophecy* (Grand Rapids, MI: Radio Bible Class, n.d.), 35.

20. M. R. DeHaan, *Who Owns Palestine?* (Grand Rapids, MI: Radio Bible Class, n.d.), 29.

21. Quoted in Darren Dochuk, *From Bible Belt to Sun Belt: Plain-Folk Religion, Grassroots Politics, and the Rise of Evangelical Conservatism* (New York: W. W. Norton, 2011), 126.

22. John Hagee, *Final Dawn over Jerusalem* (Nashville: Thomas Nelson, 1998), 9.

23. Ibid.

24. Ibid.

25. David Brog, *Standing with Israel: Why Christians Support the Jewish State* (Lake Mary, FL: FrontLine, 2006), 236.

26. John Hagee, *In Defense of Israel* (Lake Mary, FL: FrontLine, 2007), 14–15.

27. Brog, *Standing with Israel*, 236.

28. Harold Ockenga quoted in George Marsden, *Reforming Fundamentalism: Fuller Seminary and the New Evangelicalism* (Grand Rapids, MI: Wm. B. Eerdmans, 1987), 146.

29. Grant Wacker, *America's Pastor: Billy Graham and the Shaping of a Nation* (Cambridge, MA: Belknap, 2014), 192–94.

30. Wilbur M. Smith, *World Crises and the Prophetic Scriptures* (Chicago: Moody Press, 1951), 181, 183. See also Marsden, *Reforming Fundamentalism*, 173.

31. W. Smith, *World Crises and the Prophetic Scriptures*, 183.

32. Wilbur M. Smith, "Israel in Her Promised Land," *Christianity Today* 1 (December 24, 1956): 11.

33. Oswald T. Allis, "Israel's Transgression in Palestine," *Christianity Today* 1 (December 24, 1956): 9.

34. Oswald T. Allis, *Prophecy and the Church* (London: James Clark, 1945), 219.

35. Yaakov Ariel, *Evangelizing the Chosen People: Missions to the Jews in America, 1880–2000* (Chapel Hill: University of North Carolina Press), 146–49.

36. Hillary Kaell, *Walking Where Jesus Walked: American Christians and Holy Land Pilgrimage* (New York: New York University Press, 2015), 40. See also Eric R. Crouse, *American Christian Support for Israel: Standing with the Chosen People, 1948–1975* (Lanham, MD: Lexington Books, 2015), 93.

37. Billy Graham, "Men Must Be Changed Before a Nation Can," reprinted in *American Principles and Issues*, ed. Oscar Handlin (New York: Holt, Rinehart & Winston, 1961), 76.

38. Billy Graham, *Just as I Am* (New York: HarperCollins, 1997), 353–55; David Aikman, *Billy Graham: His Life and Influence* (Nashville: Thomas Nelson, 2007), 105.

39. Graham, "Men Must Be Changed Before a Nation Can," 76.

40. Ibid.

41. Shalom Goldman, "Johnny Cash: Father of Christian Zionism," *Tablet*, September 11, 2014, http://www.tabletmag.com/jewish-arts-and-culture/music/183966/johnny-cash-in-the-holy-land.

42. Leo Ribuffo, "Confessions of an Accidental (or Perhaps Overdetermined) Historian," in *Reconstructing History: The Emergence of a New Historical Society*, ed. Elizabeth Fox-Genovese and Elisabeth Lasch-Quinn (New York: Routledge, 1999), 151. See also Andrew Preston, *Sword of the Spirit, Shield of the Faith* (New York: Anchor Books, 2012), 471–72.

43. W. Cleon Skousen, *Prophecy and Modern Times* (Salt Lake City: Deseret News Press, 1948), 71–105.

44. W. Cleon Skousen, *The Naked Communist* (Salt Lake City: Ensign, 1960), 70–71.

45. Sean Wilentz, "Confounding Fathers," *New Yorker*, October 18, 2010, http://www.newyorker.com/magazine/2010/10/18/confounding-fathers. Skousen's influence may be among the reasons that the John Birch Society contributed $300,000 to the United Jewish Appeal in 1967. See Judith A. Klinghoffer, *Vietnam, Jews, and the Middle East: Unintended Consequences* (New York: St. Martin's Press, 1999), 171.

46. Paul Boyer, *When Time Shall Be No More* (Cambridge, MA: Belknap Press, 1994), chap. 4.

47. Charles L. Feinberg, *Israel in the Spotlight* (Wheaton, IL: Scripture Press, 1956); William L. Hull, *Israel: Key to Prophecy* (Grand Rapids, MI: Zondervan, 1957); J. Dwight Pentecost, *Things to Come: A Study in Biblical Eschatology* (Findlay, OH: Dunham, 1958); Charles L. Feinberg, ed., *Focus on Prophecy* (Westwood, NJ: Revell, 1964).

48. J. A. Seiss, *The Apocalypse* (Grand Rapids, MI: Zondervan, 1962).

49. John F. Walvoord, *Israel in Prophecy* (Grand Rapids, MI: Zondervan, 1962), 26.

50. Daniel G. Hummel, "A 'Practical Outlet' to Premillennial Faith: G. Douglas Young and the Evolution of Christian Zionist Activism in Israel," *Religion and American Culture* 25, no. 1 (2015): 37–81.

51. G. Douglas Young, *The Wife and the Bride* (Minneapolis: Free Church Publications, 1959), 86–91.

52. G. Douglas Young, "Toward Arab-Israel Coexistence," *Christian Century*, December 12, 1962, 1508.

53. "Shofar, Ancient Horn, Signals Triumph," *New York Times*, June 8, 1967.

54. Michael Oren, *Six Days of War: June 1967 and the Making of the Modern Middle East* (New York: Random House, 2002), 249.

55. W. Cleon Skousen, *Fantastic Victory: Israel's Rendezvous with Destiny* (Salt Lake City: Bookcraft, 1967).

56. "War Sweeps the Bible Lands," *Christianity Today* 12 (June 23, 1967): 20.

57. Ibid., 21.

58. James L. Kelso, untitled, *Christianity Today* 12 (July 21, 1967): 35.

59. "Billy Graham Voices Staunch Support for Israel, Concern for State's Security," Jewish Telegraphic Agency, December 26, 1967, http://www.jta.org/1967/12/26/archive/billy-graham-voices-staunch-support-for-israel-concern-for-states-security.

60. Wilbur M. Smith, *Israeli-Arab Conflict and the Bible* (Glendale, CA: G/L Publications, 1967), 98–99. Smith is quoting himself from *World Crises*, 235.

61. Arnold Olson, *Inside Jerusalem: City of Destiny* (Glendale, CA: G/L Publications, 1968), 166–67.

62. Crawford Gribben, *Writing the Rapture: Prophecy Fiction in Evangelical America* (New York: Oxford University Press, 2009), 89; Stephen Sizer, *Christian Zionism: Road-Map to Armageddon* (Leicester, UK: IVP, 2004), 155.

63. The proceedings were published in Carl F. H. Henry, ed., *Prophecy in the Making* (Carol Stream, IL: Creation House, 1971), 12–13.

64. Hummel, "A 'Practical Outlet' to Premillennial Faith," 57–66.

65. Carl F. H. Henry, "Jesus Christ and the Last Days," in *Prophecy in the Making*, ed. idem, 181.

66. *His Land: A Musical Journey into the Soul of a Nation* (World Wide Pictures, 1970).

67. Wacker, *America's Pastor*, 194.

68. Judith H. Banki, *Christian Reactions to the Middle East Crisis* (New York: American Jewish Committee, 1968), 18.

69. Melani McAlister, *Epic Encounters: Culture, Media, and U.S. Interests in the Middle East, 1945–2000* (Berkeley: University of California Press, 2001), 165.

70. Hal Lindsey, *The Late Great Planet Earth* (Grand Rapids, MI: Zondervan, 1970), 43–44.

71. Walvoord, *Israel in Prophecy*, 71.

72. Lindsey, *The Late Great Planet Earth*, 50.

73. McAlister, *Epic Encounters*, 166.

74. Lindsey, *The Late Great Planet Earth*, 180–86.

75. Ibid., 84–85n5.

76. Ibid., 54.

77. Salem Kirban, *666* (Wheaton, IL: Tyndale House, 1970); Thomas S. McCall and Zola Levitt, *Satan in the Sanctuary* (Chicago: Moody Press, 1973). See also Arthur E. Bloomfield, *Before the Last Battle* (Minneapolis: Bethany Fellowship, 1971).

78. Thomas S. McCall, "How Soon the Tribulation Temple?," *Bibliotheca Sacra* 121, no. 512 (1971): 342–43.

79. Dan. 9:27, 11:31, 12:11. See also Matt. 24:15–16 and Rev. 11:1–2.

80. Leo Ribuffo, *The Old Christian Right: The Protestant Far Right from the Great Depression to the Cold War* (Philadelphia: Temple University Press, 1983), 96–97.

81. Robert C. Fuller, *Naming the Antichrist: The History of an American Obsession* (New York: Oxford University Press, 1995), 143–45.

82. Arthur Bloomfield, *How to Recognize the Antichrist* (Minneapolis: Bethany Fellowship, 1975), 125.

83. Oral Roberts, *The Drama of the End Time* (Tulsa: self-published, 1963), 93. Cf. Lindsey, *The Late Great Planet Earth*, 153.

84. Kirban, *666*, 201.

85. A 1978 symposium on Israel, for example, balanced contributions from Young with an essay by the missionary and Israel critic Elisabeth Elliott. See G. Douglas Young, "Israel: The Unbroken Line," and Elliott, "The Furnace of the Lord," both in *Christianity Today* 23 (October 6, 1978). Elliott's essay was based on her book *Furnace of the Lord: Reflections on the Redemption of the Holy City* (New York: Doubleday, 1969).

86. Wilbur M. Smith, "Signs of the Second Advent of Christ," in *Prophecy in the Making*, ed. Henry, 198–99.

87. Harold John Ockenga, "Fulfilled and Unfulfilled Prophecy," in *Prophecy in the Making*, ed. Henry, 304.

88. Boyer, *When Time Shall Be No More*, 226.

89. James H. Brookes, *Maranatha: or the Lord Cometh* (Chicago: Fleming H. Revell, 1889), 388.

90. William L. Hull, *The Fall and Rise of Israel* (Grand Rapids, MI: Zondervan, 1954), 385. Hull describes his encounters with Eichmann in *The Struggle for a Soul* (New York: Doubleday, 1963).

91. John F. Walvoord, *The Nations in Prophecy* (Grand Rapids, MI: Zondervan, 1967), 174.

92. Ibid., 175.

93. Rimmer, *The Coming War and the Rise of Russia*, 79–80.

94. Ockenga, "Fulfilled and Unfulfilled Prophecy," 308.

95. Walvoord, *The Nations in Prophecy*, 175.

96. Steven P. Miller, *Billy Graham and the Rise of the Republican South* (Philadelphia: University of Pennsylvania Press, 2009), 146.

97. John F. Walvoord and John E. Walvoord, *Armageddon, Oil, and the Middle East Crisis* (Grand Rapids, MI: Zondervan, 1974), 35.

98. See Wilson, *Armageddon Now!*, 24–28.

99. *Scofield Reference Bible*, 881–82.

100. Thomas S. McCall and Zola Levitt, *The Coming Russian Invasion of Israel* (Chicago: Moody Press, 1974), 14.

101. Jack Van Impe, *Israel's Final Holocaust* (Nashville: Thomas Nelson, 1979), 55.

102. David Allen Lewis, *Magog 1982: Canceled* (Harrison, AR: New Leaf, 1982), 138. On the NCLCI, see Paul Charles Merkley, *Christian Attitudes Toward the State of Israel* (Montreal: McGill-Queen's University Press, 2001), 180–81.

103. On the earliest uses of the term, see Nahum Sokolow, *History of Zionism, 1600–1918* (London: Longman, 1919), 198; Shalom Goldman, *Zeal for Zion: Jews, Christians, and the Idea of the Promised Land* (Chapel Hill: University of North Carolina Press, 2009), 90.

104. Stephen Spector, *Evangelicals and Israel* (New York: Oxford University Press, 2009), 2.

105. David K. Shipler, "1,000 Christian 'Zionists' in Jerusalem," *New York Times*, September 25, 1980, cited in Spector, *Evangelicals and Israel*, 2.

106. Falwell, *Listen, America!*, 215–23.

107. The term "new Christian Right" assumes that conservative Christian movements have been a recurring feature of American politics, at least since the early twentieth century. In specific connection with Israel, see Michael Lienesch, *Redeeming America: Piety and Politics in the New Christian Right* (Chapel Hill: University of North Carolina Press, 1993), 229.

108. Falwell, *Listen, America!*, 98, and Jerry Falwell, ed., *The Fundamentalist Phenomenon* (New York: Doubleday, 1981), 215–16.

109. Jerry Falwell, *Armageddon and the Coming War with Russia* (undated pamphlet), 31–33. See also Robert Scheer, "The Prophet of Worldly Methods," *Los Angeles Times*, March 4, 1981.

110. Quoted in Warren L. Vinz, *Pulpit Politics: Faces of Protestant Nationalism in the Twentieth Century* (Albany: State University of New York Press, 1997), 170.

111. E.g., Grace Halsell, *Prophecy and Politics: The Secret Alliance Between Israel and the U.S. Christian Right* (Chicago: Lawrence Hill, 1986), 40–50.

112. Ed Dobson and Ed Hindson, "Apocalypse Now?," *Policy Review* 38 (Fall 1986): 21.

113. Tim LaHaye, *The Coming Peace in the Middle East* (Grand Rapids, MI: Zondervan, 1984), 167.

114. Mike Evans, *Israel: America's Key to Survival* (Plainfield, NJ: Logos, 1981), xv.

115. John S. Feinberg, "Why Christians Should Support Israel," *Fundamentalist Journal* 1 (September 1982): 17.

116. Cal Thomas, "Looking for the Reason of Lebanon," *Fundamentalist Journal* 2 (January 1983): 61. Cf. Lewis, *Magog 1982*, 44–53, 99.

117. Thomas S. Kidd, *American Christians and Muslims: Evangelical Culture from the Colonial Period to the Age of Terrorism* (Princeton, NJ: Princeton University Press, 2009), 135–36.

118. Hal Lindsey, *The 1980's: Countdown to Armageddon* (New York: Bantam, 1981), 86.

119. Ibid.,158.

120. Quoted in Vinz, *Pulpit Politics*, 172. Strictly speaking, Falwell's suggestions applied only to the period before the Rapture. After the disappearance of the church, God's blessing of America as a Christian nation would cease.

121. M. Evans, *Israel*, 14–15, 108–18. See also Mike Evans, *Jerusalem Betrayed* (Dallas: Word, 1997), 42–46. Despite sensationalistic reports that Reagan embraced some version of Armageddon theology, eschatology left no discernible trace on his policies, except as a nightmare to avoid. See

H. W. Brands, *Reagan: The Life* (New York: Anchor, 2015), 362, 679; Steven F. Hayward, *The Age of Reagan: The Conservative Counterrevolution, 1980–1989* (New York: Random House, 2009), 331.

122. Halsell, *Prophecy and Politics*, 58. Reports of these and similar tours have remained staples of the literature on Christian Zionism. For a more recent account, see Clark, *Allies for Armageddon*.

123. Spector, *Evangelicals and Israel*, 142–44.

124. Michael Sean Winter, *God's Right Hand: How Jerry Falwell Made God a Republican and Baptized the American Right* (New York: HarperCollins, 2012), 101.

125. Shalom Goldman, *Christians, Jews, and the Idea of the Promised Land* (Chapel Hill: University of North Carolina Press, 2009), 303.

126. Kevin M. Kruse, *One Nation Under God: How Corporate America Invented Christian America* (New York: Basic Books, 2015), 77–78.

127. A. James Rudin, "Prospectus for the Future," in *Evangelicals and Jews in Conversation*, ed. Marc H. Tanenbaum, Marvin R. Wilson, and A. James Rudin (Grand Rapids, MI: Baker House, 1978), 312.

128. Falwell, *Listen, America!*, 98.

129. LaHaye, *The Coming Peace in the Middle East*, 170. See also John Hagee, *Should Christians Support Israel* (San Antonio: Dominion, 1987), 76.

130. Merrill Simon, *Jerry Falwell and the Jews* (Middle Village, NY: Jonathan David, 1984), 44. Not all Christian Zionists are so restrained. Yaakov Ariel has documented the intensity and duration of conservative Christians' interest in missions to Jews. See his *Evangelizing the Chosen People*, 275–83.

131. Brog, *Standing with Israel*, 195–96. See also Motti Inbari, *Messianic Religious Zionism Confronts Israeli Territorial Compromise* (New York: Cambridge University Press, 2012), 182–83; Spector, *Evangelicals and Israel*, 149–50.

132. Richard M. Gamble, *In Search of the City on a Hill* (New York: Continuum, 2012), 154.

Conclusion

1. "Zion's Christian Soldiers," *60 Minutes*, October 3, 2006, http://www.cbsnews.com/news /zions-christian-soldiers.

2. Ibid.

3. Ibid.

4. Kevin Phillips, *American Theocracy* (New York: Penguin, 2006), 252–61.

5. See Stephen Spector, *Evangelicals and Israel* (New York: Oxford University Press, 2009), chap. 11.

6. Walter Russell Mead, "The New Israel and the Old," *Foreign Affairs* 87, no. 4 (July–August 2008): 28–46.

7. Jean Edward Smith, *Bush* (New York: Simon & Schuster, 2016), 339.

8. William Inboden, "It's Impossible to Count the Things Wrong with the Negligent, Spurious New Biography of George W. Bush," *Foreign Policy* (August 15, 2016), http://foreignpolicy.com /2016/08/15/its-impossible-to-count-the-things-wrong-with-the-negligent-spurious-distorted -new-biography-of-george-w-bush.

9. Ross Douthat, *Bad Religion*, (New York: Free Press, 2012), 254.

10. Walter Russell Mead, "God's Country?," *Foreign Affairs* 85, no. 5 (September–October 2006): 43.

11. *Religious Landscape Study* (Washington, DC: Pew Research Center, 2014), http://www .pewforum.org/religious-landscape-study.

12. Robert P. Jones, *The End of White Christian America* (New York: Simon & Schuster, 2016), 206.

13. Robert Nicholson, "Evangelicals and Israel: What American Jews Don't Want to Know (but Need To)," *Mosaic* (October 6, 2013), http://mosaicmagazine.com/essay/2013/10/evangelicals -and-israel.

14. David Brog, "The End of Evangelical Support for Israel: The Jewish State's International Standing," *Middle East Quarterly* 21, no. 4 (Spring 2014), http://www.meforum.org/3769/israel -evangelical-support#_ftnref5.

15. On this development, see Joseph Williams, "The Pentecostalization of Christian Zionism," *Church History* 84, no. 1 (2015): 159–94.

16. Simon Romero, "Temple in Brazil Appeals to a Surge in Evangelicals," *New York Times*, July 24, 2014, http://www.nytimes.com/2014/07/25/world/americas/temple-in-brazil-appeals-to-a -surge-in-evangelicals.html?partner=rss&emc=rss&smid=tw-nytimesworld&_r=1. See also "Is Christian Zionism Flowering in Brazil," *American Interest* (July 26, 2014), http://www.the-american -interest.com/2014/07/26/is-christian-zionism-flowering-in-brazil.

Bibliography

Abbot, Abiel. *Traits of Resemblance in the People of the United States to Ancient Israel*. Haverhill, MA, 1799.

Abrams, Ray H. *Preachers Present Arms*. Eugene, OR: Wipf & Stock, 2009.

Adams, Hannah. *A Dictionary of All Religions*. London, 1824.

Adams, John. *The Diary of John Adams*. Adams Family Papers: An Electronic Archive, Massachusetts Historical Society, https://www.masshist.org/digitaladams/archive/doc?id=D18&hi=1&query=jews&tag=text&archive=diary&rec=1&start=0&numRecs=4.

Ahlstrom, Sydney. *A Religious History of the American People*. New Haven, CT: Yale University Press, 1972.

Aikman, David. *Billy Graham: His Life and Influence*. Nashville: Thomas Nelson, 2007.

Allen, John. *An Oration upon the Beauties of Liberty*. Reprinted in Sandoz, *Political Sermons of the American Founding Era, 1730–1788*, 301–26. Originally published Boston, 1773.

Allis, Oswald T. "Israel's Transgression in Palestine." *Christianity Today*, December 24, 1956.

———. *Prophecy and the Church*. London: James Clark, 1945.

American Interest. "Is Christian Zionism Flowering in Brazil?" July 26, 2014, http://www.the-american-interest.com/2014/07/26/is-christian-zionism-flowering-in-brazil.

American National Biography Online. "Austin, David," by Allen C. Guelzo. Published February 2000, http://www.anb.org/articles/08/08-00064.html.

Angell, Roger. "3:45 Flat." *New Yorker*, December 17, 1960.

Ariel, Yaakov. *Evangelizing the Chosen People: Missions to the Jews in America, 1880–2000*. Chapel Hill: University of North Carolina Press, 2000.

———. "It's All in the Bible: Evangelical Christians, Biblical Literalism, and Philosemitism in Our Times." In *Philosemitism in History*, edited by Jonathan Karp and Adam Sutcliffe, 257–88. Cambridge: Cambridge University Press, 2012.

———. *On Behalf of Israel*. New York: Carlson, 1991.

———. *An Unusual Relationship: Evangelical Christians and Jews*. New York: New York University Press, 2013.

———. "William E. Blackstone and the Petition of 1916." *Studies in Contemporary Jewry* 7 (1991): 68–85.

Asch, Scholem. *One Destiny: An Epistle to the Christians*. New York: G. P. Putnam's Sons, 1945.

Atkinson, Henry A. "'The Jewish Problem' Is a Christian Problem." *Christianity and Crisis*, June 28, 1943.

Audi, Robert, and Nicholas Wolterstorff. *Religion in the Public Square*. Lanham, MD: Rowman & Littlefield, 2007.

Augustine. *City of God*. Translated by Henry Bettenson. New York: Penguin, 1984.

Austin, David, ed. *The American Preacher, or, a Collection of Sermons from Some of the Most Eminent Preachers Now Living in the United States of Different Denominations of the Christian Church*. Vol. 4. New Haven, CT, 1793.

———. *The Millennium*. Elizabethtown, NJ, 1794.

Baehr, Karl. "The Arabs and Israel." *Christianity and Crisis*, October 3, 1949.

Banki, Judith H. *Christian Reactions to the Middle East Crisis*. New York: American Jewish Committee, 1968.

Barclay, James T. *The City of the Great King*. Philadelphia, 1857.

Barnett, Michael. *The Star and the Stripes: A History of the Foreign Policies of American Jews*. Princeton, NJ: Princeton University Press, 2016.

Bar-Simon, Yaacov. "The United States and Israel Since 1948: A 'Special Relationship'?" *Diplomatic History* 22, no. 2 (Spring 1998): 231–62.

Bar-Yosef, Eitan. "Christian Zionism and Victorian Culture." *Israel Studies* 8, no. 2 (Summer 2003): 18–44.

Bass, Warren. *Support Any Friend: Kennedy's Middle East and the Making of the U.S.-Israel Alliance*. New York: Oxford University Press, 2004.

Beinart, Peter. "The End of American Exceptionalism." *Atlantic*, February 3, 2014, http://www .theatlantic.com/politics/archive/2014/02/the-end-of-american-exceptionalism/283540.

Bellah, Robert. *The Broken Covenant: American Civil Religion in Time of Trial*. Chicago: University of Chicago Press, 1992.

Bellamy, Joseph. *The Millennium*. Boston, 1758.

Benne, Robert. "Reinhold Niebuhr's Christian Zionism." In *The New Christian Zionism: Fresh Perspectives on Israel & the Land*, edited by Gerald R. McDermott, 221–48. Downers Grove, IL: IVP, 2016.

Bennett, John C. "A Response to Rabbi Brickner." *Christianity and Crisis*, September 18, 1967.

Benson, Michael T. *Harry S. Truman and the Founding of Israel*. Westport, CT: Praeger, 1997.

Bercovitch, Sacvan. *American Jeremiad*. Madison: University of Wisconsin Press, 1978.

———. *The Rites of Assent*. New York: Routledge, 1993.

Berens, John F. *Providence and Patriotism in Early America, 1640–1815*. Charlottesville: University of Virginia Press, 1978.

Berle, A. A. *The World Significance of a Jewish State*. New York: Mitchell Kennerly, 1918.

Berlin, Michael J. "U.N. Council Condemns Israeli Raid." *Washington Post*, June 20, 1981.

Bernstein, Richard. "Evangelicals Strengthening Bonds with Jews." *New York Times*, February 6, 1983.

Bicheno, James. *The Signs of the Times*. London, 1808.

Bickersteth, Edward. *The Restoration of the Jews to Their Own Land*. London, 1841.

Bierbrier, Doreen. "The American Zionist Emergency Council: An Analysis of a Pressure Group." In *American Zionism: Missions and Politics*, vol. 8, edited by Jeffrey Gurock, 391–414. New York: Routledge, 1998.

Bishops' Committee for Ecumenical and Interreligious Affairs. "Guidelines for Catholic-Jewish Relations." U.S. National Conference of Catholic Bishops. March 1967, http://www.usccb.org /beliefs-and-teachings/ecumenical-and-interreligious/jewish/upload/Guidelines-for -Catholic-Jewish-Dialogue-1967.pdf.

Blackstone, William Eugene. *Jesus Is Coming*. Chicago: Revell, 1908.

———. *The Millennium.* New York: Fleming H. Revell, 1904.

———. "May the United States Intercede for the Jews?" In *Christian Protagonists for Jewish Restoration,* edited by Moshe Davis, 15–19. New York: Arno Press, 1977.

Blankfort, Michael. *The Juggler.* New York: Dell, 1953.

Bliss, Daniel. "Justice and Peace in the Holy Land." *Christian Century,* September 8, 1948.

Bloch, Ruth. *Visionary Republic: Millennial Themes in American Thought, 1756–1800.* New York: Cambridge University Press, 1985.

Bloomfield, Arthur E. *Before the Last Battle.* Minneapolis: Bethany Fellowship, 1971.

———. *How to Recognize the Antichrist.* Minneapolis: Bethany Fellowship, 1975.

Boudinot, Elias. *The Age of Revelation.* Philadelphia, 1801.

———. "Inaugural Address." *Constitution of the American Society for Meliorating the Condition of the Jews.* New York, 1820.

———. "Oration Before the Cincinnati." Reprinted in Mayo W. Hazeltine, *Orations from Homer to McKinley,* vol. 7. New York: Collier, 1902. Originally published July 4, 1793.

———. *The Second Advent.* Trenton, NJ, 1815.

———. *A Star in the West.* Trenton, NJ, 1816.

Boyd, George Adams. *Elias Boudinot: Patriot and Statesman, 1740–1821.* Princeton, NJ: Princeton University Press, 1952.

Boyer, Paul. *When Time Shall Be No More.* Cambridge, MA: Belknap Press, 1994.

Bozeman, Theodore Dwight. *To Live Ancient Lives: The Primitivist Dimension in Puritanism.* Chapel Hill: University of North Carolina Press, 1988.

Brands, H. W. *Reagan: The Life.* New York: Anchor, 2015.

Breitman, Richard, and Allan J. Lichtman. *FDR and the Jews.* Cambridge, MA: Belknap Press, 2013.

Brick, Howard. *Transcending Capitalism: Visions of a New Society in Modern American Social Thought.* Ithaca, NY: Cornell University Press, 2006.

Brickner, Balfour. "No Ease for Us in Zion." *Christianity and Crisis,* September 18, 1967.

Brightman, Thomas. *Revelation of the Revelation.* London, 1611.

Brodie, Fawn M. *No Man Knows My History: The Life of Joseph Smith.* New York: Knopf, 1946.

Brog, David. "The End of Evangelical Support for Israel: The Jewish State's International Standing." *Middle East Quarterly* 21, no. 4 (Spring 2014), http://www.meforum.org/3769/israel -evangelical-support#_ftnref5.

———. *Standing with Israel.* Lake Mary, FL: FrontLine, 2006.

Brookes, James H. *Israel and the Church.* New York: Revell, undated.

———. *Maranatha: or the Lord Cometh.* Chicago: Fleming H. Revell, 1889.

Brown, Charles C. *Niebuhr and His Age: Reinhold Niebuhr's Prophetic Role and Legacy.* Harrisburg, PA: Trinity Press, 2002.

Bulkeley, Peter. *The Gospel Covenant.* London, 1651.

Burge, Gary M. *Whose Land? Whose Promise? What Christians Are Not Being Told About Israel.* Cleveland: Pilgrim Press, 2013.

Burton, William L. "Protestant America and the Rebirth of Israel." In *American Jewish History: Missions and Politics,* vol. 8, edited by Jeffrey S. Gurock, 295–306. New York: Routledge, 1998.

Bush, George. *The Valley of Vision.* New York, 1844.

Bushman, Richard. *Joseph Smith: Rough Stone Rolling.* New York: Vintage, 2007.

Calhoun, Charles William. *Benjamin Harrison.* New York: Henry Holt, 2005.

Calvin, John. *Commentaries on the Epistles of Paul the Apostle.* Translated by John Owen. Grand Rapids, MI: Eerdmans, 1947.

————. *Institutes of the Christian Religion*. Vol. 2. Edited by John T. McNeill. Philadelphia: Westminster Press, 1960.

Cantor, David. *The Religious Right: The Assault on Tolerance & Pluralism in America*. New York: Anti-Defamation League, 1994.

Capp, B. S. "Extreme Millenarianism." In *Puritans, the Millennium, and the Future of Israel: Puritan Eschatology 1600 to 1660*, edited by Peter Toon, 66–90. Cambridge: James Clarke, 1970.

————. *The Fifth Monarchy Men: A Study in Seventeenth-Century English Millenarianism*. Totowa, NJ: Rowman & Littlefield, 1972.

Carenen, Caitlin. *The Fervent Embrace*. New York: New York University Press, 2012.

Carpenter, Joel A. *Revive Us Again: The Reawakening of American Fundamentalism*. New York: Oxford University Press, 1997.

Case, Shirley Jackson. *The Revelation of John: A Historical Interpretation*. Chicago: University of Chicago Press, 1919.

Ceaser, James. "The Origins and Character of American Exceptionalism." *American Political Thought* 1, no. 1 (Spring 2012): 3–28.

Chafets, Zev. *A Match Made in Heaven*. New York: HarperCollins, 2007.

————. "The Rabbi Who Loved Evangelicals (and Vice Versa)." *New York Times Magazine*, July 2005, http://www.nytimes.com/2005/07/24/magazine/the-rabbi-who-loved-evangelicals -and-vice-versa.html.

Chapman, Tim. *Imperial Russia*. New York: Routledge, 2001.

Chauncy, Charles. *Civil Magistrates Must Be Just, Ruling in the Fear of God*. Reprinted in Sandoz, *Political Sermons of the American Founding Era, 1730–1788*, 137–78. Originally published Boston, 1747.

Cherry, Conrad, ed. *God's New Israel: Religious Interpretations of American Destiny*. Chapel Hill: University of North Carolina Press, 1998.

Chicago Daily Tribune. "Pleading for the Jews: The Proposition to Reclaim Palestine for Their Use." March 7, 1891.

Christian Century. "Israel Annexes Old Jerusalem." July 12, 1967.

————. "Israel and the Christian Dilemma." July 12, 1967.

————. "The Premillennial Manifesto." December 13, 1917.

————. "Rabbi Magnes Supports a Federated Palestine." September 8, 1948.

————. "Shall We Have the Republic of Judea?" January 10, 1918.

————. "What's to Become of Arab Refugees?" February 2, 1949.

————. "Will Recommend the Admission of 100,000 Jews to Palestine." May 8, 1946.

Christian Opinion on Jewish Nationalism and a Jewish State. Philadelphia: American Council for Judaism, 1945.

A Christian Report on Israel. New York: American Christian Palestine Committee, 1949.

Christianity Today. "War Sweeps the Bible Lands." June 23, 1967.

Clark, Victoria. *Allies for Armageddon: The Rise of Christian Zionism*. New Haven, CT: Yale University Press, 2007.

Clifford, Clark. *Counsel to the President*. New York: Random House, 1991.

Clouse, Robert G. "The New Christian Right, America, and the Kingdom of God." In *Modern American Protestantism and Its World*, edited by Martin Marty, 281–94. Munich: K. G. Saur, 1993.

————. "The Rebirth of Millenarianism." In *Puritan Eschatology: Puritans, the Millennium, and the Future of Israel*, edited by Peter Toon, 42–65. Cambridge: James Clarke, 1970.

Coffin, Henry Sloane. "Perils to America in the New Jewish State." *Christianity and Crisis*, February 21, 1949.

———. "Politics and Missions." *Christianity and Crisis*, August 4, 1947.

Coffmann, Elesha J. *The Christian Century and the Rise of the Protestant Mainline*. New York: Oxford University Press, 2013.

Cohen, G. Daniel. "Elusive Neutrality: Christian Humanitarianism and the Question of Palestine, 1948–1967." *Humanity* 5, no. 2 (2014): 183–210.

Cohen, Jeremy. "The Mystery of Israel's Salvation: Romans 11:25–26 in Patristic and Medieval Literature." *Harvard Theological Review* 98, no. 3 (2005): 247–81.

Cohen, Naomi W., ed. *Essential Papers on Jewish-Christian Relations in the United States: Imagery and Reality*. New York: New York University Press, 1991.

Cohn, Norman. *The Pursuit of the Millennium*. New York: Oxford University Press, 1970.

Collet, Samuel. *Treatise of the Future Restoration of the Jews to Their Own Land*. London, 1747.

"Commitment to Israel." *America*, June 3, 1967.

Conflict over Palestine. Federal Council of Churches Information Service, October 7, 1944.

Cooper, Samuel. *A Sermon Preached Before His Excellency John Hancock, Esq.* Reprinted in Sandoz, *Political Sermons of the American Founding Era, 1730–1788*, 627–56. Originally published Boston, 1780.

Cotton, John. *A Brief Exposition of the Whole Book of Canticles*. London, 1642.

———. *A Discourse About Government in a New Plantation Whose Design Is Religion*. Cambridge, 1663.

———. "Gods Promise to His Plantation." London, 1630.

———. *Moses His Judicialls and Abstract of the Laws of New England*. Edited by Worthington Chauncy Ford. Cambridge, MA: John Wilson, 1902.

———. *The Powring Out of the Seven Vials; or an Exposition of the 16. Chapter of Revelation with an Application of It to Our Times*. London, 1642.

Cox, Daniel, Juhem Navarro-Rivera, and Robert P. Jones. "Most Are Proud to Be American." July 27, 2013. Public Religion Research Institute, http://www.prri.org/research/july-2013-prri-rns.

Cresson, Warder. *The Key of David*. Philadelphia, 1852.

Crome, Andrew. *The Restoration of the Jews: Early Modern Hermeneutics, Eschatology, and National Identity in the Works of Thomas Brightman*. New York: Springer, 2014.

Crouse, Eric R. *American Christian Support for Israel: Standing with the Chosen People, 1948–1975*. Lanham, MD: Lexington Books, 2015.

Crowther, Bosley. "Film Cameras over the Holy Land." *New York Times*, May 15, 1960.

Crum, Bartley. *Behind the Silken Curtain: A Personal Account of Anglo-American Diplomacy in Palestine and the Middle East*. New York: Simon & Schuster, 1947.

Cumming, John. *The End, or the Proximate Signs of the Close of This Dispensation*. Boston, 1855.

Daugherty, Edgar F. "The Fall of Jerusalem." *Christian Century*, December 20, 1917.

Davenport, John. "An Epistle to the Reader." In Mather, *The Mystery of Israel's Salvation*, unpaginated.

Davidson, J. W. *The Logic of Millennial Thought: Eighteenth Century New England*. New Haven, CT: Yale University Press, 1977.

Davis, Moshe. *America and the Holy Land*. Westport, CT: Praeger, 1995.

———, ed. *Christian Protagonists for Jewish Restoration*. New York: Arno Press, 1977.

Dayton, Donald W., ed. *The Prophecy Conference Movement: Fundamentalism in American Religion*. 6 vols. New York: Garland, 1988.

DeHaan, M. R. *Palestine in History and Prophecy*. Grand Rapids, MI: Radio Bible Class, n.d.

———. *Who Owns Palestine?*. Grand Rapids, MI: Radio Bible Class, n.d.

"Democratic Party Platform of 1944." American Presidency Project, University of California, Santa Barbara, http://www.presidency.ucsb.edu/ws/?pid=29598.

de Tocqueville, Alexis. *Democracy in America*. Translated by Arthur Goldhammer. New York: Library of America, 2004.

Dictionary of National Biography. Vol. 45. Edited by Sidney Lee. New York: Macmillan, 1896.

Dobson, Ed, and Ed Hindson. "Apocalypse Now?" *Policy Review* 38 (Fall 1986): 16–23.

Dochuk, Darren. *From Bible Belt to Sun Belt: Plain-Folk Religion, Grassroots Politics, and the Rise of Evangelical Conservatism*. New York: W. W. Norton, 2011.

The Doctrine and Covenants in *English Scriptures*. Salt Lake City: Church of Jesus Christ of Latter-Day Saints, 2013, https://www.lds.org/scriptures/dc-testament/dc?lang=eng.

Dodge, Bayard. "Must There Be War in the Middle East?" *Reader's Digest*, April 1947.

———. "Peace or War in Palestine." *Christianity and Crisis*, March 15, 1948.

Dorrien, Gary. *The Making of American Liberal Theology: Imagining Progressive Religion*. Vol. 1. Louisville, KY: Westminster/John Knox, 2001.

Doumani, Beshara B. "Rediscovering Ottoman Palestine: Writing Palestinians into History." *Journal of Palestine Studies* 21, no. 2 (1992): 5–28.

Douthat, Ross. *Bad Religion*. New York: Free Press, 2012.

Draxe, Thomas. *The Worldes Resurrection or the General Calling of the Iewes*. London, 1608.

Drinan, Robert F. *Honor the Promise: America's Commitment to Israel*. New York: Doubleday, 1977.

———. "The State of Israel: Theological Implications for Christians." *Conservative Judaism* 22, no. 3 (1968): 28–35.

Duffield, George. *Dissertation on the Prophecies Relative to the Second Coming of Jesus Christ*. New York, 1842.

———. *A Sermon Preached on a Day of Thanksgiving*. Reprinted in Sandoz, *Political Sermons of the American Founding Era, 1730–1788*, 771–88. Originally published Philadelphia, 1784.

Dunbar, Samuel. *The Presence of God with His People, Their Only Safety and Happiness*. Reprinted in Sandoz, *Political Sermons of the American Founding Era, 1730–1788*, 207–30. Originally published Boston, 1760.

Durbin, John P. *Observations in the East, Chiefly in Palestine, Syria, and Asia Minor*. Vol. 1. New York, 1845.

Dwight, Timothy. *The Conquest of Canäan*. Hartford, 1785.

———. *A Discourse of Some Events of the Last Century*. New Haven, CT, 1801.

Eckardt, A. Roy. *Christianity and the Children of Israel*. New York: King's Crown, 1948.

———. "Israeli 'Aggression.'" *New York Times*, July 13, 1967.

Eckardt, A. Roy, and Alice Eckardt. "Again, Silence in the Churches." *Christian Century*, August 8, 1967.

———. *Encounter with Israel: A Challenge to Conscience*. New York: Association Press, 1970.

Edwards, Jonathan. "Blank Bible." In *Works of Jonathan Edwards Online*, vol. 24, *The Blank Bible*, edited by Stephen J. Stein. Jonathan Edwards Center, Yale University.

———. "An Humble Attempt to Promote the Agreement and Union of God's People Throughout the World." In *Works of Jonathan Edwards Online*, vol. 5, *Apocalyptic Writings*, edited by Stephen J. Stein. Jonathan Edwards Center, Yale University.

———. Letter of June 28, 1751, to the Rev. John Erskine. In *Letters and Personal Writings* in *Online Works of Jonathan Edwards*, vol. 16, *Letters and Personal Writings*, edited by George S. Claghorn. Jonathan Edwards Center, Yale University.

———. "Notes on the Apocalypse." In *Works of Jonathan Edwards Online*, vol. 5, *Apocalyptic Writings*, edited by Stephen J. Stein. Jonathan Edwards Center, Yale University.

———. "Some Thoughts Concerning the Present Revival of Religion in New England." In *Works of Jonathan Edwards Online*, vol. 4, *The Great Awakening*, edited by C. C. Goen, 289–530. Jonathan Edwards Center, Yale University.

Edwards, Jonathan, Jr. *Observations on the Language of the Muhhekaneew Indians*. New Haven, CT, 1788.

Eisen, Robert. *The Peace and Violence of Judaism: From the Bible to Modern Zionism*. New York: Oxford University Press, 2011.

Elazar, Daniel J. *Community and Polity: The Organizational Dynamics of American Jewry*. Philadelphia: Jewish Publication Society, 1995.

Eliot, John. *The Christian Commonwealth*. London, 1659.

———. *The Eliot Tracts: With Letters from John Eliot to Thomas Thorowgood and Richard Baxter*. Edited by Michael P. Clark. Westport, CT: Prager, 2003.

Elliott, Elisabeth. *Furnace of the Lord: Reflections on the Redemption of the Holy City*. New York: Doubleday, 1969.

———. "The Furnace of the Lord." *Christianity Today*, October 6, 1978.

Elliott, Emory. "From Father to Son: The Evolution of Typology in Puritan New England." In *Literary Uses of Typology from the Late Middle Ages to the Present*, edited by Earl Miner, 204–27. Princeton, NJ: Princeton University Press, 1977.

Ellis, Arthur B. *History of the First Church in Boston, 1630–1880*. Boston, 1881.

Ellwood, Robert S. *1950: Crossroads of American Religious Life*. Louisville, KY: Westminster/John Knox, 2000.

Evans, Christopher Hodge. *The Kingdom Is Always but Coming: A Life of Walter Rauschenbusch*. Grand Rapids, MI: William B. Eerdmans, 2004.

Evans, Mike. *Israel: America's Key to Survival*. Plainfield, NJ: Logos, 1981.

———. *Jerusalem Betrayed: Ancient Prophecy and Modern Conspiracy*. Dallas: Word, 1997.

Faber, George Stanley. *A General and Connected View of the Prophecies*. London, 1808.

Falwell, Jerry. *Armageddon and the Coming War with Russia*. n.d.

———. *An Autobiography*. Lynchburg, VA: Liberty House, 1996.

———. *Listen, America! The Conservative Blueprint for America's Moral Rebirth*. New York: Bantam, 1980.

———, ed. *The Fundamentalist Phenomenon*. New York: Doubleday, 1981.

Fea, John. "Does America Have a Biblical Heritage?" In *The Bible in the Public Square*, edited by Mark A. Chancey, Carol Meyers, and Eric M. Meyers, 65–80. Atlanta: SBL Press, 2014.

Feinberg, Charles L. *Israel in the Spotlight*. Wheaton, IL: Scripture Press, 1956.

———, ed. *Focus on Prophecy*. Westwood, NJ: Revell, 1964.

Feinberg, John S. "Why Christians Should Support Israel." *Fundamentalist Journal* 1 (September 1982): 10–17.

Feinstein, Marnin. *American Zionism, 1884–1904*. New York: Herzl Press, 1965.

Feldblum, Esther Yolles. *The American Catholic Press and the Jewish State*. New York: Ktav, 1977.

Feldman, Egal. "American Protestant Theologians on the Frontiers of Jewish-Christian Relations, 1922–82." In *Anti-Semitism in American History*, edited by David A. Gerber, 363–85. Urbana: University of Illinois Press, 1986.

———. *Dual Destinies: The Jewish Encounter with Protestant American*. Champaign: University of Illinois Press, 1990.

Ferguson, Robert A. *Reading the Early Republic*. Cambridge, MA: Harvard University Press, 2004.

Finch, Henry. *The Calling of the Iewes, or the World's Great Restauration.* London, 1621.

Finestein, Israel. "Early and Middle 19th-Century British Opinion on the Restoration of the Jews: Contrasts with America." In *Themes and Sources in the Archives of the United States, Great Britain, Turkey, and Israel,* vol. 2, *With Eyes Toward Zion,* edited by Moshe Davis. New York: Praeger, 1986.

Fischer, David Hackett. *Albion's Seed: Four British Folkways in America.* New York: Oxford University Press, 1989.

Fishman, Herzl. *American Protestantism and a Jewish State.* Detroit: Wayne State University Press, 1973.

Flannery, Edward H. *The Anguish of the Jews: Twenty-Three Centuries of Anti-Semitism.* New York: Macmillan, 1965.

———. "Theological Aspects of the State of Israel." *Bridge* 3 (1958): 301–24.

Fosdick, Harry Emerson. *Christianity and Progress.* Chicago: Revell, 1922.

———. *A Pilgrimage to Palestine.* New York: Macmillan, 1927.

Fox, Frank. "Quaker, Shaker, Rabbi: Warder Cresson, the Story of a Philadelphia Mystic." *Pennsylvania Magazine of History and Biography* (April 1971).

Fox, Richard. *Reinhold Niebuhr: A Biography.* New York: Pantheon, 1985.

Frederiksen, Paula. *Augustine and the Jews.* New York: Doubleday, 2008.

Freedman, David Noel. "Another View of the Middle East Crisis." *Presbyterian Life,* September 15, 1967.

Frey, Joseph Samuel C. F. *Judah and Israel, or, the Restoration and Conversion of the Jews and the Ten Tribes.* New York, 1840.

Friedman, Lee B. *Cotton Mather and the Jews.* New York: American Jewish Historical Society, 1918.

Fromkin, David. *A Peace to End All Peace: The Fall of the Ottoman Empire and the Creation of the Modern Middle East.* New York: Holt, 2009.

Fuller, Robert C. *Naming the Antichrist: The History of an American Obsession.* New York: Oxford University Press, 1995.

Gaebelein, Arno. *The Conflict of the Ages.* New York: Our Hope, 1933.

———. "Prophecy Fulfilled: A Potent Argument for the Bible." In *The Fundamentals: A Testimony to the Truth,* vol. 11, edited by R. A. Torrey, 55–86. Chicago: Testimony, 1915.

Gamble, Richard M. *In Search of the City on a Hill: The Making and Unmaking of an American Myth.* New York: Continuum, 2012.

———. *The War for Righteousness: Progressive Christianity, the Great War, and the Rise of the Messianic Nation.* Wilmington, DE: ISI Books, 2003.

Garfinkle, Adam M. "On the Origin, Meaning, Use and Abuse of a Phrase." *Middle Eastern Studies* 27, no. 4 (1991): 539–50.

Gazit, Mordecai. "Israeli Military Procurement from the United States." In *Dynamics of Dependence: U.S. Israeli Relations,* edited by Gabriel Sheffer, 83–124. Boulder, CO: Westview Press, 1987.

The Geneva Bible: A Facsimile of the 1560 Edition. Madison: University of Wisconsin Press, 1967.

"A Gentle Fundamentalist." *Time,* December 11, 1964.

Gilboa, Eytan. *American Public Opinion Toward Israel and the Arab-Israeli Conflict.* Lexington, MA: Lexington Books, 1987.

Gill, Jill K. *Embattled Ecumenism: The National Council of Churches, the Vietnam War, and the Protestant Left.* DeKalb: Northern Illinois University Press, 2011.

Glaude, Eddie S., Jr. *Exodus! Religion, Race, and Nation in Early Nineteenth-Century Black America.* Chicago: University of Chicago Press, 2000.

Global Survey of Evangelical Protestant Leaders. Washington, DC: Pew Forum on Religion and Public Life, 2011.

Goldish, Matt. *The Sabbatean Prophets.* Cambridge, MA: Harvard University Press, 2004.

Goldman, Samuel. "A Glorious Spiritual and Political Achievement: Reinhold Niebuhr on Zionism, Israel, and Realism." *American Political Thought* 6, no. 2 (2017): 432–54.

Goldman, Shalom. *Christians, Jews, and the Idea of the Promised Land.* Chapel Hill: University of North Carolina Press, 2009.

———. *God's Sacred Tongue: Hebrew and the American Imagination.* Chapel Hill: University of North Carolina Press, 2004.

———. "The Holy Land Appropriated: The Careers of Selah Merrill, Nineteenth-Century Hebraist, Palestine Explorer, and U.S. Consul in Jerusalem." *American Jewish History* 85, no. 2 (1997): 151–67.

———. "Johnny Cash: Father of Christian Zionism." *Tablet,* September 11, 2014, http://www.tabletmag.com/jewish-arts-and-culture/music/183966/johnny-cash-in-the-holy-land.

———. *Zeal for Zion: Jews, Christians, and the Idea of the Promised Land.* Chapel Hill: University of North Carolina Press, 2009.

Goodstein, Laurie. "Percentage of Protestant Americans in Steep Decline." *New York Times,* October 9, 2012, http://www.nytimes.com/2012/10/10/us/study-finds-that-percentage-of-protestant-americans-is-declining.html.

Gorenberg, Gershom. *The End of Days: Fundamentalism and the Struggle for the Temple Mount.* New York: Oxford University Press, 2000.

Graham, Billy. "I Have Never Felt Called to Single Out Jews." *Christianity Today,* November 1, 1999, http://www.christianitytoday.com/ct/1999/novemberweb-only/53.0d.html.

———. *Just as I Am.* New York: HarperCollins, 1997.

———. "Men Must Be Changed Before a Nation Can." In *American Principles and Issues,* edited by Oscar Handlin, 75–80. New York: Holt, Rinehart & Winston, 1961.

Green, Abigail. *Moses Montefiore: Jewish Liberator, Imperial Hero.* Cambridge, MA: Belknap Press, 2010.

Greenberg, Gershon. *The Holy Land in American Religious Thought, 1620–1948.* Lanham, MD: University Press of America, 1994.

Gribben, Crawford. *Writing the Rapture: Prophecy Fiction in Evangelical America.* New York: Oxford University Press, 2009.

Grose, Peter. *Israel in the Mind of America.* New York: Knopf, 1983.

Guyatt, Nicholas. *Providence and the Invention of the United States.* New York: Cambridge University Press, 2007.

Haberski, Raymond, Jr. *God and War: American Civil Religion Since 1945.* New Brunswick, NJ: Rutgers University Press, 2012.

Hagee, John. *The Beginning of the End: The Assassination of Yitzhak Rabin and the Coming Antichrist.* Nashville: Thomas Nelson, 1996.

———. *Final Dawn over Jerusalem.* Nashville: Thomas Nelson, 1998.

———. *In Defense of Israel.* Lake Mary, FL: Frontline, 2007.

———. *Jerusalem Countdown: A Warning to the World.* Lake Mary, FL: Frontline, 2006.

———. *Should Christians Support Israel.* San Antonio: Dominion, 1987.

———. "Why Christians Should Support Israel." John Hagee Ministries, http://www.jhm.org/Home/About/WhySupportIsrael.

Hall, Michael G. *The Last American Puritan: The Life of Increase Mather.* Middletown, CT: Wesleyan University Press, 1988.

Halsell, Grace. *Prophecy and Politics: The Secret Alliance Between Israel and the U.S. Christian Right.* Chicago: Lawrence Hill, 1986.

Harrison, Benjamin. "Third Annual Message." December 9, 1891. Miller Center, University of Virginia, http://millercenter.org/president/speeches/detail/3767.

Haselby, Sam. *The Origins of American Religious Nationalism.* New York: Oxford University Press, 2015.

Hatch, Nathan O. *The Sacred Cause of Liberty: Republican Thought and the Millennium in Revolutionary New England.* New Haven, CT: Yale University Press, 1977.

Hauerwas, Stanley. *Resident Aliens: Life in the Christian Colony.* Nashville: Abingdon Press, 2014.

Hayward, Steven F. *The Age of Reagan: The Conservative Counterrevolution, 1980–1989.* New York: Random House, 2009.

Hazony, Yoram. "Nationalism and the Future of Western Freedom." *Mosaic,* September 6, 2016, http://mosaicmagazine.com/essay/2016/09/nationalism-and-the-future-of-western-freedom.

Henry, Carl F. H., ed. *Prophecy in the Making.* Carol Stream, IL: Creation House, 1971.

Henry, Patrick. "'And I Don't Care What It Is': The Tradition-History of a Civil Religion Proof Text." *Journal of the American Academy of Religion* 49 (1981): 35–49.

Herberg, Will. *Judaism and Modern Man: An Interpretation of Jewish Religion.* New York: Farrar, Straus and Young, 1951.

———. *Protestant, Catholic, Jew: An Essay in American Religious Sociology.* Chicago: University of Chicago Press, 1983.

Heschel, Abraham Joshua. "Conversation with Martin Luther King." *Conservative Judaism* 22, no. 3 (1968): 1–19.

———. "Reinhold Niebuhr: A Last Farewell." *Conservative Judaism* 25 (1971): 62–63.

Hoberman, Michael. *New Israel/New England: Jews and Puritans in Early America.* Amherst: University of Massachusetts Press, 2011.

Hobsbawm, Eric. *Primitive Rebels.* New York: W. W. Norton, 1965.

Hollinger, David. A. "Christianity and Its American Fate: Where History Interrogates Secularization Theory." In *The Worlds of American Intellectual History,* edited by Joel Isaac et al., 280–303. New York: Oxford University Press, 2016.

Holmes, Abiel. *The Life of Ezra Stiles.* Boston, 1798.

Holmes, John Haynes. *Palestine To-Day and To-morrow: A Gentile's Survey of Zionism.* New York: Macmillan, 1929.

Horowitz, Craig. "Israel's Christian Soldiers." *New York,* September 29, 2003, http://nymag.com/nymetro/news/religion/features/n_9255.

Howe, Daniel Walker. *What Hath God Wrought: The Transformation of America, 1815–1848.* New York: Oxford University Press, 2007.

Huebner, Theodore, and Carl Hermann Voss. *This Is Israel: Palestine: Yesterday, Today, and To-morrow.* New York: Philosophical Library, 1956.

Huie, James A. *The History of the Jews: From the Taking of Jerusalem by Titus to the Present Time.* Andover, MA, 1843.

Hull, William L. *Israel: Key to Prophecy.* Grand Rapids, MI: Zondervan, 1957.

———. *The Fall and Rise of Israel.* Grand Rapids, MI: Zondervan, 1954.

———. *The Struggle for a Soul.* New York: Doubleday, 1963.

Hulsether, Mark. *Building a Protestant Left: Christianity and Crisis Magazine, 1941–1993.* Knoxville: University of Tennessee Press, 1999.

Hummel, Daniel G. "A 'Practical Outlet' to Premillennial Faith: G. Douglas Young and the Evolution of Christian Zionist Activism in Israel." *Religion and American Culture* 25, no. 1 (2015): 37–81.

Inbari, Motti. *Messianic Religious Zionism Confronts Israeli Territorial Compromise*. New York: Cambridge University Press, 2012.

Inboden, William. "It's Impossible to Count the Things Wrong with the Negligent, Spurious, Distorted New Biography of George W. Bush." *Foreign Policy*, August 15, 2016, https://foreignpolicy.com/2016/08/15/its-impossible-to-count-the-things-wrong-with-the-negligent-spurious-distorted-new-biography-of-george-w-bush.

———. *Religion and American Foreign Policy, 1945–1960*. New York: Cambridge University Press, 2008.

Inhofe, James. "Peace in the Middle East." March 4, 2002, http://www.inhofe.senate.gov/newsroom/speech/peace-in-the-middle-east-speech.

Irenaeus. *Against Heresies*. Edited by Alexander Roberts and James Donaldson. Lexington, KY: Ex Fontibus, 2010.

Ironside, Harry. *Looking Backward over a Third of a Century of Prophetic Fulfillment*. New York: Loizeaux Bros., 1930.

Israel, Menasseh ben. *The Hope of Israel*. London, 1650.

Jerusalem Post. "Hagee, Falwell Deny Endorsing 'Dual Covenant.'" March 2, 2006, http://www.jpost.com/Jewish-World/Jewish-News/Hagee-Falwell-deny-endorsing-dual-covenant.

Jew and Gentile: Being a Report of a Conference of Israelites and Christians. Chicago: Fleming H. Revell, 1890.

Jewish Telegraphic Agency. "Billy Graham Voices Staunch Support for Israel, Concern for State's Security." December 26, 1967, http://www.jta.org/1967/12/26/archive/billy-graham-voices-staunch-support-for-israel-concern-for-states-security.

———. "Reagan Urges GOP Platform to Declare Need for Compromises to Settle Mideast Conflict." August 12, 1976.

Johnson, Edward. *A History of New-England*. London, 1651.

Johnson, Lyndon. Remarks at the 125th Anniversary Meeting of B'nai B'rith. September 10, 1968. American Presidency Project, http://www.presidency.ucsb.edu/ws/?pid=29109.

Johnson, Paul E., and Sean Wilentz. *The Kingdom of Matthias: A Story of Sex and Salvation in Nineteenth-Century America*. New York: Oxford University Press, 1994.

Jones, David W., and Russell S. Woodbridge. *Health, Wealth, and Happiness: Has the Prosperity Gospel Overshadowed the Gospel of Christ?* Grand Rapids, MI: Kregel, 2011.

Jones, Edgar DeWitt. "Palestine, the Jews, and the World War." *Christian Century*, July 12, 1917.

Jones, Robert P. *The End of White Christian America*. New York: Simon & Schuster, 2016.

Judis, John. *Genesis: Truman, American Jews, and the Origins of the Arab-Israeli Conflict*. New York: Farrar, Straus and Giroux, 2014.

Kaell, Hillary. *Walking Where Jesus Walked: American Christians and Holy Land Pilgrimage*. New York: New York University Press, 2015.

Kahn, Paul. *Political Theology: Four New Chapters on the Concept of Sovereignty*. New York: Columbia University Press, 2012.

Katz, David S. *Philo-Semitism and the Readmission of the Jews to England, 1603–1655*. Oxford, UK: Oxford University Press, 1982.

———, and Richard Popkin. *Messianic Revolution*. New York: Hill & Wang, 1998.

Kelso, James L. Untitled. *Christianity Today*, July 21, 1967.

Kennedy, John F. "City upon a Hill." January 9, 1961. Miller Center, University of Virginia, http://millercenter.org/president/kennedy/speeches/speech-3364.

Kidd, Thomas S. *American Christians and Islam: Evangelical Culture and Muslims from the Colonial Period to the Age of Terrorism*. Princeton, NJ: Princeton University Press, 2009.

Kiracofe, Clifford, Jr. *Dark Crusade: Christian Zionism and U.S. Foreign Policy*. New York: I. B. Tauris, 2009.

Kirban, Salem. *666*. Wheaton, IL: Tyndale House, 1970.

Klinghoffer, Judith A. *Vietnam, Jews, and the Middle East*. New York: St. Martin's Press, 1999.

Kobler, Franz. *Vision Was There: A History of the British Movement for the Restoration of the Jews to Palestine*. London: Lincolns-Prager, 1956.

Kolsky, Thomas A. *Jews Against Zionism: The American Council for Judaism, 1942–1948*. Philadelphia: Temple University Press, 1990.

Kotzin, Daniel P. *Judah L. Magnes: The American Jewish Nonconformist*. Syracuse, NY: Syracuse University Press, 2010.

Kramer, Martin. *The War on Error: Israel, Islam, and the Middle East*. New Brunswick, NJ: Transaction, 2016.

Kreiger, Barbara, and Shalom Goldman. *Divine Expectations: An American Woman in Nineteenth-Century Palestine*. Athens: Ohio University Press, 1999.

Kruse, Kevin M. *One Nation Under God: How Corporate America Invented Christian America*. New York: Basic Books, 2015.

Kyle, Richard. *The Last Days Are Here Again*. Grand Rapids, MI: Baker, 1998.

LaHaye, Tim. *The Coming Peace in the Middle East*. Grand Rapids, MI: Zondervan, 1984.

Lapide, Pinchas. *Three Popes and the Jews*. New York: Hawthorn, 1967.

Laqueur, Walter. *The History of Zionism*. London: I. B. Tauris, 2003.

LaSor, William Sanford. *Israel: A Biblical View*. Grand Rapids, MI: Eerdmans, 1975.

———. *The Truth About Armageddon: What the Bible Says About the End Times*. New York: Harper & Row, 1982.

Laud, William. *A Sermon Preached Before His Majesty*. London, 1621.

Lerner, Robert E. *The Feast of Saint Abraham: Medieval Millenarians and the Jews*. Philadelphia: University of Pennsylvania Press, 2000.

Lewis, David Allen. *Magog 1982: Canceled*. Harrison, AR: New Leaf, 1982.

Lewis, Donald M. *The Origins of Christian Zionism: Lord Shaftesbury and Evangelical Support for a Jewish Homeland*. New York: Cambridge University Press, 2010.

Lienesch, Michael. *Redeeming America: Piety and Politics in the New Christian Right*. Chapel Hill: University of North Carolina Press, 1993.

Lilla, Mark. *The Stillborn God*. New York: Vintage, 2008.

Lincoln, Abraham. "Address to the New Jersey Senate at Trenton, New Jersey." In *The Language of Liberty: The Political Speeches and Writings of Abraham Lincoln*, edited by Joseph R. Fornieri, 577–78. Washington, DC: Regnery, 2009.

Lindsey, Hal. *The Late Great Planet Earth*. Grand Rapids, MI: Zondervan, 1970.

———. *The 1980's: Countdown to Armageddon*. New York: Bantam, 1981.

———. *Planet Earth 2000 A.D.* Palos Verdes, CA: Western Front, 1994.

Lipstadt, Deborah. *Beyond Belief: The American Press and the Coming of the Holocaust, 1933–1945*. New York: Free Press, 1986.

Littell, Franklin. "Reinhold Niebuhr and the Jewish People." *Holocaust and Genocide Studies* 6, no. 1 (1991): 45–61.

Littell, Franklin H. *The Crucifixion of the Jews*. New York: Harper & Row, 1975.

———. "Israel and the Jewish-Christian Dialogue." In *The Religious Dimension of Israel: The Challenge of the Six-Day War*, edited by David Polish et al., 41–46. New York: Synagogue Council of America, 1968.

Littell, Norman. "The Christian Heritage." In *The Voice of Christian America*, 6–9. Washington, DC: American Palestine Committee, 1944.

Little, David. "Basis for U.S. Commitments in Asia." *New York Times*, June 25, 1967.

Little, Douglas. *American Orientalism: The United States and the Middle East Since 1945*. Chapel Hill: University of North Carolina Press, 2004.

Locke, John. *The Works of John Locke*. Vol. 7. London, 1824.

Los Angeles Times. "'Conscience Statement' on Middle East Issued." July 26, 1967.

Lowance, Mason I., Jr. *Increase Mather*. New York: Twayne, 1974.

———. *The Language of Canaan: Metaphor and Symbol in New England from the Puritans to the Transcendentalists*. Cambridge, MA: Harvard University Press, 1980.

Luther, Martin. *Commentary on Romans*. Translated by J. Theodore Mueller. Grand Rapids, MI: Kregel, 1976.

Lutz, Donald S. "The Relative Influence of European Writers on Late Eighteenth-Century American Political Thought." *American Political Science Review* 78, no. 1 (March 1984): 189–97.

MacKaye, William R. "Middle East War Issue Fractures Bond Linking Liberal Protestants." *Washington Post*, May 6, 1972.

Maclear, J. B. "New England and the Fifth Monarchy." *William and Mary Quarterly* 32, no. 2 (1975): 223–60.

Malachy, Yona. *American Fundamentalism and Israel: The Relation of Fundamentalist Churches to Zionism and the State of Israel*. Jerusalem: Institute of Contemporary Jewry, 1978.

Malcolmson, Scott. *One Drop of Blood: The American Misadventure of Race*. New York: Farrar, Straus and Giroux, 2000.

Maritain, Jacques. "On Anti-Semitism." *Commonweal*, September 25, 1942.

Marley, David John. *Pat Robertson: An American Life*. Lanham, MD: Rowman & Littlefield, 2007.

Marsden, George M. *Fundamentalism and American Culture*. New York: Oxford University Press, 2006.

———. *Fundamentalism and Evangelicalism*. Grand Rapids, MI: Eerdmans, 1991.

———. *Reforming Fundamentalism: Fuller Seminary and the New Evangelicalism*. Grand Rapids, MI: Wm. B. Eerdmans, 1987.

Mart, Michelle. "The 'Christianization' of Israel and Jews in 1950s America." *Religion and American Culture* 14, no. 1 (2004): 109–47.

———. *Eye on Israel: How Americans Came to View the Jewish State as an Ally*. Albany: State University of New York Press, 2006.

Marty, Martin. *Modern American Religion: Under God, Indivisible 1941–1960*. Chicago: University of Chicago Press, 1996.

Martyr, Justin. *The First Apology, The Second Apology, Dialogue with Trypho, Exhortation to the Greeks, Discourse to the Greeks, the Monarchy or the Rule of God*. Translated by Thomas B. Falls. Washington, DC: Catholic University of America Press, 1948.

Mather, Cotton. *Parentator: Memoirs of Remarkables in the Life and Death of the Ever-Memorable Dr. Increase Mather*. In *Two Mather Biographies: Life and Death and Parentator*, edited by William J. Scheick. Cranbury, NJ: Associated University Presses, 1989. Originally published Boston, 1723.

———. *Theopolis Americana: An Essay on the Golden Street of the Holy City*. Boston, 1710.

Mather, Increase. *A Brief History of the Warr with the Indians in New England*. Boston, 1676.

———. *A Dissertation Concerning the Future Conversion of the Jewish Nation*. London, 1709.

———. *The Mystery of Israel's Salvation, Explained and Applyed*. London, 1669.

Mather, Samuel. *Figures and Types of the Old Testament*. London, 1683.

Matthews, Shailer. *Will Christ Come Again?* Chicago: American Institute of Sacred Literature, 1917.

Mayo, Louise. *Ambivalent Image: Nineteenth-Century America's Perception of the Jew*. Rutherford, NJ: Fairleigh Dickinson University Press, 1988.

McAlister, Melani. *Epic Encounters: Culture, Media, and U.S. Interests in the Middle East, 1945– 2000*. Berkeley: University of California Press, 2001.

McCall, Thomas S. "How Soon the Tribulation Temple?" *Bibliotheca Sacra* 121, no. 512 (1971): 341–51.

———, and Zola Levitt. *Satan in the Sanctuary*. Chicago: Moody Press, 1973.

———. *The Coming Russian Invasion of Israel*. Chicago: Moody Press, 1974.

McClymond, Michael J., and Gerald R. McDermott. *The Theology of Jonathan Edwards*. New York: Oxford University Press, 2012.

McCracken, Brett. "The Birth of Blackstone Hall." *Biola Magazine* (Winter 2016): 9–11, http://magazine.biola.edu/static/media/downloads/pdf/Biola_Magazine_Winter_2016_web.pdf.

McCullough, David. *Truman*. New York: Touchstone, 1992.

McDermott, Gerald R. "A History of Christian Zionism." In *The New Christian Zionism: Fresh Perspectives on Israel and the Land*, edited by idem, 44–75. Downers Grove, IL: IVP, 2016.

———. *Jonathan Edwards Confronts the Gods*. New York: Oxford University Press, 2000.

———. *One Holy and Happy Society: The Public Theology of Jonathan Edwards*. State College, PA: Penn State University Press, 1992.

McDonald, James G. "Toward Middle East Peace." *New York Times*, March 4, 1956.

McDonald, John. *Isaiah's Message to the American Nation*. Photographically reproduced in *Call to America to Build Zion*, edited by Moshe Davis. New York: Arno Press, 1977. Originally published Albany, NY, 1814.

McKanan, Dan. *Prophetic Encounters: Religion and the American Radical Tradition*. Boston: Beacon Press, 2011.

Mead, Walter Russell. *Arc of a Covenant: The United States, Israel, and the Fate of the Jewish People*. New York: Knopf, 2017.

———. "God's Country." *Foreign Affairs* 85, no. 5 (September–October 2006): 24–43.

———. "The New Israel and the Old." *Foreign Affairs* 87, no. 4 (July–August 2008): 28–46.

Mearsheimer, John J., and Stephen M. Walt. *The Israel Lobby and U.S. Foreign Policy*. New York: Farrar, Straus and Giroux, 2007.

Mede, Joseph. *The Works of the Pious and Profoundly Learned Joseph Mede, B.D.* London, 1664.

Medoff, Rafael. "A Further Note on the 'Unconventional Zionism' of Reinhold Niebuhr." *Studies in Zionism* 12, no. 1 (1991): 85–88.

Melville, Herman. *Clarel: A Poem and Pilgrimage in the Holy Land*. Edited by Harrison Hayford et al. Evanston, IL: Northwestern University Press, 1991.

———. *Redburn, White-Jacket, Moby-Dick*. New York: Library of America, 1983.

Mendieta, Eduardo, ed. *The Power of Religion in the Public Square*. New York: Columbia University Press, 2011.

Merkley, Paul Charles. *American Presidents, Religion, and Israel*. Westport, CT: Praeger, 2004.

———. *Christian Attitudes Toward the State of Israel*. Montreal: McGill-Queens University Press, 2001.

———. *The Politics of Christian Zionism, 1891–1948*. Portland, OR: Frank Cass, 1998.

Meyer, Isidore S., ed. *Early History of Zionism in America*. New York: American Jewish Historical Society, 1958.

Middlekauff, Robert. *The Mathers: Three Generations of Puritan Intellectuals, 1596–1728.* Berkeley: University of California Press, 1999.

Miller, Perry. *Errand into the Wilderness.* Cambridge, MA: Harvard University Press, 2000.

———. *The New England Mind: From Colony to Province.* Cambridge, MA: Belknap Press, 1953.

Miller, Robert Moats. *Harry Emerson Fosdick: Preacher, Pastor, Prophet.* New York: Oxford University Press, 1985.

Miller, Steven P. *Billy Graham and the Rise of the Republican South.* Philadelphia: University of Pennsylvania Press, 2009.

Minor, Clorinda S. *Meshullam, or Tidings from Jerusalem.* Philadelphia, 1850.

Moorhead, James H. *World Without End: Mainstream American Protestant Visions of the Last Things, 1880–1925.* Bloomington: Indiana University Press, 1999.

Moorhead, Jonathan. "The Father of Zionism: William E. Blackstone?" *Journal of Evangelical Theological Studies* 53, no. 4 (2010): 787–800.

Moots, Glenn A. *Politics Reformed: The Anglo-American Legacy of Covenant Theology.* Columbia: University of Missouri Press, 2010.

Morrison, S. A. "Israel and the Middle East." *Christianity and Crisis,* July 11, 1949.

Munk, Linda. *The Devil's Mousetrap: Redemption and Colonial American Literature.* New York: Oxford University Press, 1997.

National Security Council. "Statement of Policy by the National Security Council." In *Foreign Relations of the United States, 1952–1954. The Near and Middle East (in Two Parts),* vol. 9, pt. 1, no. 145. NSC 155/1, S/P–NSC files, lot 61 D 167, Near East (NSC 155), https://history.state .gov/historicaldocuments/frus1952-54v09p1/d145.

Nelson, Eric. *The Royalist Revolution: Monarchy and the American Founding.* Cambridge, MA: Harvard University Press, 2014.

"New Low of 52% 'Extremely Proud' to Be Americans." July 1, 2016. Gallup, http://www.gallup .com/poll/193379/new-low-extremely-proud-americans.aspx.

New York Times. "Israel as Ally of West." May 8, 1951.

———. "Israel's Illusion." June 9, 1981.

———. "Jerusalem Should Remain Unified." July 12, 1967.

———. "The Moral Responsibility in the Middle East." Advertisement. June 4, 1967.

———. "President-Elect Says Soviet Demoted Zhukov Because of Their Friendship." December 23, 1952.

———. "Rabbinical Leaders Criticize Christians." June 27, 1967.

———. "Shofar, Ancient Horn, Signals Triumph." June 8, 1967.

Nichols, J. Bruce. *The Uneasy Alliance: Religion, Refugee Work, and U.S. Foreign Policy.* New York: Oxford University Press, 1988.

Nicholson, Robert. "Evangelicals and Israel: What American Jews Don't Want to Know (but Need To)." *Mosaic,* October 6, 2013, http://mosaicmagazine.com/essay/2013/10/evangelicals-and -israel.

Niebuhr, Gustav, and Elisabeth Sifton. *Huffington Post,* May 7, 2014, http://www.huffingtonpost .com/gustav-niebuhr/why-reinhold-niebuhr-supp_b_5280958.html.

Niebuhr, Reinhold. "Anglo-American Destiny and Responsibility." In *Love and Justice: Selections from the Shorter Writings of Reinhold Niebuhr,* edited by D. B. Robertson, 183–88. Louisville, KY: Westminster/John Knox, 1957.

———. *Faith and Politics.* New York: George Braziller, 1968.

———. "Germany Must Be Told." *Christian Century,* June 28, 1933.

———. *The Irony of American History.* Chicago: University of Chicago Press, 2008.

———. "Jews After the War." *Nation*, pt. 2 (February 28, 1942): 253–55.

———. "Judah Magnes and the Zionists." *Detroit Times*, December 28, 1929.

———. *Leaves from the Notebook of a Tamed Cynic*. Louisville, KY: Westminster/John Knox, 1980.

———. *Moral Man and Immoral Society*. New York: Charles Scribner, 1960.

———. "My Sense of Shame." *Hadassah Newsletter* 19, no. 3 (December 1938): 59–60.

———. "Our Stake in the State of Israel." *New Republic*, February 3, 1957.

———. "The Partition of Palestine." *Christianity and Society* 13, no. 1 (Winter 1948): 3–4.

———. *Pious and Secular America*. New York: Charles Scribner's Sons, 1958.

———. *The Self and the Dramas of History*. New York: Charles Scribner's Sons, 1955.

———. "Seven Great Errors of U.S. Foreign Policy." *New Leader*, December 24–31, 1956.

———. "Statement to the Anglo-American Committee of Inquiry." *Jewish Frontier* 13 (February 1946): 38–44.

———. "Toward a Program for the Jews." *Contemporary Jewish Record*, June 1942.

———, and Alan Heimert. *A Nation So Conceived: Reflections on the History of America from Its Early Visions to Its Present Power*. London: Faber & Faber, 1963.

Nirenberg, David. *Anti-Judaism: The Western Tradition*. New York: W. W. Norton, 2003.

Noah, Mordecai Manuel. *Discourse Delivered at the Consecration of the Synagogue Shearith Israel*. New York, 1818.

———. *Discourse on the Evidence of the American Indians Being the Descendants of the Lost Tribes of Israel*. New York, 1837.

———. *Travels in England, France, Spain, and the Barbary States*. New York, 1819.

Noll, Mark A. *America's God: From Jonathan Edwards to Abraham Lincoln*. New York: Oxford University Press, 2002.

———. *Princeton and the Republic, 1768–1822*. Vancouver: Regent College Publishing, 2004.

———. *The Scandal of the Evangelical Mind*. Grand Rapids, MI: Eerdmans, 1994.

Noyes, Nicholas. *New-Englands Duty and Interest to Be an Habitation of Justice and Mountain of Holiness Containing Doctrine, Caution, & Comfort*. Boston, 1698.

Numbers, Ronald L. *The Creationists*. Berkeley: University of California Press, 1993.

O'Brien, Conor Cruise. *God Land: Reflections on Religion and Nationalism*. Cambridge, MA: Harvard University Press, 1988.

Obenzinger, Hilton. *American Palestine: Melville, Twain, and the Holy Land Mania*. Princeton, NJ: Princeton University Press, 1999.

———. "Holy Lands, Restoration, and Zionism in *Ben-Hur*." In *Bigger than Ben-Hur: The Book, Its Adaptations, and Their Audiences*, edited by Barbara Ryan and Millette Shamir, 74–90. Syracuse, NY: Syracuse University Press, 2016.

———. "In the Shadow of 'God's Sun-Dial.'" *Stanford Humanities Review* 5, no. 1 (February 27, 1996), https://web.stanford.edu/group/SHR/5-1/text/obenzinger.html.

Ockenga, Harold. "Fulfilled and Unfulfilled Prophecy." In *Prophecy in the Making*, edited by Carl F. H. Henry. Carol Stream, IL: Creation House, 1971.

Oesterreicher, John M. *The Rediscovery of Judaism: A Re-Examination of the Conciliar Statement on the Jews*. South Orange, NJ: Institute for Judaeo-Christian Studies, 1971.

Olson, Arnold. *Inside Jerusalem: City of Destiny*. Glendale, CA: G/L Publications, 1968.

Oren, Michael B. *Power, Faith, and Fantasy: America in the Middle East, 1776 to the Present*. New York: W. W. Norton, 2007.

———. *Six Days of War: June 1967 and the Making of the Modern Middle East*. New York: Random House, 2002.

Oxtoby, Willard G. "What Is the Christian Stake in a Jewish Dream?" *Presbyterian Life*, July 1, 1967.

Pace, Eric. "The Rev. Edward Flannery, 86, Priest Who Fought Anti-Semitism." *New York Times*, October 22, 1998.

Pagels, Elaine. *Revelations: Visions, Prophecy, and Politics in the Book of Revelation*. New York: Penguin, 2013.

Paine, Thomas. *Political Writings*. Edited by Bruce Kuklick. New York: Cambridge University Press, 2000.

Parins, James W. *Elias Cornelius Boudinot: A Life on the Cherokee Border*. Lincoln: University of Nebraska Press, 2008.

Parsons, Levi. *The Dereliction and Restoration of the Jews: A Sermon Preached in Park-Street Church Boston, Sabbath, Oct. 31, 1819, Just Before the Departure of the Palestine Mission*. Photographic reprint in *Holy Land Missions and Missionaries*. New York: Arno Press, 1977.

Patterson, Richard S., and Richardson Dougall. *The Eagle and the Shield: A History of the Great Seal of the United States*. Washington, DC: Department of State, 1976.

Paul VI. *Nostra Aetate* ("Declaration on the Relation of the Church to Non-Christian Religions"). October 28, 1965. Vatican, http://www.vatican.va/archive/hist_councils/ii_vatican_council/documents/vat-ii_decl_19651028_nostra-aetate_en.html.

Pawlikowksi, John T. *Cathechetics and Prejudice: How Catholic Teaching Materials View Jews, Protestants, and Racial Minorities*. New York: Paulist Press, 1973.

Pentecost, J. Dwight. *Things to Come: A Study in Biblical Eschatology*. Findlay, OH: Dunham, 1958.

Pew Research Center. "Public Uncertain; Divided over America's Place in the World." May 5, 2016, http://www.people-press.org/2016/05/05/public-uncertain-divided-over-americas-place-in-the-world.

———. *Religious Landscape Study*. Washington, DC: Pew Research Center, 2014, http://www.pewforum.org/religious-landscape-study.

Phillips, Kevin. *American Theocracy*. New York: Penguin, 2006.

Philo. "Against Flaccus." In *Philo*, vol. 9, translated by F. H. Colson. Cambridge, MA: Harvard University Press, 1995.

Pipes, Daniel. "Israel's Best Weapon?" *New York Post*, July 15, 2003. Archived at http://www.danielpipes.org/1148/christian-zionism-israels-best-weapon.

Poling, Daniel. "Our Good Faith at Stake." In *The Voice of Christian America*, 32–34. Washington, DC: American Palestine Committee, 1944.

Popkin, Richard H. "The Rise and Fall of the Jewish Indian Theory." In *Menasseh ben Israel and His World*, edited by Yosef Kaplan, Henry Méchoulan, and Richard H. Popkin, 63–82. Leiden: Brill, 1989.

Pratt, Orson. *The New Jerusalem; or, the Fulfillment of Modern Prophecy*. Liverpool, 1849.

Preston, Andrew. *Sword of the Spirit, Shield of the Faith*. New York: Anchor Books, 2012.

Prime, William Cowper. *Tent Life in the Holy Land*. New York, 1857.

Prothero, Steven. *The American Bible*. New York: HarperOne, 2012.

———. *Religious Literacy: What Every American Needs to Know*. New York: HarperCollins, 2008.

Rader, Paul. *Round the Round World: Some Impressions of a World Tour*. Chicago: Revell, 1922.

Radosh, Ronald, and Allis Radosh. *A Safe Haven: Harry S. Truman and the Founding of Israel*. New York: Harper Perennial, 2010.

Ravitsky, Avi. *Messianism, Zionism, and Jewish Religious Radicalism*. Chicago: University of Chicago Press, 1996.

Rausch, David A. "Arno C. Gaebelein." *American Jewish History* 68 (September 1978): 43–55.

———. "Proto-Fundamentalism's Attitudes Toward Zionism, 1878–1918." In *American Zionism: Missions and Politics*, vol. 8, edited by Jeffrey Gurock, 13–28. New York: Routledge, 1998.

Rauschenbusch, Walter. *A Theology for the Social Gospel*. New York: Macmillan, 1917.

Rawls, John. "The Idea of Public Reason Revisited." *University of Chicago Law Review* 64, no. 3 (Summer 1997): 765–807.

———. *Political Liberalism*. New York: Columbia University Press, 2005.

Read, Hollis. *The Coming Crisis of the World*. Columbus, OH, 1861.

———. *The Hand of God in History*. Hartford, 1849.

Reed, Ralph. "We People of Faith Stand Firmly with Israel." *Los Angeles Times*, April 21, 2002, http://articles.latimes.com/2002/apr/21/opinion/oe-reed21.

Reeves, Marjorie. *The Influence of Prophecy in the Later Middle Ages: A Study in Joachimism*. South Bend, IN: University of Notre Dame Press, 2011.

Reissig, Herman F. "Another Look at the Arab-Israeli Problem." *Christianity and Crisis*, April 16, 1956.

Republican Party Platform of 1964. July 13, 1946. American Presidency Project, http://www.presidency.ucsb.edu/ws/?pid=25840.

Ribuffo, Leo. "Confessions of an Accidental (or Perhaps Overdetermined) Historian." In *Reconstructing History: The Emergence of a New Historical Society*, edited by Elizabeth Fox-Genovese and Elisabeth Lasch-Quinn, 143–63. New York: Routledge, 1999.

———. *The Old Christian Right: The Protestant Far Right from the Great Depression to the Cold War*. Philadelphia: Temple University Press, 1983.

Richard, Carl J. *The Founders and the Classics: Greece, Rome, and the American Enlightenment*. Cambridge, MA: Harvard University Press, 1994.

Ricks, Steven D. "From Joseph to Joseph." In *Covenant and Chosenness in Judaism and Mormonism*, edited by Raphael Jospe, Truman G. Madsen, and Seth Ward, 91–102. Cranbury, NJ: Associated University Presses, 2001.

Rimmer, Harry. *The Coming War and the Rise of Russia*. Grand Rapids, MI: Wm. Eerdmans, 1943.

———. *The Shadow of Coming Events*. Grand Rapids, MI: Wm. Eerdmans, 1946.

Robbins, Chandler. *History of the Second Church, or Old North Church, in Boston*. Boston, 1852.

Roberts, Oral. *The Drama of the End Time*. Tulsa: self-published, 1963.

Robertson, Pat. *The New World Order*. Dallas: Word Publishing, 1991.

Robinson, Edward. *Biblical Researches in Palestine, Mount Sinai, and Arabia Petraea*. Excerpted in *The Holy Land in American Protestant Life, 1800–1948: A Documentary History*, by Robert T. Handy, 3–36. New York: Arno Press, 1981. Originally published Boston, 1856.

Rogers, Stephanie Stidman. *Inventing the Holy Land: American Protestant Pilgrimage to Palestine*. Lanham, MD: Rowman & Littlefield, 2011.

Romero, Simon. "Temple in Brazil Appeals to a Surge in Evangelicals." *New York Times*, July 24, 2014, http://www.nytimes.com/2014/07/25/world/americas/temple-in-brazil-appeals-to-a-surge-in-evangelicals.html?partner=rss&emc=rss&smid=tw-nytimesworld&_r=1.

Rorty, Richard. *Philosophy and Social Hope*. New York: Penguin, 1999.

Rosenbaum, Stuart. "Must Religion Be a Conversation-Stopper?" *Harvard Theological Review* 102, no. 4 (2009): 393–409.

Ross, Jack. *Rabbi Outcast: Elmer Berger and American Jewish Anti-Zionism*. Washington, DC: Potomac Books, 2011.

Rovner, Adam. *In the Shadow of Zion: Promised Lands Before Israel*. New York: New York University Press, 2014.

Rudin, A. James. *Israel for Christians*. Philadelphia: Fortress Press, 1983.

————. "Prospectus for the Future." In *Evangelicals and Jews in Conversation*, edited by Marc H. Tanenbaum, Marvin R. Wilson, and A. James Rudin, 311–13. Grand Rapids, MI: Baker House, 1978.

Russell, Charles Taze. "Zionism in Prophecy." Reprinted in *Pastor Russell's Sermons*. Brooklyn, NY: International Bible Students Association, 1917.

Rynhold, Jonathan. *The Arab-Israeli Conflict in American Political Culture*. New York: Cambridge University Press, 2015.

Sandoz, Ellis, ed. *Political Sermons of the American Founding Era, 1730–1788*. Vol. 1, *Political Sermons of the American Founding Era, 1730–1805*. Indianapolis: Liberty Fund, 1991.

Santorum, Rick. *American Patriots: Answering the Call to Freedom*. Carol Stream, IL: Tyndale, 2012.

Sarna, Jonathan. *Jacksonian Jew: The Two Worlds of Mordecai Noah*. New York: Holmes & Meier, 1981.

Saum, Lewis O. *The Popular Mood of America, 1860–1890*. Lincoln: University of Nebraska Press, 1990.

Saxon, Wolfgang. "Balfour Brickner, Activist Reform Rabbi, Dies at 78." *New York Times*, September 1, 2005, https://query.nytimes.com/gst/fullpage.html?res=9801E1DB1731F932A3 575AC0A9639C8B63.

Scheer, Robert. "The Prophet of Worldly Methods." *Los Angeles Times*, March 4, 1981.

Schlesinger, Arthur, Jr. "Niebuhr's Shadow." *New York Times*, June 22, 1992, http://www.nytimes .com/1992/06/22/opinion/reinhold-niebuhr-s-long-shadow.html.

Scholem, Gershom. *Sabbatai Sevi: The Mystical Messiah*. Princeton, NJ: Princeton University Press, 1976.

Schram, Martin. "Jerry Falwell Vows Amity with Israel." *Washington Post*, September 12, 1981.

Schroth, Raymond A. *Bob Drinan: The Controversial Life of the First Catholic Priest Elected to Congress*. New York: Fordham University Press, 2010.

Schuldiner, Michael, and Daniel J. Kleinfeld, eds. *The Selected Writings of Mordecai Manuel Noah*. Westport, CT: Praeger, 1999.

The Scofield Reference Bible. New York: Oxford University Press, 1909.

Seiss, Joseph A. *The Apocalypse*. Grand Rapids, MI: Zondervan, 1962.

————. *The Last Times and the Great Consummation*. Philadelphia, 1863.

Sewall, Samuel. *Phaenomena quaedam Apocalyptica*. Boston, 1697.

Shachar, Yoram. "Jefferson Goes East: The American Origins of the Israeli Declaration of Independence." *Theoretical Inquiries in Law* 10, no. 2 (2009): 589–618.

Shalev, Eran. *American Zion: The Old Testament as a Political Text from the Revolution to the Civil War*. New Haven, CT: Yale University Press, 2013.

————. *Rome Reborn on Western Shores: Historical Imagination and the Creation of the American Republic*. Charlottesville: University of Virginia Press, 2009.

Shimeall, Robert C. *Christ's Second Coming: Is It Pre-Millennial or Postmillennial?* New York, 1866.

Shimoni, Gideon. *The Zionist Ideology*. Hanover, NH: University Press of New England, 1995.

Shipler, David K. "1,000 Christian 'Zionists' in Jerusalem." *New York Times*, September 25, 1980.

Silk, Mark. "Notes on the Judeo-Christian Tradition in America." *American Quarterly* 36, no. 1 (1984): 65–85.

————. *Spiritual Politics: Religion and America Since World War II*. New York: Simon & Schuster, 1988.

Simon, Merrill. *Jerry Falwell and the Jews*. Middle Village, NY: Jonathan David, 1984.

Singer, David G. "American Catholic Attitudes Toward the Zionist Movement and the Jewish State." *Commonweal*, September 25, 1942.

Sizer, Stephen. *Christian Zionism: Road-Map to Armageddon?* Leicester, UK: IVP, 2004.

Skillen, James W. "Evangelicals and American Exceptionalism." *Review of Faith & International Affairs* 4, no. 3 (2006): 45–46.

Skousen, W. Cleon. *Fantastic Victory: Israel's Rendezvous with Destiny.* Salt Lake City: Bookcraft, 1967.

———. *The Naked Communist.* Salt Lake City: Ensign, 1960.

———. *Prophecy and Modern Times.* Salt Lake City: Deseret News Press, 1948.

Smith, Ethan. *A View of the Hebrews.* Poultney, VT, 1823.

Smith, Jean Edward. *Bush.* New York: Simon & Schuster, 2016.

Smith, Joseph Fielding. *Essentials in Church History.* Salt Lake City: Deseret News Press, 1922.

Smith, Robert O. "Jewish-Christian Difficulties in Challenging Christian Zionism." *Journal of Lutheran Ethics* (May 2007), https://www.elca.org/JLE/Articles/512.

———. *More Desired than Our Owne Salvation: The Roots of Christian Zionism.* New York: Oxford University Press, 2013.

Smith, Wilbur M. *Israeli-Arab Conflict and the Bible.* Glendale, CA: G/L Publications, 1967.

———. "Israel in Her Promised Land." *Christianity Today,* December 24, 1956.

———. *World Crises and the Prophetic Scriptures.* Chicago: Moody Press, 1951.

Smolinski, Reiner. "Apocalypticism in Colonial North America." In *The Continuum History of Apocalypticism,* edited by Bernard J. McGinn, John J. Collins, and Seymour J. Stein, 441–66. New York: Continuum, 2003.

———. "Israel Redivivus: The Eschatological Limits of Puritan Typology in New England." *New England Quarterly* 63, no. 3 (1990): 357–95.

Sokolow, Nahum. *History of Zionism, 1600–1918.* London: Longman, 1919.

Spector, Stephen. *Evangelicals and Israel: The Story of American Christian Zionism.* New York: Oxford University Press, 2009.

Spence, Martin. *Heaven on Earth.* Eugene, OR: Pickwick, 2015.

Spiegel, Irving. "8 Church Leaders Ask Aid to Israel." *New York Times,* May 28, 1967.

———. "Rabbis Score Christians for Silence on Mideast." *New York Times,* June 23, 1967.

Sprague, William Buell. "Austin, David." Vol. 1, *Annals of the American Pulpit.* New York, 1859.

"Statement by the President Following the Adjournment of the Palestine Conference in London." American Presidency Project, University of California, Santa Barbara, http://www.presidency.ucsb.edu/ws/?pid=12520.

"Statement of the President re: Recognition of Israel, May 14, 1948." Correspondence file, 1916–50. Harry S. Truman Library, http://www.trumanlibrary.org/exhibit_documents/index.php?tldate=1948-05-14&groupid=3429&pagenumber=1&collectionid=ROIexhibit.

Stendahl, Krister. "Judaism and Christianity II: After a Colloquium and a War." *Harvard Divinity Bulletin* (Fall 1967): 2–9.

Stevens, Jason W. *God-Fearing and Free.* Cambridge, MA: Harvard University Press, 2010.

Stiles, Ezra. "The United States Elevated to Glory and Honor." New Haven, CT, 1783.

Stout, Jeffrey. *Democracy and Tradition.* Princeton, NJ: Princeton University Press, 2004.

Stowe, Harriet Beecher. *Oldtown Folks.* Boston: Houghton Mifflin, 1911.

Street, Nicholas. *The American States Acting over the Part of the Children of Israel in the Wilderness.* New Haven, CT, 1777.

Sugrue, Thomas. *Watch for the Morning: The Story of Palestine's Jewish Pioneers and Their Battle for the Birth of Israel.* New York: Harper, 1950.

Sutton, Matthew Avery. *American Apocalypse: A History of Modern Evangelicalism.* Cambridge, MA: Harvard University Press, 2014.

Sykes, Christopher. *Crossroads to Israel*. London: Collins, 1965.

———. *Orde Wingate: A Biography*. Cleveland: World Publishing, 1959.

Tacitus. *The Histories*. Translated by Kenneth Wellesley. New York: Penguin, 1995.

Taft, Robert A. "Address at Testimonial Dinner for Dr. Abba Hillel Silver." In *The Papers of Robert A. Taft*, edited by Clarence E. Wunderlin, 3:32–37. Kent, OH: Kent State University Press, 2003.

Tanenbaum, Marc H. "Israel's Hour of Need and Jewish-Christian Dialogue." *Conservative Judaism* 22, no. 2 (1968): 1–18.

Taylor, Alan. *William Cooper's Town: Power and Persuasion on the Frontier of the Early American Republic*. New York: Vintage, 1996.

Thomas, Cal. "Looking for the Reason of Lebanon." *Fundamentalist Journal* 2 (January 1983): 60–61.

Thorowgood, Thomas. *Digitus Dei*. London, 1652.

———. *Jews in America*. London, 1650.

Tillich, Paul. "Is There a Judeo-Christian Tradition?" *Judaism* 1, no. 2 (1952): 106–9.

Tooley, Mark. "Mainline Protestant Zionism and Anti-Zionism." In *The New Christian Zionism*, edited by Gerald R. McDermott, 198–219. Downers Grove, IL: IVP, 2016.

Torrey, Reuben. *Will Christ Come Again: An Exposure of the Foolishness, Fallacies, and Falsehoods of Shailer Matthews*. Los Angeles: Bible Institute of Los Angeles, 1918.

Truman, Harry. "Address in Columbus at a Conference of the Federal Council of Churches." March 6, 1946. Truman Library, http://www.trumanlibrary.org/publicpapers/index.php?pid=1494.

Truth About Palestine. New York: Christian Council on Palestine, 1946.

Tuchman, Barbara. *Bible and Sword: England and Palestine from the Bronze Age to Balfour*. New York: New York University Press, 1956.

———. "U.S. Role in the Mideast." *New York Times*, May 30, 1967.

Tuveson, Ernest. *Redeemer Nation: The Idea of America's Millennial Role*. Chicago: University of Chicago Press, 1968.

Twain, Mark. *The Innocents Abroad*. Edited by Guy Cardwell. New York: Penguin, 2002.

Tyng, Stephen Higginson. *Recollections of England*. London, 1847.

Urofsky, Melvin I. *American Zionism from Herzl to the Holocaust*. Lincoln, NE: Bison, 1995.

Van Dusen, Henry P. "'Silence' of Church Leaders on Mideast." *New York Times*, July 7, 1967.

Van Impe, Jack. *Israel's Final Holocaust*. Nashville: Thomas Nelson, 1979.

Verdon, Lexie. "2-Minute Raid: Planning, Technology, and Subterfuge Aided in Pinpoint Bombing Mission." *Washington Post*, June 10, 1981.

Vinz, Warren L. *Pulpit Politics: Faces of Protestant Nationalism in the Twentieth Century*. Albany: State University of New York Press, 1997.

Vital, David. *The Origins of Zionism*. Oxford: Clarendon Press, 1975.

Vogel, Lester I. *To See a Promised Land: Americans and the Holy Land in the Nineteenth* Century. University Park, PA: Penn State University Press, 1993.

The Voice of Christian America. Washington, DC: American Palestine Committee, 1944.

Voss, Carl Hermann. *A Christian Looks at the Jewish Problem*. New York: American Christian Palestine Committee, 1946.

———. *The Palestine Problem Today: Israel and Its Neighbors*. Boston: Beacon Press, 1953.

———. *Questions and Answers on Palestine*. New York: American Christian Palestine Committee, 1947.

———. *Rabbi and Minister: The Friendship of Stephen S. Wise and John Haynes Holmes*. Amherst, NY: Prometheus Books, 1980.

———, and David A. Rausch. "American Christians and Israel." *American Jewish Archives* 40, no. 2 (1988): 41–81.

Wacker, Grant. *America's Pastor: Billy Graham and the Shaping of a Nation*. Cambridge, MA: Belknap, 2014.

Walls, Jerry L. "Introduction." In *The Oxford Handbook of Eschatology*, edited by idem, 3–18. New York: Oxford University Press, 2008.

Walvoord, John F., and John E. Walvoord. *Armageddon, Oil, and the Middle East Crisis*. Grand Rapids, MI: Zondervan, 1974; rev. 1990.

———. *Israel in Prophecy*. Grand Rapids, MI: Zondervan, 1962.

———. *The Nations in Prophecy*. Grand Rapids, MI: Zondervan, 1967.

Washington Post. "Let Them Live in Peace." March 6, 1891.

———. "President Bush Addresses the Nation." September 20, 2001, http://www.washington-post.com/wp-srv/nation/specials/attacked/transcripts/bushaddress_092001.html.

Weber, Timothy P. *Living in the Shadow of Armageddon: American Premillennialism, 1875–1982*. Chicago: University of Chicago Press, 1987.

———. "Millennialism." In *The Oxford Handbook of Eschatology*, edited by Jerry L. Walls, 365–83. New York: Oxford University Press, 2008.

———. *On the Road to Armageddon: How Evangelicals Became Israel's Best Friend*. Grand Rapids, MI: Baker Academic, 2004.

Wellcome, Isaac. *History of the Second Advent Message*. Boston, 1874.

Whalen, Robert K. "'Christians Love the Jews!' The Development of American Philo-Semitism, 1790–1860." *Religion and American Culture* 6, no. 2 (Winter 1996): 225–59.

Wilentz, Sean. "Confounding Fathers." *New Yorker*, October 18, 2010, http://www.newyorker.com/magazine/2010/10/18/confounding-fathers.

Wilford, Hugh. *America's Great Game: The CIA's Secret Arabists and the Shaping of the Modern Middle East*. New York: Basic Books, 2013.

Wilken, Robert L. *The Land Called Holy: Palestine in Christian History and Thought*. New Haven, CT: Yale University Press, 1992.

Wilkinson, Paul Richard. *For Zion's Sake: Christian Zionism and the Role of John Nelson Darby*. Eugene, OR: Wipf & Stock, 2008.

Willard, Samuel. *The Fountain Opened*. Boston, 1700.

Willett, Herbert L., Jr. "The Holy Land in the War." *Christian Century*, December 20, 1917.

Williams, Joseph. "The Pentecostalization of Christian Zionism." *Church History* 84, no. 1 (March 2015): 159–94.

Wilsey, John D. *American Exceptionalism and Civil Religion: Reassessing the History of an Idea*. Downers Grove, IL: IVP, 2015.

Wilson, Dwight. *Armageddon Now! The Premillenarian Response to Russia and Israel Since 1917*. Grand Rapids, MI: Baker House, 1977.

Winchester, Elhanan. *A Century Sermon on the Glorious Revolution*. Reprinted in Sandoz, *Political Sermons of the American Founding Era, 1730–1788*, 969–1000. Originally published London, 1788.

———. *A Course of Lectures on the Prophecies That Remain to Be Fulfilled*. London, 1789.

Wingfield, Marshall. "Arab and Israeli." *Christianity and Crisis*, October 29, 1951.

Winter, Michael Sean. *God's Right Hand: How Jerry Falwell Made God a Republican and Baptized the American Right*. New York: HarperCollins, 2012.

Winthrop, John. "A Modell of Christian Charitie." In *God's New Israel: Religious Interpretations of American Destiny*, edited by Conrad Cherry, 37–41. Chapel Hill: University of North Carolina Press, 1998.

Wise, Stephen. *Challenging Years: The Autobiography of Stephen Wise.* New York: Putnam's Sons, 1949.

Wood, Gordon. *The Radicalism of the American Revolution.* New York: Vintage, 1991.

Wood, Michael. *America in the Movies.* New York: Columbia University Press, 1989.

Wuthnow, Robert. *The Restructuring of American Religion: Society and Faith Since World War II.* Princeton, NJ: Princeton University Press, 1990.

Wysner, Gloria M. "Dilemma in Palestine." *Bulletin of the Committee on Work Among Moslems* (November 1944): 1–8.

Young, G. Douglas. "Israel: The Unbroken Line." *Christianity Today,* October 6, 1978.

———. "Toward Arab-Israel Coexistence." *Christian Century,* December 12, 1962.

———. *The Wife and the Bride.* Minneapolis: Free Church Publications, 1959.

Zakai, Avihu. *Jonathan Edwards's Philosophy of History: The Reenchantment of the World in the Age of Enlightenment.* Princeton, NJ: Princeton University Press, 2003.

Zionism in Prophecy. New York: Pro-Palestine Federation of America, 1936.

"Zion's Christian Soldiers." *60 Minutes,* October 2, 2003. CBS News, http://www.cbsnews.com/news/zions-christian-soldiers.

Index

Acknowledgments

If I had realized what I was getting into, I might not have written this book. The vastness of the primary sources and the quality of the existing scholarship should have served as warnings to an inexperienced voyager. But I did not notice them and ventured heedless into the unknown. I sat up more than one night wondering whether I had ventured too far from home and wouldn't be better off reversing course.

It is due to generous assistance from colleagues and friends that I remained more or less on track. An exhaustive list of the people and institutions that helped me would exceed reasonable limits. Those named here deserve particular mention.

The journey began at Princeton. I am grateful to Leora Batnitzky and the Tikvah Project in Jewish Thought for giving me the opportunity to undertake an intellectual reorientation during my fellowship there. The faculty, fellows, and staff of Princeton's Religion Department and Center for the Study of Religion provided an intellectual home for two productive years. Among others, I thank Jeffrey Stout and John Gager for leading seminars in philosophy of religion and cultural history in which I began to pursue my interest in Christian Zionism.

Work continued at the George Washington University, where I received unfailing support and encouragement. Successive chairs of the Political Science Department—Paul Wahlbeck and Bruce Dickson—made sure that I had the time and resources to write. Departmental colleagues read the manuscript and participated in a workshop on an early draft. I might have remained stuck without the insights I received from Michael Barnett, Ingrid

Creppell, Eric Gyrnaviski, and Nathan Brown. Beyond the Political Science Department, members of the GW faculty including Denver Brunsman, Arie Dubnov, Robert Eisen, and Leo Ribuffo read and commented on parts of the manuscript.

At GW, two undergraduate research assistants helped me locate primary sources, collate documents, and copyedit. Seth Harrison and Paul Neumann saved me from much confusion and many errors. In addition, Neumann did yeoman's work compiling the index.

I also owe a debt of gratitude to Robert Nicholson and the Philos Project, which generously supported a second manuscript workshop. The participants—Daniel G. Hummel, Matthew Franck, Robert Wilken, and John Wilsey—offered sage advice and reassured me that I was fairly representing Christian perspectives. Yaakov Ariel and Gerald McDermott were unable to attend in person but read the manuscript and suggested important revisions.

Not everyone who helped me with this book had a professional responsibility to do so. I relied shamelessly on friends. Jonathan Bronitsky, Angus Burgin, David Grewal, Sara Henary, and James Patterson took time out of busy schedules to read and respond to a flurry of drafts.

At the University of Pennsylvania Press, Damon Linker expertly led me through the editorial process, answering a first-time author's stupid questions with unfailing patience. Two anonymous reviewers offered discerning critiques and valuable advice. The production staff made frustrating tasks as painless as they could possibly be. I am grateful for their efforts.

Above all, I thank my wife, Sarah. Her love and friendship are my greatest supports in all things.